# THEODORE THOMAS
## A Musical Autobiography

# THEODORE THOMAS

## A Musical Autobiography

Edited by
GEORGE P. UPTON

With a New Introduction by
LEON STEIN

Da Capo Press
NEW YORK
1964

*A Da Capo Reprint Edition*

*Da Capo Press wishes to express its appreciation to A. C. McClurg & Co., Chicago, Illinois, whose cooperation made possible this reprint edition, based on their original 2-volume work of 1905. Pages 35 through 356 of Volume II, an enumeration of Thomas' "Concert Programmes 1855-1905," were omitted in order to include the new introduction and appendices.*

*Library of Congress Catalog Card No. 64-18990*

*Printed in the United States of America*

# CONTENTS

# INTRODUCTION

A MONUMENT IN CHICAGO, a statue in Cincinnati, and a mountain in New Hampshire bear his name. Revered at the time of his death as the man to whom America owed more "for its musical taste and knowledge than it can ever owe to another," and as "the most conspicuous figure in the modern history of music in America," he is, after scarcely two generations, all but forgotten. Week after week, it is true, Chicago Symphony Orchestra subscribers see on the covers of their program books "Founded by Theodore Thomas in 1891," but for most, this is a kind of expletive sentence; beyond its use in association with the words "founded by," the name signifies little. Thomas, himself, would have been least troubled by this turn. "Others will reap what I have sown," he had said, and that this would be so gave him a sufficient sense of accomplishment.

There is no surety for immortality, but of all activities in the arts the most ephemeral, the least enduring is that of performance. We may be captivated by the moment but how vain it is to attempt to recover that moment. An aesthetic event can only be directly experienced; its impress can never be recalled. This being so, how can one transmit to another the essence of a past performance and

A7

how much less can one generation convey to another what, in a literal sense, it has "lived through." So the names of performers, however famous, become more and more faded letters on the pages of history until, with time, they become almost completely obliterated.

If the life and career of Thomas were those of a performer alone, however great, the republication of his *Autobiography* might be of some limited interest but hardly of any essential significance. But the story of his life is not only coeval with the growth and development of orchestral music in the United States, it *is* that development, truly its "evolutionary history" as John H. Mueller wrote in *The American Symphony Orchestra.* Yet, as interesting and important as the Thomas biography may be from the historical viewpoint, for us and for succeeding generations it is most meaningful as the saga of a man possessing unique qualities rarely found in combination; a man who, storm-tossed and buffeted, still held firmly to a great plan, whose vision and determination never faltered, despite setbacks and disappointments.

Not that the story is easy to come by. This "sound kernel in a rough shell" as Thomas was described by Lilli Lehmann *(My Pathway Through Life),* indeed encased himself within a husk, but it is characteristic of his effect on kindred spirits that almost in the same breath Frau Lehmann declares, "Thomas was a man, take him all in all, to whom I should like to erect a monument." The "rough shell" is in evidence in much of the *Autobiography*. The writing is not "literary" nor does it seek to be ingratiating, but it has, above all, the salient characteristic of its writer—it is completely honest. This is no ghost-written work. As Thomas would not attach his name to anything to which he could not subscribe personally, he could never allow another's writing to pass as his own. The directness, the terseness even to brusqueness— these were his characteristic traits, in behavior as well as in this narration. Note how in one brief paragraph he disposes of his family, concluding, "This is the end of my knowledge of my family history. Both my parents were refined and honest people." In *The American Orchestra and Theodore Thomas,* Charles E. Russell writes, "I once asked him to tell me the story of the American Opera Company. He told it. He said: 'Good intentions, bad management, no money.' "

In other respects, also, the *Autobiography* is a paradoxical work. It is undoubtedly the most reticent example of its type. It was not written out of a desire to impart the story of the writer's life nor to share with his readers insights which the author felt were of significance. Much interesting and valuable information is either omitted or touched upon in the most casually oblique manner. George P. Upton's *Reminiscence and Appreciation,* which follows the autobiography, very obviously was added in order to fill the outline. Rose Fay Thomas' *Memoirs of Theodore Thomas* with its more than five hundred pages and Russell's book of some three hundred pages are certainly more complete, and yet they remain ancillary works. Concise as it is, in the *Autobiography* the essential Thomas is still to be found—though often he must be sought out. As communicative as he could be in his letters and in conversations with close friends, in his public utterances, written or spoken, he was often the leader "ohne Worte."

As Thomas indicates in his preface, the *Autobiography* was an outgrowth of Upton's suggestion concerning "the necessity of adding some historical matter . . . without which these volumes [the compilation of Thomas' programs] would be incomplete." From some correspondence with the composer Horatio Parker (1903), it is evident that the thought of compiling and publishing his programs apparently had been in Thomas' mind for some time. Parker had volunteered to approach G. Schirmer, but whatever the reason, nothing came of this effort. In Upton, Thomas found an ideal collaborator. The former was among the first to grasp not only the scope and significance of Thomas' work, but also the nature of his character. The music editor of the *Chicago Tribune*, he was a gifted and prolific writer. In an article in *The Star Magazine* of 1873, written but four years after Upton's first encounter with Thomas (and the term "encounter" is used advisedly) and eighteen years before the founding of the Chicago Orchestra, it is interesting to note the accuracy and discernment of Upton's evaluation of the conductor.

Upon completing Thomas' account of his life the reader may be suddenly startled by the realization that the period of the narration coincides with America's most critical hour. Yet, not once is the Civil War mentioned, neither is there a single reference to Lincoln nor to any other historical personage of the time. One's first reaction is that here is an unparalleled example of the detached musician's insularity, of the artist whose occupational blinders shut from his vision all matters extraneous to his art. But to what degree are matters extraneous? What of Thomas' family life, wife, children? Why are these not mentioned at all?

The answer is surprisingly simple. In her *Memoirs,* Rose Fay Thomas wrote of "the mantle of reserve in which he habitually wrapped his inner thoughts and feelings before the world." Even more revealing is an incident related by Upton in his *Musical Memories:* "I met him one day alone in his library when he was looking through the score of the "Domestic Symphony" [i.e., *Symphonia Domestica*] which he had just received from Richard Strauss. I asked him what he thought of it. He replied: 'I do not care to express an opinion about the music itself, but how can a composer thrust his personality and family affairs upon people? What do they care for him or his wife and babies and relatives, or for what is going on in his home?' "

Thomas, it is clear, felt that the distinctly and intensely personal events were his concern only; and the more deeply he was affected, the more closely he "wrapped his inner thoughts and feelings." And the *Autobiography* was written "before the world." Apparently respecting this desire for personal and domestic privacy, Upton does not disturb the "mantle of reserve" embracing these areas.

Because Thomas does not wish "to thrust his family affairs upon people," we are not informed that as a member of the Mason-Thomas ensemble which performed at Miss Porter's School for young women at Farmington, Connecticut, he first met Minna L. Rhodes, a member of a New York family, who was a student at the school. The acquaintance continued after Miss Rhodes left Farmington and in 1864 they were married. Nor are we told of their three sons and two daughters. From all evidences it appears that Thomas was an exemplary father and husband.

In some instances his reserve coupled with a stern sense of duty could become almost frightening. During the intermission of the concert of Thursday evening, December 20, 1901, he was brought word of the sudden death of his eldest son, Franz, in Pensacola, Florida. Lest this news disturb an orchestra party scheduled for that evening, he requested of the manager, Wessels, that the orchestra should not be informed of the tragedy. The funeral was to take place the following afternoon in New York. To Wessels' suggestion that he cancel the Friday afternoon concert and attend the funeral—for there was no official assistant conductor—Thomas replied, "I have no right to make the public mourn with me. . . . My duty is to remain here."

Behind the immobile countenance of this *Autobiography* are hidden chambers, each containing a key to some integral component of its author's character. We will have occasion to discuss three incidents, each revealing some important facet of his nature and concepts. The first, concerned with the commissioning of Wagner's *Centennial March,* and the third, involving an invitation to conduct at the Paris Exhibition of 1900 are mentioned in neither the *Autobiography* nor Upton's *Appreciation.* Of the second, revolving around the Chicago fire and its aftermath, there are but the briefest intimations in the *Autobiography.*

In order to place these events in their proper context, it will prove helpful to trace his early development and simultaneously to correct a prevalent misconception. Because most nineteenth-century American conductors were foreigners who had come to the United States as established artists, there is often a mistaken assumption that Thomas, too, was in this category. Actually, he was but a boy of ten when he arrived in the United States. There are overtones of the Lincoln legend in the story of this youth whose formal education stopped at the equivalent of the fourth grade, but who somehow became informed not only in a factual sense, but cultured in a general one, and so proficient in his chosen art that his national leadership in music was universally acknowledged.

In the manner of its attainment, that proficiency was something to marvel at. That he was something of a prodigy is suggested by his recollection that members of his father's band amused themselves by trying to find something he could not read at sight. He was all of seven years of age at the time. As a wonder child he played in concerts in his native Friesland, once even before the King of Hanover. After his arrival in the United States there are no records of systematic violin study, though he does mention two theory teachers. His interest in composition must have been quite strong at one time, for the collection of his books left to the Newberry Library includes a surprising number of various composition and form texts. We have some hint of how he applied the lessons of his musical experiences to his own work. His contact with the finest singers—Patti, Sontag, Jennie Lind—helped set his standards of tone production, taste, and execution. In his time, the typical "German tone" of string players was firm, accurate—and somewhat coarse. Thomas consciously attempted to impart to his violin playing and eventually to the string players in his orchestras the vibrant tonal beauty of the great vocalists. "The right influence," he writes, "came to me at the right time . . . and shaped my future as no other influence could have done."

But in both areas, the specifically musical and the broadly cultural, it was not enough that the seeds of influence existed; these needed fertile soil in which to take root and an empathy to nourish them. Both were provided by the inherent qualities in Thomas' nature. He recognized that in the great singers it was not voice and technique alone which accounted for their preeminence, but the combining of these factors "with the single aim—that of truthful expression."

He was constantly learning and expanding his musical horizons. No matter what the height of his achievement, complacency was never for him. He not only met challenges, he deliberately set them up. His first European trip in 1867 was in the nature of a self-examination—a comparison of *his* standards with those prevailing in the great musical centers. His notebook reveals his honest and objective evaluation of conductors and performers— and what he saw and heard gave him added confidence and reassurance in the rightness of his path and of his methods.

In one respect, a pattern is established quite early in his career: the young violinist who put up posters announcing his appearance, sold tickets, collected them at the door, and then appeared from backstage to play his program, was the prototype of the later conductor who for so many years was organizer, business manager, tour arranger, and fund raiser as well as musical director. He was enabled to assume these diverse duties and responsibilities by a capacity for work which amounted virtually to a compulsion, and a stamina and endurance which sometimes surprised even himself. Between 1869 and 1891 when he crossed and recrossed the continent, east and west, north and south, over what he termed "The Great Highway," the schedule of performances, including orchestra concerts and the management and direction of huge festivals in New York, Chicago, Cincinnati, Philadelphia, and San Francisco is incredible. Two seasons within this period, those of 1872-73 and 1885-86, are of particular interest. During the 1872-73 season Thomas and his orchestra made four trips from New York to Chicago. He gave in all eighty-five concerts outside New York, including programs in Boston, St. Louis, and Cincinnati. Seventeen times he returned to New York, itself, to conduct the New York Symphony and Brooklyn Philharmonic Orchestras, and, at the end of April, 1873, a week-long festival at Steinway Hall, including a large chorus, orchestra, and soloists. This was followed by the first Cincinnati Festival, May 6–9, 1873. On September 17, 1872, Thomas conducted the first all-Wagner program and used the occasion to found the first Wagner-Verein in the United States, raising ten thousand dollars for the Bayreuth Festival. On October 15, 1872, Wagner sent him a personal letter acknowledging this contribution. Curiously, while he was an avid promoter of Wagner, he never became embroiled in the so-called "Brahms–Wagner" controversy, for he performed numerous American premieres of works by both composers.

Four years later he was instrumental in commissioning Wagner to compose a march to inaugurate the Philadelphia Centennial Exhibition of 1876. Few events touched him in a more sensitive area than those associated with this commission, so much so that, as we have noted, it is not mentioned at all in his *Autobiography*. The complete story and the correspondence between Wagner and Thomas (and the latter's designated representative, a Mr. Federlein) is detailed in Rose Fay Thomas' *Memoirs*. (Wagner's part of this correspondence is also in the Thomas collection at the Newberry Library.)

Since our principal concern here is not the incident itself but those aspects of Thomas' character and concepts which are brought into relief by this episode, it will suffice merely to outline the events. On the suggestion of Mrs. E. D. Gillespie, President of the Women's Centennial Committee of the Philadelphia Centennial Exposition, Thomas, authorized to commission a famous European to compose an inaugural march for the opening ceremonies of May 10, immediately wrote to Wagner. The latter, delaying his reply so that it would be impossible to approach another composer, finally assented, stipulating a—for that time—staggering fee of $5,000. The composer had promised to withhold European publication in any form until six months after publication in America by the Women's Committee. But even before the score reached Thomas, a published piano four-hand arrangement by Joseph Rubinstein had arrived in America. (Thomas himself prepared a piano arrangement published by John Church in Cincinnati, also in 1876, with the title *Grand Festival March* on the cover and *Centennial March* on the first page of music. This may have been prepared because of his knowledge of the Rubinstein arrangement.) Finally, when the full score did come, it turned out to be a quite mediocre work, one which the embarrassed Thomas felt was a reflection both on his recommendation and on the occasion for which it was commissioned.

The manner of delivery stipulated by Wagner was hardly flattering to either Thomas or the Centennial Committee: the manuscript was to be sent to a German bank stipulated by Thomas, from which it was to be sent to America after the deposit of the five-thousand-dollar fee to Wagner's account. However, Wagner was not altogether ungenerous in the matter. In requesting a reply from Thomas concerning the acceptance of the composer's terms, Wagner wrote, "I authorize you to deduct the cost of the telegram from my honorarium." Nor was he ungallant. "A few soft and tender passages," he wrote, "are meant to depict the beautiful and talented women of North America as they take part in the cortege. I am glad to say that it was my intention to have these noble hearted women take the first place in the procession rather than the men because they were the chief promoters and most energetic workers for my composition."

What troubled Thomas deeply, however, was not that he, the foremost Wagner protagonist in the United States, had been somewhat shabbily treated in this affair, but something much more fundamental. To grasp the nature of his disappointment it is necessary that we understand his basic attitude toward music.

For Thomas, the most significant aspect of music was its ethical content. He considered the art to be a "powerful character-building force . . . the strongest influence of any art if properly controlled." In a letter to a Miss Twombly he wrote ". . . the best music elevates the mind, purifies the thought and yet provides without sinking into the insignificance of an amusement a healthful and enjoyable recreation for all classes alike." In the article, "Music in Chicago" *(Chicago Tribune,* January 23, 1894) he speaks of that "deeper joy and . . . nobler spirituality to be gained from familiarity with the higher art forms."

The composer of great music necessarily, therefore, should be as noble in his concepts and behavior as his music was elevated. The dichotomy of Wagner the creator and Wagner the man was difficult for him to reconcile, all the more since it shook one of his essential convictions.

After the episode of the *Centennial March* (or as Wagner called it, *Grosser Festmarsch),* he never corresponded with Wagner again. "The wound rankled all the rest of Thomas' life," wrote Russell. "Twenty-eight years after, happening to mention it to him, I was astonished to find that it was still painful." On the other hand, he continued to perform Wagner's music as much as ever. In this respect, there is an interesting coincidence. In his biography of Wagner (Volume IV), discussing the *Centennial March,* Ernest Newman wrote, "The mysterious psychology of the creative genius is well illustrated by the fact that while he was working at the march one day there came to him the theme of the chorus—Komm, holder Knabe—of the Flower Maidens in *Parsifal."* The first performance of this chorus in America was given by Thomas in Philadelphia, February 24, 1887.

His final evaluation of Wagner's music (in his essay on "Programme Making," included in the present edition) was that his "effective scoring makes the desired climax. Wagner excites his hearers, especially the younger generation, and interests the less musical. . . . Wagner's music is effective only at a distance, and only under certain conditions." Twice Thomas uses the term "without soul" in referring to this music. "Wagner . . .," he continues, "made a great impression on the world by his combination of intellect and passion, or sensuousness. He touched greatness in "Siegfried's Death March," but even in this chiefly by his intellect. Wagner did not care for humanity. . . ."

In comparison with the schedule of 1872-73, the season of 1885-86 was even more astonishing. This was the year in which the ill-fated American Opera Company was established. Between January 4 and June 4, 1886, Thomas directed one hundred and twenty-six performances of eight different operas—all in English, in cities between New York and Chicago. During the same season there were subscription concerts by the New York Philharmonic, Brooklyn Philharmonic, twenty-four Young People's Concerts in New York, eight popular concerts in Brooklyn, two Liederkranz concerts of choral music, and the seventh biennial Cincinnati Festival, immediately followed by the summer nights concerts in Chicago.

It might seem that this number of performances would have assured him, at the least, a comfortable income. On the contrary, it was not until he assumed the direction of the Chicago Orchestra that he was finally free of the debts that had plagued him for some twenty years. On the one hand, we must remember that he himself carried the financial burden of his orchestra, which was almost entirely dependent on box-office receipts. Secondly, his normal expenses were compounded by a series of financial mishaps that would have broken a lesser man.

From the time he had organized his orchestra in 1862 there had been the expected vicissitudes and problems, but by 1871, writes Thomas, "For the first time, everything, even from the business point of view, looked very promising." Then, on a never-to-be-forgotten Monday, October 9, 1871, fate brought him to Chicago. "On this morning," wrote Philo A. Otis in *The Chicago Symphony Orchestra,* "I left my home, which was then at 369 (now 1216) Michigan Avenue to go over to State Street to watch the progress of the conflagration, and there I observed a line of men walking north, carrying violins, cellos, trombones and other instruments. I learned, on inquiring, that they were members of the Thomas orchestra who had just arrived at the Twenty-second Street Station of the Lake Shore Road."

"We got away from the burning city as best we could," writes Thomas, "and spent the time intervening before our next engagement which was at St. Louis, October 21, in rehearsals. . . . It is sufficient to say that I became so involved financially by this disaster and the consequent interruption of our tour that it was many years before I recovered from my losses."

With typical reticence, Thomas neglects to inform us that, though exempted from responsibility by the usual "Act of God" clause in the contracts with members of his organization, he voluntarily assumed the total expenses for the two weeks of enforced idleness, involving not only his orchestra, but soloists, managers, and other functionaries. His financial problems were increased by the poor attendance at the concerts of the Philadelphia Centennial. Finally, in 1876, the Sheriff of Philadelphia seized and advertised for sale "The entire musical library of Theodore Thomas," listing instruments and equipment down to the last ink-stand. Almost in the manner of a nineteenth-century melodrama, a devoted friend, Dr. Franz Zinzer, hearing of this sale, rushed from New York to Philadelphia to rescue the library, ink-stand, and all, leaving it in the possession of the Thomases, and two years later presenting it to Mrs. Thomas for her husband's use.

Thomas' advisors had urged him to declare bankruptcy and he actually had pen in hand, ready to sign, when, he writes, "I threw down the pen and refused to sign. I said to myself that for the sake of my family and my profession, I would not make a bankrupt of myself voluntarily, although I did not see any possibility of ever making enough money to buy up all the claims against me. However, eventually I succeeded. But twelve years of experience with sheriffs and scoundrels have made their impression on the nerves and I cannot hear the door-bell today, yet, without being startled" (*Memoirs,* Rose Fay Thomas).

In a letter to a Mr. Seymour Eaton concerning remuneration for some musical project, he wrote, "Money has never been an object with me in working for the cause of art." While many have given lip service to this doctrine, with Thomas it was a dogma. In his twelve years as conductor of the New York Philharmonic, which, under his leadership reached an unprecedented level of prosperity, he voluntarily relinquished part of his salary, although entitled to it by contract. His engagement as Director of the Cincinnati College of Music came shortly after the seizure of his property by the Sheriff of Philadelphia. Obviously, he was in desperate need of money. Where a lesser person would have found ample excuse to rationalize and compromise his essential principles in order to retain a much needed position, Thomas resolutely and immovably held to his basic convictions though it was soon evident that this stand must lead to his resignation. Two years after his departure he was tardily vindicated when the school was reorganized in accordance with his original precepts.

The year 1889 marked the nadir of his fortunes. His already dwindling resources were swept away by the necessity of defending himself against the lawsuits which resulted from the collapse of the American Opera Company. The courts decided that he was neither liable nor responsible for the organization's debts, but by this time his reserves were gone. On April 4, 1889, his wife died and, to multiply his sorrows, he was forced to disband his orchestra. In the summer of 1889 he wrote to Rose Fay, "Artistically there is nothing for me to do in this world. . . . I am tired . . . tired of everything. . . . I do not know myself. . . . The world is so tedious to me, but I must go on for the sake of my children for a few years yet."

But this was the proverbial darkness before dawn. Within less than two years, he was to realize his most cherished ambition—the direction of an orchestra with a full season of programs, subsidized by a dedicated Board of Directors. A prospectus setting forth the specific plan of organization was issued. Of particular moment for Thomas was the clause under "The rights, powers and duties of the Musical Director:" . . . "The Musical Director is to determine the character and standard of all performances given by the Association, and to that end make all programmes, select all soloists, and take the initiative in arranging for choral and festival performances. The intention of the Association being to lodge in the hands of the Director the power and responsibility for the attainment of the highest standard of artistic excellence in all performances given by the Association." Despite deficits, temporary discouragements, and the humiliating experiences associated with the World Columbian Exposition, the next fourteen years were to prove, relatively, the most serene of his life and the crowning achievement of his career.

If any one person is to be singled out for initiating and working for the establishment of the Chicago Orchestra, that person would have to be Charles Norman Fay. An executive of various power and utility companies of the Chicago area, he was the brother of pianist and writer Amy Fay, and of Rose Fay, who became Thomas' wife May 7, 1890. During the summer railroad strike of 1877, Fay had come to Chicago from Marquette, Michigan, out of concern for his business interests. Quite accidentally, as he was strolling near the Exposition Building he was drawn by the sound of an orchestra concert from within the hall; here Thomas was conducting one of his summer programs. He entered the hall; almost miraculously, his cares vanished, and the visitor carried away with him an indelible impression of a new world of music. Shortly afterward, his business interests brought him to Chicago permanently, and on September 23, 1879, he wrote a letter to Thomas proposing a Philharmonic Society of Chicago using local musicians, with Thomas as conductor. For various reasons, this proposal was not feasible at the time and Thomas declined. Nevertheless, what had begun as a casual acquaintance ripened into a devoted friendship.

One April day in 1889, Fay was walking down Fifth Avenue in New York, and, for the second time in his life, accidentally encountered Thomas. In *Outlook Magazine* of January 22, 1910, he tells the story of this chance meeting which was destined to be so consequential. ". . . we turned into the old Delmonicos. He looked worn and worried, and I asked him why. There were reasons enough . . . almost worst of all he had been obliged to give up his orchestra. . . .

"For a moment, so bitter was his tone, I had nothing to reply, but finally I said: 'Is there no one, no rich and generous man to do here as Major Higginson has done in Boston—keep your orchestra going and pay the deficit?'

'No one,' he answered . . . .

'Would you come to Chicago if we could give you a permanent orchestra?'

"The answer, grim and sincere, and entirely destitute of humor, came back like a flash:

'I would go to hell if they gave me a permanent orchestra.'

"Then and there," continues Fay, "were roughed out in talk the general principles on which the orchestra was to be established."

Not long afterward the Orchestral Association was organized. Literally going from door to door, Fay secured the necessary guarantors from among his wealthy acquaintances. Modestly, he took the post of Vice-President (and "factotum" as he later described himself), from which he continued for many years to direct the activities of the Association. The contract with Thomas was signed in December, 1890, and the Chicago Orchestra became a reality. Suddenly, his supporters in New

York awakened to their impending loss. Three separate groups approached Thomas, promising to raise any guarantee he would name if he would but remain. It was too late.

The decision to leave New York did not come easily. It meant the division of his family, with two of his sons remaining in the East. He was not too confident of Chicago's capacity to support an orchestra year after year. Problems, anticipated and unanticipated, did arise. There were times when, disheartened by tiring and badly arranged tours, newspaper attacks on his programs, mounting deficits and empty seats in the cavernous Auditorium Theater, the conductor spoke of resigning; on November 14, 1899, he actually submitted a written resignation. It is to their everlasting credit that on these occasions the officers of the Orchestral Association tactfully withheld any serious consideration of his avowed intentions, assuring him in the latter instance, "We do not wish to think of your resignation. . . . You are engaged to play only the great works of ancient and modern times. If there are any deficits in giving the concerts we will take care of them."

A combination of circumstances, some indirectly rather than directly related, finally brought to realization another of Thomas' dreams—a permanent home for his orchestra. For the various reasons cited in the *Autobiography,* it was becoming more and more evident that the Auditorium was too large for the regular series of subscription concerts. At the same time, the continuing and mounting deficits did not make feasible the added expense of a new building. Because of these deficits, the possibility of a liaison with a music school to be established at the University of Chicago, with orchestra and school to share a million-dollar endowment, was suggested by the University's President Harper. Eventually these negotiations were dropped, principally because President Harper would not accept Thomas' reservation that voice and piano should not be taught at the school. But while the school was under consideration, Leroy Payne's livery stable on south Michigan Avenue was considered a possible site. When it became evident that the joint enterprise was not to be established, it was nevertheless decided to purchase the land for a hall which would house the orchestra. Accordingly, on November 26, 1902, Bryan Lathrop, acting for the Board, purchased the Michigan Avenue site for $450,000 and here Orchestra Hall was built.

During his tenure as conductor of the Chicago Orchestra, Thomas twice declined an invitation to become Musical Director of the Boston Symphony. As with the New York offer of 1890, he could have named his own salary. A principal factor in his decision to remain was his conviction that he had committed not only himself but also the Orchestral Association, and he would not betray this obligation. His decision to remain is also an attest of the mutual confidence which existed between the conductor and the Board.

One other invitation he declined. Over a half-century was to pass before the full implications of this refusal would be understood.

On August 15, 1899, Edouard Colonne, the eminent French conductor, invited Thomas to be one of a number of conductors at the Paris Exposition of 1900, either with his orchestra or as guest conductor with Colonne's own orchestra. A New York correspondent, somehow learning of this invitation, interviewed a number of eminent French musicians, including the conductor Lamoreux and the organist-composer Widor; all hailed the anticipated visit of the famous American conductor with great praise.

On September 14, 1899, Thomas replied from his Felsengarten summer home in Bethlehem, New Hampshire. (He evidently took some care in the phrasing of this letter, because a preliminary draft was written, one of the few copies of his own letters among the hundreds in the Thomas collection at the Newberry Library.) After apologizing for his seeming tardiness in answering Colonne's friendly invitation, Thomas continues: "I regret sincerely that circumstances have so changed of late—that I as an American, who love justice and liberty, am prevented from visiting the Metropolis of France next summer.

"If I can render to you as a colleague, any assistance perhaps in this country please do not hesitate to command me."

This is the complete letter. The explanation of this cryptic refusal fortunately is provided by Rose Fay Thomas in the *Memoirs*. "This invitation," she writes, "Thomas declined for a reason which seems very inadequate now, but which moved him strongly at the time; namely, the trial and condemnation of Dreyfus by the French government. Thomas considered it a piece of monumental injustice and was so indignant about it that he was unwilling to accept an invitation which came to him, even indirectly, from a government institution. . . . It was a pity he felt thus about the matter, for there was much interest in Paris over his proposed visit with his orchestra."

As much as Thomas, at the very height of his power and reputation, would have welcomed the opportunity to conduct in Europe, his refusal of Colonne's invitation revealed one of his most important qualities—he would never sacrifice principle to expediency. The same cannot be said for those—not only musicians, but statesmen and spiritual leaders—who, a generation later, were to face a similar crisis of decision and were to be found sadly wanting.

It is noteworthy and typical that in his letter to Colonne there is no sermonizing, nor any of that implicit self-righteousness which so often seeks to direct attention to itself when a moral stand is taken. He had reached a conclusion consistent with his principles, and the most important of these is stated in his own preface to the *Autobiography:* "I have been compelled by truth without which the whole world would have been worthless"—and this is sufficient for him. It is also of some moment that his decision was reached and adhered to despite his wife's opinion that "it was a pity he felt thus about the matter," an opinion, we may feel quite certain, she did not leave unexpressed, but in this instance, without effect.

In his fourteen seasons as conductor of the Chicago Orchestra, the 274 subscription programs he conducted included works by 170 composers. Of these, 64 did not remain in the repertoire after his death. One hundred and eight, or forty percent of the programs, included compositions by Beethoven, while 164, or sixty percent, included compositions by Wagner; a corroboration of his consideration of these composers as "pillars" of the orchestra repertoire. Four Beethoven-Wagner, five all-Wagner, and twelve all-Beethoven programs were given. The eighteenth program of the first season, devoted to works of living American composers, included compositions by Paine, Chadwick, Gleason, and Shelley. Otis reported that this concert had the smallest attendance of the season, with a box office of $598.00. In contrast, the fifth program of the season, featuring Paderewski as soloist, yielded $4,373.75.

In the course of his lifetime, hundreds of works by 146 different composers were given their first American performances by Thomas. These include large numbers of compositions which became staples of the orchestral repertoire. During Thomas' later years, Richard Strauss, Sibelius, and Elgar began to replace Wagner in the Chicago Orchestra repertoire. (It may be pointed out that in the list of first American performances, Upton mistakenly lists Beethoven's Ninth Symphony. This work, however, was first played in the United States by the New York Philharmonic Orchestra, directed by George Loder, on May 20, 1846.)

On the nineteenth program of the 1893-94 season, Thomas performed Beethoven's Ninth Symphony. "Mr. Thomas," wrote Philo Otis, "had the choral part of the symphony transposed from D major to C major, one whole tone lower. This made it easier for the singers; less strain on the voices; but much of the life and brightness of the music was gone." Apparently this was the first and last time such a mutation was attempted. While this was the most radical alteration ever made by Thomas, there are other instances which may be noted. His scores of Bach's *B Minor Mass*, Handel's *Israel in Egypt*, and the opera scores of Mozart and Gluck performed by the American Opera Company also reveal instances of editing. In the *presto* introduction to the Finale of Beethoven's Ninth, the trumpets are altered generally to double the clarinet parts. Thomas was not nearly as radical in altering scores as was his successor, Frederick Stock; nevertheless, even the occasional alterations are surprising in view of his essentially objective approach. But in the end, he turned away from all changes. He is quoted by Rose Fay Thomas as saying, "I have at last come to the conclusion that no one has a right to alter in any particular the work of a composer. It is the duty of the executant musician to interpret a work exactly as the composer intended it should be interpreted, and he should not change or embellish it to suit the taste of another generation."

It may seem surprising that, contradictory as editing and not editing a score may seem in principle, in Thomas' case, both approaches spring from a common purpose—an attempt to protect the content of a work. In the beginning, he mistakenly assumed that "updating" the orchestration would make a work more accessible to his audience; in the end, he realized that any kind of marked change is, at best, presumptuous. That he could change his mind and admit his error is an indication of that flexibility which explains a great part of his accomplishment. He was not content to accept an established norm when his independent judgment urged otherwise. So he was among the first to seat his orchestra, to use uniform bowings, and to schedule complete symphonies. His conclusions were reached not through any external influence, but through his own evolving convictions.

So, gradually, in respect to his career as a conductor, a sense of ordainment evolves, and one can trace in the *Autobiography* the step-by-step realization of his manifest destiny. In writing of his early years, Thomas refers to "the opportunities to prepare myself for my later-day task." One by one, the experiences which were to shape various facets of his work succeed each other, finally to become integrated in the mature conductor. His violin study gave him an understanding of strings; the horn player on the battleship *Pennsylvania,* "damn bad" as by his own description he might have been, gained an insight into the brass; the player in Jullien's orchestra heard woodwinds which were to set a standard for him forever after; his early contact with the greatest singers, as we have noted, gave him a lasting sense of both vocal and musical values; his ensemble experience gave him an awareness of finish and refinement that only chamber music may impart; under Arditi he became cognizant of the responsibilities of both concertmaster and contractor. All of these experiences were fused by an innate sense of musical and artistic values, together with a probity that never deserted him. With characteristic simplicity, he states the decision which was to mean so much for the development of music in America: "In 1862 I concluded to devote my energies to the public taste for instrumental music. . . . What this country needed most of all to make it musical was a good orchestra and plenty of concerts within reach of the people." In the beginning, the principal reason for the travels on which he embarked was the very practical one of providing a means for maintaining his orchestra intact. Only gradually as he traveled over "The Great Highway" did the full import of his "later-day task" become manifest. His programs were not planned as single detached units, but as a series intended progressively to elevate the public taste. Where there had been none before, he established standards, not only for his own orchestra, but for other orchestras which were resident in one or another of the cities on his itinerary. He taught his audiences how to distinguish between music as an art and music as mere entertainment. His objective of enlarging the repertoire of the public and broadening its conceptions constituted the broad outline of what Russell so well refers to as the "Grand Design." In a letter to Rose Fay, Thomas wrote, "I believe I am laying a good foundation for what is to come after me." He brought to his hearers an awareness that music could transfigure their lives.

Though he was often referred to as an "educator," he himself was quickest to disavow the didactic and pedantic aspects so often associated with the term. In the essay on "Programme Making," he wrote, "I have never wished to pose as an educator or a philanthropist, except in so far as I might help the public to get beyond certain so-called 'popular music'—which represents nothing more than sweet sentimentalism and rhythm, on the level of the dime novel." His carefully planned programs were consistently enough ahead of his audience to constitute a not unwelcome challenge. Though some of the audience protested and some critics complained, his judgment was eventually proved right.

He believed there was a place for music as an "amusement," but since others could do this adequately enough, it was not his place. He was by no means musically snobbish, nor did he at any time in his career eschew so-called "light" music; it was simply that he considered this type peripheral to his essential repertoire. It was not the attempted intimidations (which frightened him not at all), nor the maliciously false insinuations of commercially minded harp and piano manufacturers which led to his resignation as Music Director of Chicago's World Columbian Exposition. It was rather the discouraging conclusion that, presumably, the Exposition audiences were not attracted to the type of programs he had projected. The harassment no doubt hastened his resignation; it is possible that had circumstances permitted him to wait until the improvement of conditions increased the attendance, he would have found a responsive audience.

For Thomas, conducting was never an end in itself. He was most depressed when circumstances made it impossible for him to exercise his own special talents. In one of his letters written to Rose

Fay during the bleak fall of 1889, he complains bitterly, "What I am doing now others can do as well. What I am good for and my talents and experience have ripened me for and others cannot do, I have no longer any opportunity for. . . . Circumstances force me to prostitute my art and my talent."

Obviously enough, to have accomplished what he did took an enormous ambition—but it was an ambition tempered by vision. Because he saw himself as an instrumentality, and because sympathetic associates recognized the vision as well as the drive, he evoked the deepest friendships and loyalties. On the other hand, because in every sense of the word he kept his own counsel, he often provoked animosity on the part of those who misjudged his reserve. Especially in Chicago, his capacity to fire the imagination and secure the cooperation of people of stature led to a mutually stimulating relationship. Revealing in this respect is a letter of October 26, 1901, from the great architect, Daniel H. Burnham. Both, the architect and the conductor, were builders. Their further kinship was emphasized by a concept and vision common to both, epitomized in Burnham's affirmation, "Make no little plans, they have no magic to stir men's blood . . ." (*Christian Science Monitor,* January 16, 1927).

"I am here in Washington," writes Burnham, ". . . with Olmstead, McKim and St. Gaudens. We have talked of you constantly and wish you were with us and you have come in and taken part almost as if present in body as well as in spirit.

"The Senate appointed us to improve the park system. . . . Again has come the old joy of creating noble things . . . altogether we have risen where I never hoped to tread in this existence. And you have been with us and we all think of how much of our power to dream truly we owe to you, dear friend and comrade."

A few years later, Thomas was to work diligently with Burnham on specific details of the architecture and acoustics of Orchestra Hall. These were matters to which he had given much thought throughout his life. His *Notes on the Construction of Music Halls* written at the request of the architectural writer, Russell Sturgis, was incorporated in a *Dictionary of Architecture* edited by Sturgis and published by the Macmillan Company (1901).

There had been the usual inevitable delays in the construction of the new building; these were complicated by the replanning made necessary by newly-passed ordinances called into being as a result of the Iroquois Theater holocaust of December 30, 1903. Once the building was approximately ready for occupancy, the impatient Thomas began rehearsals there, despite a cold which soon became aggravated by the dampness and drafts of the not-yet-completed structure. In all, he was to conduct but five programs in the new hall. The dedicatory program was given December 14, 1904, the annual Beethoven programs on December 16 and 17, rehearsals resumed on December 19, and on December 23 and 24 two popular concerts were performed. He was by now quite ill; rehearsals, performances, and festivities attendant upon the opening of the new hall allowed but little rest. The cold quickly developed into a grippe, then into a fatal pneumonia. The end came on Wednesday morning, January 4, 1905.

The funeral services were held at St. James Episcopal Church in Chicago on January 6. The final interment was described in a letter from Mrs. Thomas to the then-interim conductor, Frederick Stock: "Will you kindly tell the orchestra for me that we buried Mr. Thomas' remains this noon— Saturday, March 4—in the beautiful cemetery of Mt. Auburn, about three miles from Boston, in the suburb Cambridge.

"There were present only myself, Mr. Thomas' children and a few of his intimate friends. We had no services except the prayers appointed to be read at the grave by the Episcopal Church. . . . There was no music."

During some forty years as a conductor, Thomas had led his troupe across the musical deserts of America, fighting false gods, often disheartened by the misunderstanding of the very people he sought to guide. That he died so shortly after entering the so long dreamt of promised land —a permanent home for his orchestra—was tragic in a personal sense. In a larger sense, he had triumphed; his work had been accomplished, his precepts of taste, repertoire, and performance had become accepted and exemplary standards throughout the land. He had taught his generation, which transmitted this lesson to succeeding generations, that "The greatest enemy is mediocrity." Important as was the work of earlier conductors in America—Hill, Eckert, Eisfeld, Bergmann, Balatka—the accomplishments of his predecessors and most of his contemporaries are dwarfed by the achievements of Thomas. The immigrant youth, left to his own resources from the age of ten, had indeed become a giant among men. Sustained by an indomitable faith and a relentless resolution, he never lost sight of his principal objective. As he grew, so did music in America, through his ten-thousand concerts and twice ten-thousand rehearsals, grow with him. As Mueller points out, "At the time he mounted the podium in Chicago on October 17, 1891, he had behind him a broader disciplined experience, and was intimately familiar with a more extended repertoire than any European conductor of comparable prestige ever accumulates in a lifetime."

Constantly occupied though he was, in the area of his professional activities he still remained the most approachable of men. Amidst letters from Wagner, Strauss, Saint-Saëns, Elgar, MacDowell, Paine, Chadwick, and Parker, one encounters an extensive correspondence with an obscure organist of Bethlehem, Pennsylvania, who had solicited advice concerning a local presentation of Bach's *B Minor Mass,* or with a now-forgotten music instructor in New York who had asked and received assistance in his professional work. Numberless letters from composers, performers, and associates express gratitude for his generosity and aid, admiration for his talent, and from those who had known him many years, the warmth of lasting friendship. Most eloquent is a letter to Thomas from the American violinist Maude Powell, dispatched from England December 16, 1899: ". . . as much as we Americans appreciate and love our Theodore Thomas, we need to spend a time over here . . . in order to arrive at an adequate appreciation of the stupendous work he has done for us. The results are so far-reaching and will continue to be so through so many generations to come that a mighty spiritual monument of appreciation and love and veneration will be built up to stand through all the centuries. . . ."

So was a Great Highway traversed, a Grand Design accomplished. Across the vast continent, wherever he had passed, music was to flourish. Though his very name might be forgotten by many, this was to be his great memorial. For those who would read, there would be, in addition, the record of an inspired and inspiring life.

The republication of the *Autobiography* with Upton's *Reminiscence and Appreciation,* a reminder of our indebtedness to an intrepid pioneer, is a wreath placed in remembrance. But more than this, it is a means of vivifying a monument in Chicago, a statue in Cincinnati—of scaling a mountain called Thomas.

LEON STEIN

*June 30, 1964*

# ACKNOWLEDGMENTS

I AM INDEBTED TO Dr. Lawrence W. Towner and Dr. Donald Krummel of the Newberry Library for making available the letters, scores, and books of the Thomas Collection. I appreciate, also, the cooperation of Silas Edman, Seymour Raven and the Orchestral Association of the Chicago Symphony Orchestra, and the libraries of De Paul and Northwestern Universities for the use of their facilities.

Appreciation is extended to the publishers and copyright holders for permission to quote material from the following books:

**The American Orchestra and Theodore Thomas**
Charles Edward Russell
*Doubleday, Page & Co., Inc., New York (1927)*
**Memoirs of Theodore Thomas**
Rose Fay Thomas
*Moffat, Yard and Co., New York (1911)*
**The Life of Richard Wagner**
Ernest Newman
*Alfred A. Knopf, Inc., New York (1946)*
**The American Symphony Orchestra**
John H. Mueller
*Indiana University Press, Bloomington, Indiana (1951)*
**My Pathway Through Life**
Lilli Lehmann
*G. P. Putnams' Sons, New York (1914)*
**The Chicago Symphony Orchestra**
Philo A. Otis
*Summy-Birchard Co., Evanston, Illinois (1925)*

Unless otherwise identified or attributed, all letters quoted in the Introduction are from the Thomas Collection in the Newberry Library.

LEON STEIN

# CHICAGO SYMPHONY ORCHESTRA*

**Conductors**
Theodore Thomas, 1891-1905
Frederick Stock, 1905-1942
Désiré Defauw, 1943-1947
Artur Rodzinski, 1947-1948
Rafael Kubelik, 1950-1953
Fritz Reiner, 1953-1963
Jean Martinon, 1963-

**Associate Conductors**
Arthur Mees, 1896-1898
Frederick Stock, 1899-1905
Eric De Lamarter, 1918-1936
Hans Lange, 1936-1946
Tauno Hannikainen, 1947-1950
George Schick, 1950-1956
Walter Hendl, 1958-1964
Irwin Hoffman
    *Assistant Conductor,* 1964-

**Managers**
Milward Adams, 1891-1894
George H. Wilson, 1894-1895
Anna Millar, 1895-1899
Frederick J. Wessels, 1899-1926
Henry E. Voegeli
    *Assistant Manager,* 1900-1926
    *Manager,* 1927-1943
George A. Kuyper, 1944-1959
Seymour S. Raven, 1960-1962
    *General Manager,* 1962-1964
Silas Edman, *General Manager,* 1964-

*When it was founded in 1891 the orchestra was called "The Chicago Orchestra." On January 28, 1905, the name was changed to "The Chicago Orchestra founded by Theodore Thomas," and on April 11, 1905, to "The Theodore Thomas Orchestra." Since February 21, 1913, the name "The Chicago Symphony Orchestra founded by Theodore Thomas" has been used.

# THE ORCHESTRAL ASSOCIATION
## OFFICERS OF THE BOARD OF TRUSTEES

## 1912-1913

Bryan Lathrop, *President*
Clyde M. Carr, *First Vice-President*
C. Norman Fay, *Second Vice-President*
Philo A. Otis, *Secretary*
Frederick J. Wessels, *Treasurer*
Henry E. Voegeli, *Assistant Treasurer*

## 1913-1916

Bryan Lathrop, *President*
Clyde M. Carr, *First Vice-President*
Charles H. Hamill, *Second Vice-President*
Philo A. Otis, *Secretary*
Frederick J. Wessels, *Treasurer*
Henry E. Voegeli, *Assistant Treasurer*

## 1916-1919

Clyde M. Carr, *President*
Charles H. Hamill, *First Vice-President*
Joseph Adams, *Second Vice-President*
Philo A. Otis, *Secretary*
Frederick J. Wessels, *Treasurer*
Henry E. Voegeli, *Assistant Treasurer*

## 1919-1923

Clyde M. Carr, *President*
Charles H. Hamill, *Vice-President*
Joseph Adams, *Second Vice-President*
Horace S. Oakley, *Third Vice-President*
Philo A. Otis, *Secretary*
Frederick J. Wessels, *Treasurer*
Henry E. Voegeli, *Assistant Treasurer*

## 1923-1924

Charles H. Hamill, *President*
Horace S. Oakley, *First Vice-President*
Joseph Adams, *Second Vice-President*
Philo A. Otis, *Secretary*
Frederick J. Wessels, *Treasurer*
Henry E. Voegeli, *Assistant Treasurer*

## 1924-1927

Charles H. Hamill, *President*
Horace S. Oakley, *Vice-President*
Joseph Adams, *Second Vice-President*
Augustus S. Peabody, *Third Vice-President*
Philo A. Otis, *Secretary*
Frederick J. Wessels, *Treasurer*
  (resigned Dec. 31, 1926; replaced by Henry E. Voegeli)
Henry E. Voegeli, *Assistant Treasurer*

## 1927-1929

Charles H. Hamill, *President*
Horace S. Oakley, *Vice-President*
Joseph Adams, *Second Vice-President*
Augustus S. Peabody, *Third Vice-President*
Philo A. Otis, *Secretary*
Henry E. Voegeli, *Treasurer*

## 1929-1931

Charles H. Hamill, *President*
Joseph Adams, *Vice-President*
Augustus S. Peabody, *Second Vice-President*
Ezra J. Warner, *Third Vice-President*
Philo A. Otis, *Secretary* (died Sept. 23, 1930)
Chalkley J. Hambleton, *Secretary* (elected Oct. 10, 1930)
Henry E. Voegeli, *Treasurer*
Charles F. Bostetter, *Assistant Secretary*

## 1931-1933

Charles H. Hamill, *President*
Joseph Adams, *Vice-President*
Augustus S. Peabody, *Second Vice-President*
Ezra J. Warner, *Third Vice-President* (died May 9, 1933)
Chalkley J. Hambleton, *Secretary*
Henry E. Voegeli, *Treasurer*
Charles F. Bostetter, *Assistant Secretary*

## 1933-1934

Charles H. Hamill, *President*
Joseph Adams, *Vice-President*
Augustus S Peabody, *Second Vice-President*
  (died April 27, 1934)

Charles H. Swift, *Third Vice-President*
Chalkley J. Hambleton, *Secretary*
Henry E. Voegeli, *Treasurer*
Charles F. Bostetter, *Assistant Secretary*

## 1934-1938

Charles H. Hamill, *President*
Albert A. Sprague, *Vice-President*
Edward L. Ryerson, *Second Vice-President*
Charles H. Swift, *Third Vice-President*
Chalkley J. Hambleton, *Secretary*
Henry E. Voegeli, *Treasurer*
Charles F. Bostetter, *Assistant Secretary*

## 1938-1941

Charles H. Hamill, *Honorary President*
  (died August 10, 1941)
Edward L. Ryerson, *President*
Albert A. Sprague, *Vice-President*
Charles H. Swift, *Second Vice-President*
Arthur G. Cable, *Third Vice-President*
Chalkley J. Hambleton, *Secretary*
Henry E. Voegeli, *Treasurer*
Charles F. Bostetter, *Assistant Secretary*

## 1941-1945

Edward L. Ryerson, *President*
Albert A. Sprague, *Vice-President*
Charles H. Swift, *Vice-President*
Arthur G. Cable, *Vice-President* (died April 12, 1945)
Chalkley J. Hambleton, *Secretary*
Francis M. Knight, *Treasurer*
Henry E. Voegeli, *Assistant Treasurer*
  (died December 28, 1943)
Charles F. Bostetter, *Assistant Secretary*
  (died February 2, 1943)
Ruth H. Carroll, *Assistant Secretary*

## 1945-1946

Edward L. Ryerson, *President*
Cyrus H. Adams, *Vice-President*
Albert A. Sprague, *Vice-President*

Charles H. Swift, *Vice-President*
Chalkley J. Hambleton, *Secretary*
Francis M. Knight, *Treasurer*

**1946-1948**
Edward L. Ryerson, *President*
Cyrus H. Adams, *Vice-President*
Arthur B. Hall, *Vice-President*
Charles H. Swift, *Vice-President*
Chalkley J. Hambleton, *Secretary*
Francis M. Knight, *Treasurer*
Ruth H. Carroll, *Assistant Secretary*

**1948-1952**
Edward L. Ryerson, *President*
Cyrus H. Adams, *Vice-President*
Eric Oldberg, *Vice-President*
Charles H. Swift, *Vice-President, Honorary*
    (died Sept. 30, 1948)
Chalkley J. Hambleton, *Secretary*
Francis M. Knight, *Treasurer*
Ruth H. Carroll, *Assistant Secretary*

**1952-1956**
Eric Oldberg, *President*
Edward L. Ryerson, *Honorary President*
Daniel H. Burnham, *Vice-President*
Arnold Horween, *Vice-President*
Edward D. McDougal, Jr., *Vice-President*
Donald F. McClure, *Secretary*
Francis M. Knight, *Treasurer*

**1956-1957**
Eric Oldberg, *President*
Graham Aldis, *Vice-President*
Arnold Horween, *Vice-President*
Edward D. McDougal, Jr., *Vice-President*
Donald F. McClure, *Secretary*
Francis M. Knight, *Treasurer*

**1957-1958**
Eric Oldberg, *President*
Edward D. McDougal, Jr., *Vice-President*

Graham Aldis, *Vice-President*
Leigh B. Block, *Vice-President*
Donald F. McClure, *Secretary*
Francis M. Knight, *Treasurer*

**1958-1963**

Eric Oldberg, *President*
Edward D. McDougal, Jr., *Vice-President*
Graham Aldis, *Vice-President*
Leigh B. Block, *Vice-President*
Merrill Shepard, *Secretary*
Donald F. McClure, *Treasurer*

**1963-**

Merrill Shepard, *President*
Edward D. McDougal, Jr., *Vice-President*
Leigh B. Block, *Vice-President*
Theodore Tieken, *Vice-President*
Rosecrans Baldwin, *Secretary*
James C. Hemphill, *Treasurer*

# CHICAGO SYMPHONY ORCHESTRA
### SEVENTY-FOURTH SEASON · · · 1964-1965

**JEAN MARTINON, Music Director**

SILAS EDMAN, General Manager

CHARLES O. BOARDMAN, Manager, Operations

LEIF THORNE-THOMSEN, Manager,
Community Affairs

RUTH H. CARROLL, Assistant Secretary

**Violins**

Steven Staryk
Victor Aitay
Francis Akos
Paul Kahn
Josef Faerber
Frank Fiatarone
Perry Crafton
Victor Charbulak
Theodore Silavin
Edward Gradman
Raymond Niwa
Jerry Sabransky
Charles Zika
Samuel Siegel
Otakar Sroubek
Joseph Michalek
Edgar Muenzer
Samuel Magad

John Weicher
Leon Brenner
Royal Johnson
Sol Spector
William Faldner
Morris Monitz
Philip Scharf
Max Wexler

Joseph Golan
Michael Rill
Adrian Daprato
James Hansen
Joseph Kovacs
Norbert Mueller
Bohuslav Harvanek
Sol Turner
Arnold Brostoff

**Violas**

Milton Preves
William York
Robert Glazer
Isadore Zverow
Sheppard Lehnhoff
Harold Sorin
Samuel Feinzimer
Robert Alexa
Donald Evans
Guido Rizzo
Robert Coleman

**Cellos**

Frank Miller
Leonard Chausow
Joseph Sciacchitano
Robert Smith

A51

Joseph Saunders
Alois Trnka
Philip Blum
David Greenbaum
Nicolai Zedeler
Margaret Evans
Leonore Glazer

**Basses**
Joseph Guastafeste
James Vrhel
Warren Benfield
Radivoj Lah
Wayne Balmer
Vladimir Kalina
Alfred Kovar
James Palecek
Nathan Zimberoff

**Harps**
Edward Druzinsky
Lynne Turner

**Flutes**
Donald Peck
Joane Bennett
Ralph Johnson
Walfrid Kujala

**Oboes**
Ray Still
Grover Schiltz
Richard Kanter
De Vere Moore

**Clarinets**
Clark Brody
Jerome Stowell
Walter Wollwage
George Weber

**Bassoons**
Willard Elliot
John Raitt
Wilbur Simpson
Richard Lottridge

**Horns**
Clarendon Van Norman
Frank Brouk
Clyde Wedgwood
Joseph Mourek
Richard Oldberg

**Trumpets**
Adolph Herseth
Vincent Cichowicz
Frank Kaderabek
William Scarlett

**Trombones**
Robert Lambert
Frank Crisafulli
Edward Kleinhammer
Jay Friedman

**Tuba**
Arnold Jacobs

**Timpani**
Donald Koss

**Percussion**
Gordon Peters
James Ross
Sam Denov
Albert Payson

**Librarian**
John Klima

**Custodian**
  **of Library**
Lionel Sayers

## CHICAGO SYMPHONY ORCHESTRA
### WORLD PREMIERES — 1906-1964
*(Regular Subscription Concerts)*
For a listing of works introduced into this country by Mr. Thomas see page 353.

| Composer | Composition | Conductor | Date |
| --- | --- | --- | --- |
| Stock | Symphonic Poem, *Eines Menschenlebens Morgen, Mittag und Abend* | Stock | Apr. 7-8, 1906 |
| Stock | Festival March | Stock | Oct. 14-15, 1910 |
| Smith, D. S. | Symphony, F Minor, Op. 28 | Stock | Dec. 13-14, 1912 |
| Oldberg | Theme and Variations for Orchestra, Op. 19 | Stock | Jan. 10-11, 1913 |
| De Lamarter | Symphony, D Major | Stock | Jan. 23-24, 1914 |
| Oldberg | Symphonic Variations for Organ and Orchestra, Op. 35 | Stock | Feb. 6-7, 1914 |
| Stock | Overture, *Life's Spring-Tide* | Stock | Mar. 27-28, 1914 |
| Weidig | Symphonic Suite | Stock | Dec. 18-19, 1914 |
| Carpenter | Suite, *Adventures in a Perambulator* | Stock | Mar. 19-20, 1915 |
| Oldberg | Rhapsody, *June* | Stock | Apr. 16-17, 1915 |
| Stock | *Festival Prologue* | Stock | Oct. 15-16, 1915 |
| Carpenter | Concertino for Pianoforte and Orchestra | Stock | Mar. 10-11, 1916 |
| Brune | *Overture to a Drama* | Stock | Apr. 14-15, 1916 |

| Composer | Composition | Conductor | Date |
|---|---|---|---|
| Otterstrom | Suite, *American Negro* | Stock | Dec. 15-16, 1916 |
| Borowski | Overture to *Anacréon* | Stock | Mar. 9-10, 1917 |
| De Lamarter | *Fable of the Hapless Folk Tune* | Stock | Apr. 6-7, 1917 |
| Oldberg | Fantasy, *At Night*, Op. 38 | Stock | Apr. 13-14, 1917 |
| Borowski | *Peintures* | Stock | Jan. 25-26, 1918 |
| Sowerby | *A Set of Four*, "Suite of Ironics" | Stock | Feb. 15-16, 1918 |
| Stock | Overture to a Romantic Comedy | Stock | Mar. 15-16, 1918 |
| Mason, D. G. | *Russians*, for Baritone and Orchestra | Stock | Nov. 15-16, 1918 |
| Avery | Overture, *The Taming of the Shrew* | Smith | Feb. 7-8, 1919 |
| Borowski | Suite from the Ballet-Pantomime, *Boudour* | Borowski | Feb. 14-15, 1919 |
| Stock | *March and Hymn to Democracy* | Stock | Feb. 28-Mar. 1, 1919 |
| Cole, R. | *Pioneer Overture (1818-1918)* | Stock | Mar. 14-15, 1919 |
| Brune | A Fairy Tale | Stock | Mar. 19-20, 1920 |
| De Lamarter | Concerto for Organ, E Major | Stock | Apr. 2-3, 1920 |
| Bax | Symphonic Poem, *The Garden of Fand* | Stock | Oct. 29-30, 1920 |
| Mason, D. G. | *Prelude and Fugue*, for Piano and Orchestra | Stock | Mar. 4-5, 1921 |

| Composer | Work | Conductor | Date |
| --- | --- | --- | --- |
| Liszt | Concerto Pathètique for Two Pianos (orchestration by Lee Pattison) | Stock | Nov. 25-26, 1921 |
| Prokofiev | Concerto No. 3 in C Major, for Pianoforte and Orchestra | Prokofiev | Dec. 16-17, 1921 |
| Carpenter | Krazy Kat | Stock | Dec. 23-24, 1921 |
| De Lamarter | Concerto No. 2, A Major, for Organ | Stock | Feb. 24-25, 1922 |
| Sowerby | Symphony No. 1 | Stock | Apr. 7-8, 1922 |
| Stock | Elegy | Stock | Oct. 12-13, 1923 |
| Glière | Symphony No. 3, B Minor, Ilya Murometz | Stock | Mar. 21-22, 1924 |
| Collins | Mardi Gras | Stock | Mar. 28-29, 1924 |
| Collins | Concerto for Pianoforte, E flat major | Stock | Mar. 27-28, 1925 |
| Borowski | Tone Poem, Semiramis | Stock | Nov. 13-14, 1925 |
| Wald | Retrospectives | Stock | Jan. 15-16, 1926 |
| Whithorne | Poem for Piano and Orchestra | Stock | Feb. 4-5, 1927 |
| Oldberg | Symphony No. 3, F. Minor, Op. 41 | Stock | Mar. 18-19, 1927 |
| Brune | Allegro Assai, from Symphony No. 2, E Minor, Op. 29 | Stock | Apr. 1-2, 1927 |
| Noelte | Suite for String Orchestra and Kettledrums | Stock | Mar. 23-24, 1928 |
| Schoenefeld | Concerto for Violoncello, Op. 80 | Stock | Mar. 30-31, 1928 |
| La Violette | Penetrella, for String Orchestra | Stock | Nov. 30-Dec. 1, 1928 |

| Composer | Composition | Conductor | Date |
| --- | --- | --- | --- |
| Bloch | *America,* an Epic Rhapsody in Three Parts (simultaneous premiere with New York, Boston, Philadelphia, San Francisco, and Cincinnati) | Stock | Dec. 21-22, 1928 |
| Stock | Concerto for Violoncello and Orchestra, D Minor | Stock | Jan. 25-26, 1929 |
| Lockwood, N. | Suite, *Odysseus* | Stock | Mar. 22-23, 1929 |
| Sowerby | Symphony No. 2, B Minor | Stock | Mar. 29-30, 1929 |
| Bach, J. S. | Passacaglia and Fugue, C Minor (transcribed for modern orchestra by Frederick Stock) | Stock | Jan. 3-4, 1930 |
| Rameau | Suite from *Dardanus* <br> Minuet <br> Rondeau Tendre <br> Tambourin I and II | De Lamarter | Feb. 27-28, 1931 |
| De Lamarter | Suite from *The Dance of Life* | De Lamarter | Feb. 27-28, 1931 |
| Bach, J. S. | Prelude and Fugue ("St. Anne's"), E Flat Major (transcribed for modern orchestra by Frederick Stock) | Stock | Apr. 3-4, 1931 |
| Brune | Overture to a Tragedy, Op. 62 | Stock | Apr. 17-18, 1931 |
| Whithorne | Concerto for Violin | Stock | Nov. 12-13, 1931 |

| Composer | Work | Conductor | Date |
|---|---|---|---|
| La Violette | *Dedications,* Concerto for Violin and Orchestra | Stock | Nov. 26-27, 1931 |
| Collins | Concert Piece for Piano and Orchestra, A Minor | Stock | Dec. 3-4, 1931 |
| Froberger, J. | Suite, E Minor (17th Century) (arranged for orchestra by Eric De Lamarter) | Stock | Jan. 7-8, 1932 |
| Bloch, E. | *Helvetia, the Land of Mountains and its People: A Symphonic Freso,* for Orchestra | Stock | Feb. 18-19, 1932 |
| Mueller, F. | *Two Symphonic Sketches* | Stock | Mar. 10-11, 1932 |
| Stock | *A Musical Self-Portrait* | Stock | Apr. 14-15, 1932 |
| Carpenter | *Song of Faith,* for Chorus and Orchestra | Stock | Feb. 23, 1932 |
| Rosales | Three Spanish Dances | Stock | Dec. 15-16, 1932 |
| Glazunov | *Concerto-Ballata,* for Violoncello and Orchestra | Stock | Dec. 15-16, 1932 |
| Kieter | Concerto for Pianoforte and Orchestra, B Minor | Stock | Feb. 2-3, 1933 |
| De Lamarter | Symphony No. 3, E Major | Sanders, R. | Feb. 16-17, 1933 |
| Borowski | Symphony No. 1 | Stock | Mar. 16-17, 1933 |
| Carpenter | *Sea Drift* | Stock | Nov. 30-Dec. 1, 1933 |

| Composer | Composition | Conductor | Date |
|---|---|---|---|
| Sowerby | Passacaglia, Interlude, and Fugue | Stock | Feb. 22-23, 1934 |
| Whitney, R. | *Concerto Grosso* | Stock | Apr. 5-6, 1934 |
| Bach, J. S. | Fantasia and Fugue, G Minor (transcribed for modern orchestra by Frederick Stock) | Stock | Nov. 1-2, 1934 |
| Zemachson | Concerto Grosso, E Minor, Op. 8 | Stock | Nov. 29-30, 1934 |
| Lieberson, G. | Suite, *In a Winter Garden* | Stock | Mar. 14-15, 1935 |
| Brune | Tone Poem, *At Bernina Falls*, Op. 83 | Stock | Apr. 4-5, 1935 |
| Van Vactor | *Concerto Grosso*, for Three Flutes, Harp, and Orchestra | Stock | Apr. 4-5, 1935 |
| Lockwood, N. | Symphony, *A Year's Chronicle* | Stock | Apr. 4-5, 1935 |
| Gruenberg, L. | *Serenade to a Beauteous Lady* | Stock | Apr. 4-5, 1935 |
| Haubiel | *Rittrati (Portraits)* | Stock | Dec. 12-13, 1935 |
| Cole, R. | Suite from *The Maypole Lovers* | Stock | Jan. 9-10, 1936 |
| Sanders, R. | *The Tragic Muse — Five Impressions* (now known as *Scenes of Poverty and Toil*) | Sanders | Jan. 30-31, 1936 |
| Zimbalist, E. | *American Rhapsody* | Zimbalist | Mar. 5-6, 1936 |

| | | | |
|---|---|---|---|
| Schumann, R. | *Fantasie* for Violin and Orchestra, A Minor, Op. 131 (freely transcribed by Fritz Kreisler) | Stock | Oct. 29-30, 1936 |
| Tchaikovsky | Trio, for Pianoforte, Violin, and Violoncello, A Minor, Op. 50 (transcribed for modern orchestra by Frederick Stock) | Stock | Nov. 12-13, 1936 |
| Noelte | *Four Symphonic Impressions*, Op. 29 | Stock | Feb. 18-19, 1937 |
| Oldberg | Symphonic Poem, *The Sea*, Op. 47 | Lange | Mar. 11-12, 1937 |
| Carpenter | Concerto for Violin and Orchestra | Stock | Nov. 18-19, 1937 |
| Kurthy | Symphonic Rhapsody, *Puszta* | Lange | Jan. 13-14, 1938 |
| Bach, J. S. | Canzona and Fugue, G Minor (transcribed for modern orchestra by Frederick Stock) | Lange | Feb. 3-4, 1938 |
| Bach, J. S. | Prelude, C Sharp Minor, from *The Well-Tempered Clavier* (arranged for orchestra by Frederick Stock) | Stock | Apr. 14-15, 1938 |
| Bach, J. S. | Chorale Prelude, "A Mighty Fortress Is Our God" (freely transcribed for orchestra by Frederick Stock) | Stock | Oct. 13-14, 1938 |
| Stringham, E. | *Nocturne* for Orchestra, No. 2 | Lange | Mar. 30-31, 1939 |
| Jacobi | Concerto for Violin and Orchestra | Stock | Mar. 14, 1939 |

| Composer | Composition | Conductor | Date |
| --- | --- | --- | --- |
| Martin, C. | Nocturno | Stock | Mar. 14, 1939 |
| Dumler, M. | Suite for Orchestra, No. 1 | Stock | Apr. 15, 1939 |
| Bach, J. S. | Prelude and Fugue, B Minor (transcribed for modern orchestra by Gardner Read) | Stock | Nov. 2-3, 1939 |
| Stock | Festival Fanfare* | Stock | Oct. 10-11, 1940 |
| Milhaud | Symphony No. 1* | Milhaud | Oct. 17-18, 1940 |
| Carpenter | Symphony in C* | Stock | Oct. 24-25, 1940 |
| Harris, R. | American Creed, for Chorus and Orchestra* | Stock | Oct. 31-Nov. 1, 1940 |
| Stravinsky | Symphony in C* | Stravinsky | Nov. 6-7, 1940 |
| Gassman | Symphonic Overture, G Major | Lange | Dec. 13-14, 1940 |
| Miaskovsky | Symphonie Fantasie, F Sharp Minor (now known as Symphony No. 21)* | Stock | Dec. 26-27, 1940 |
| Noelte | Prologue to a Romantic Drama, Op. 35 | Stock | Jan. 16-17, 1941 |
| Kodály | Concerto for Orchestra* | Stock | Feb. 6-7, 1941 |
| Eppert, C. | Two Symphonic Impressions* (First prize winner in Chicago Symphony's Golden Jubilee Contest for American Composers) | Stock | Feb. 13-14, 1941 |

| Ganz, R. | Concerto for Piano, E Flat Major, Op. 32 (now known as *Konzertstück*)* | Stock | Feb. 20-21, 1941 |
|---|---|---|---|
| Sowerby | Symphony No. 3, F Sharp Minor* | Stock | Mar. 6-7, 1941 |
| Glière | Overture, *Fête Ferganaise*, Op. 75 | Stock | Mar. 20-21, 1941 |
| Casella, A. | Symphony No. III, Op. 63* | Stock | Mar. 27-28, 1941 |
| Walton | *Scapino*, A Comedy Overture* | Stock | Apr. 3-4, 1941 |
| Milhaud | Concerto No. 2 for Pianoforte and Orchestra | Lange | Dec. 18-19, 1941 |
| Zádor | Pastorale and Tarantella | Stock | Feb. 5-6, 1942 |
| Mueller, F. | *Five Symphonic Etudes*, Based on the American Folk Song, "El-A-Noy" | Stock | Feb. 5-6, 1942 |
| Van Vactor | *Gothic Impressions* (now known as *Variazioni Solenne*) | Stock | Feb. 26-27, 1942 |
| Lévy, H. | *Twenty-four Variations on an Original Theme* | Stock | Apr. 9-10, 1942 |
| Oldberg | Symphony No. 4, B Minor, Op. 50 | Lange | Dec. 31, 1942-Jan. 1, 1943 |
| Collins | Concerto for Pianoforte, No. 3, B Minor | Lange | Mar. 25-26, 1943 |

*Dedicated to and written for the Chicago Symphony Orchestra on the occasion of its Golden Jubilee Season.

| Composer | Composition | Conductor | Date |
|---|---|---|---|
| Schubert, F. | Quintet for Strings, C Major, Op. 163 (arranged for orchestra by Frederick Stock) | Defauw | Oct. 14-15, 1943 |
| Zádor | Biblical Triptych in Three Movements for Grand Orchestra | Lange | Dec. 9-10, 1943 |
| Borowski | Requiem for a Child | Defauw | Mar. 15-16, 1945 |
| de Bourguignon | Concerto Grosso, Op. 82 | Defauw | Oct. 17-18, 1946 |
| Oldberg | Concerto for Violin, D Minor, Op. 46 | Defauw | Nov. 7-8, 1946 |
| Still | Wood Notes | Rodzinski | Apr. 22-23, 1948 |
| Britten | Five French Folk Songs, for Baritone and Orchestra | F. Busch | Dec. 23-24, 1948 |
| Oldberg | Symphony No. 5, E Minor, Op. 54 | Szell | Jan. 19-20, 1950 |
| Tcherepnin, A. | Symphony No. 2, E Flat Major, Op. 77 | Kubelik | Mar. 20-21, 1952 |
| Harris, R. | Symphony No. 7 (in one movement) | Kubelik | Nov. 20-21, 1952 |
| Bloch, E. | Suite Hébraïque, for Viola and Orchestra | Kubelik | Jan. 1-2, 1953 |
| Read, G. | The Temptation of St. Anthony, Dance Symphony in One Movement and Four Scenes, Op. 56 | Kubelik | Apr. 9-10, 1953 |
| Barber, S. | Souvenirs, Op. 28 | Reiner | Nov. 12-13, 1953 |

| | | | |
|---|---|---|---|
| Schreiber, F. C. | Concerto Grosso for Four Solo Instruments and Orchestra | Reiner | Mar. 3-4, 1955 |
| Turner, C. | Encounter | Reiner | Oct. 18-19, 1956 |
| Tcherepnin, A. | Divertimento | Reiner | Nov. 14-15, 1957 |
| Copland, A. | Suite from The Tender Land | Reiner | Apr. 10-11, 1958 |
| Bennett, R. | Symphony | Reiner | Apr. 11-12, 1963 |

## CHICAGO SYMPHONY ORCHESTRA

### AMERICAN PREMIERES — 1908-1964

*(Regular Subscription Concerts)*

For a listing of works introduced into this country by Mr. Thomas see page 353.

| Composer | Composition | Conductor | Date |
|---|---|---|---|
| Noren | *Kaleidoscope*, Op. 30 | Stock | Oct. 30-31, 1908 |
| Sinigaglia | Overture, *Le Baruffe Chiozzotte*, Op. 32 | Stock | Dec. 11-12, 1908 |
| Klose | Prelude and Double Fugue, on a Theme by Bruckner, for Organ, Four Trumpets, and Four Trombones | Stock | Jan. 8-9, 1909 |
| Widor | *Sinfonia Sacra*, Op. 81, for Organ and Orchestra | Stock | Jan. 8-9, 1909 |
| Schumann, G. | Overture, *Lebensfreude* | Stock | Mar. 8-9, 1912 |
| Bach-Busoni | *Fantasia Contrappuntistica* (arranged for orchestra by Frederick Stock) | Stock | Mar. 29-30, 1912 |
| Straesser | Symphony, G Major, Op. 22 | Stock | Nov. 15-16, 1912 |
| Mraczek | "Symphonic Burleske" after Wilhelm Busch's *Max und Moritz* | Stock | Dec. 20-21, 1912 |
| Kaun | *On the Rhine (Wanderings of Jolly Fellows)*, Op. 90 | Stock | Jan. 31-Feb. 1, 1913 |

| Composer | Work | Conductor | Date |
|---|---|---|---|
| Schoenberg | Five Pieces for Orchestra, Op. 16 | Stock | Oct. 31-Nov. 1, 1913 |
| Delius | Life's Dance | Stock | Nov. 7-8, 1913 |
| Glière | Symphonic Poem, The Sirens, Op. 33 | Stock | Dec. 5-6, 1913 |
| Noren | Concerto for Violin, A Minor, Op. 38 | Stock | Dec. 5-6, 1913 |
| Casella | Rhapsody, Italia, Op. 11 | Stock | Dec. 26-27, 1913 |
| Korngold | Sinfonietta, Op. 5 | Stock | Apr. 3-4, 1914 |
| Stephan | Music for Orchestra, in One Movement | Stock | Jan. 8-9, 1915 |
| Scriabin | Prometheus, or The Poem of Fire, Op. 60 | Stock | Mar. 5-6, 1915 |
| Granados, E. | Symphonic Poem, Dante | Stock | Nov. 5-6, 1915 |
| Alfvén | Symphony No. 3, E Major | Stock | Nov. 19-20, 1915 |
| Strauss, R. | Aria, "Grossmächtige Prinzessin," from Ariadne auf Naxos | Stock | Nov. 16-17, 1917 |
| Widor | Salvum Fac Populum Tuum | Stock | Dec. 14-15, 1917 |
| Glière | Symphony No. 3, B Minor, Op. 42 | Stock | Jan. 18-19, 1918 |
| Tommasini | Moonlights | Stock | Mar. 7-8, 1919 |
| d'Indy | La Queste de Dieu | Stock | Oct. 31-Nov. 1, 1919 |
| Roussel | Les Evocations, Op. 15, No. 2 (La Ville Rose) | Stock | Nov. 28-29, 1919 |

| Composer | Composition | Conductor | Date |
|---|---|---|---|
| Holst | The Planets, Op. 32 | Stock | Dec. 31-Jan. 1, 1921 |
| Mahler | Symphony No. 7, E Minor | Stock | Apr. 15-16, 1921 |
| Malipiero | Symphonic Illustrations, "For a Knightly Story" | Stock | Jan. 20-21, 1922 |
| Mraczek | Symphonic Poem, Eva | Stock | Feb. 10-11, 1922 |
| Respighi | Ballata delle gnomidi | Stock | Mar. 3-4, 1922 |
| Bax | Symphonic Poem, November Woods | Stock | Nov. 3-4, 1922 |
| Goossens, E. | The Eternal Rhythm | Stock | Nov. 17-18, 1922 |
| Pick-Mangiagalli | Symphonic Poem, Op. 39 | Stock | Feb. 23-24, 1923 |
| Panizza | Tema con Variaciones | Panizza | Jan. 25-26, 1924 |
| Bach, C.P.E. | Concerto | Stock | Feb. 15-16, 1924 |
| Bax | Symphony, E Flat Minor | Stock | Mar. 14-15, 1924 |
| Perinello | Symphonic Poem, The Dying Swan | Stock | Apr. 11-12, 1924 |
| Respighi | Concerto Gregoriano, for Violin and Orchestra | Stock | Oct. 31-Nov.1, 1924 |
| Bartók | Dance Suite [for orchestra] | Stock | Nov. 20-21, 1925 |
| Castaldi | Symphonic Poem, Marsyas | Stock | Dec. 18-19, 1925 |
| Strauss, R. | Interlude Waltz Scene from Intermezzo, Op. 72 | Stock | Oct. 22-23, 1926 |

| Composer | Work | Conductor | Date |
|---|---|---|---|
| Ibert | Concerto for Cello and Wind Instruments | Stock | Nov. 12-13, 1926 |
| Schumann, G. | Variations and Gigue on a Theme by Handel | Stock | Feb. 11-12, 1927 |
| Tartini | Pastorale, A Major, for Violin and String Orchestra | Stock | Oct. 28-29, 1927 |
| Vladigerov | Concerto for Violin and Orchestra, Op. 11 | Stock | Oct. 28-29, 1927 |
| Reger | Variations and Fugue on a Theme by Bach for Piano and Orchestra | Stock | Dec. 30-31, 1927 |
| Inghelbrecht | For the Day of the First Snow in Old Japan [ballet] | Stock | Jan. 25-26, 1929 |
| Casella | Concerto for Violin and Orchestra, A Minor | Stock | Feb. 1-2, 1929 |
| Giuranna | Marionette | Stock | Feb. 8-9, 1929 |
| Giuranna | Suite, Apina Stolen by the Dwarfs of the Mountain | Stock | Feb. 8-9, 1929 |
| Prokofiev | Divertissement, Op. 43 | Prokofiev | Feb. 25, 1930 |
| Pedrotti | Nocturne | De Lamarter | Jan. 13, 1931 |
| Ferroud | Symphony, A Major | Stock | Oct. 22-23, 1931 |
| Trapp | Symphony No. 4, B Minor, Op. 24 | Stock | Mar. 10-11, 1932 |
| Miaskovsky | Symphony No. 12, G Minor, Op. 35 | Stock | Dec. 22-23, 1933 |

| Composer | Composition | Conductor | Date |
| --- | --- | --- | --- |
| Handel | Concerto, D Major, for orchestra with organ (transcribed by Sir Hamilton Harty) | Harty | Jan. 9, 1934 |
| Miaskovsky | Symphony No. 13, B Flat Minor, Op. 36 | Stock | Nov. 15-16, 1934 |
| Trapp | Concerto for Pianoforte, D Major, Op. 26 | Stock | Nov. 29-30, 1934 |
| Walton | Symphony No. 1 | Harty | Jan. 23-24, 1936 |
| Golestan | *Concerto Moldave*, for Violoncello and Orchestra | Lange | Feb. 8, 1938 |
| Kreutzer, R. | *Perpetuum Mobile* (based on a Kreutzer etude, arranged by Max Schönherr) | Stock | Oct. 13-14, 1938 |
| Miaskovsky | Symphony No. 15, D Minor, Op. 38 | Stock | Oct. 20-21, 1938 |
| Höller | *Hymns on Four Gregorian Melodies* | Stock | Nov. 3-4, 1938 |
| Bartók | Concerto for Pianoforte and Orchestra, No. 2 | Stock | Mar. 2-3, 1939 |
| Brusselmans | Suite after the Caprices by Paganini | Stock | Oct. 12-13, 1939 |
| Babin | Concerto for Two Pianos and Orchestra | Lange | Nov. 23-24, 1939 |
| Muradeli | Symphony No. 1, B Minor | Stock | Feb. 15-16, 1940 |

| Composer | Work | Conductor | Date |
|---|---|---|---|
| Rossi, S. | Symphonia for Double Orchestra (newly scored and arranged by Max Sinzheimer) | Lange | Dec. 21-22, 1944 |
| Miaskovsky | Homage Overture, Op. 48 | Defauw | Oct. 4-5, 1945 |
| Franck | Chorale and Variations, B Minor (transcribed for orchestra by Désiré Defauw) | Defauw | Oct. 3-4, 1946 |
| Braga | Variation on a Brazilian Theme | Carvalho | Feb. 12-13, 1948 |
| Martin, F. | Symphonie Concertante, for piano, harpsichord, and harp, with double small string orchestra | Ansermet | Feb. 19-20, 1948 |
| Siqueira | "Tango, Toada, Côco" from the First Suite, Nordestina | Carvalho | Feb. 10, 1948 |
| Rieti | Symphony No. 5 | Kubelik | Oct. 19-20, 1950 |
| Jirák | Symphony No. 5, Op. 60 | Kubelik | Dec. 13-14, 1951 |
| Rosenberg, H. | Concerto for Orchestra | Kubelik | Oct. 30-31, 1952 |
| Ibert | Le Chevalier Errant (Suite Symphonique) [ballet] | Schick | Nov. 27-28, 1952 |
| Vaughan Williams | Sinfonia Antartica | Kubelik | Apr. 2-3, 1953 |
| Arnold, M. | Symphony No. 2, Op. 40 | Reiner | Dec. 13-14, 1956 |
| Henze | Five Neapolitan Songs | Hendl | Nov. 24-25, 1960 |
| Martinon | Concerto for Violin, No. 2, Op. 51 | Martinon | Nov. 14-15, 1963 |

# THEODORE THOMAS
## A MUSICAL AUTOBIOGRAPHY

THEODORE THOMAS

*From a photograph taken in 1896*

# THEODORE THOMAS
## A MUSICAL AUTOBIOGRAPHY

EDITED BY
## GEORGE P. UPTON

In Two Volumes, with Portraits and Views

### VOL. I.
*LIFE WORK*

WITH AN APPRECIATION AND PERSONAL RECOLLECTION, AND A DETAILED
ACCOUNT OF HIS MORE IMPORTANT WORK, BY MR. UPTON,
AND AN APPENDIX

### VOL. II.
*CONCERT PROGRAMMES*

WITH AN INTRODUCTION BY MR. THOMAS, SETTING FORTH HIS SYSTEM OF
PROGRAMME-MAKING, AND COMMENTING ON HABITUAL LATE-
COMERS AND MODERN ORCHESTRA TECHNIQUE

CHICAGO
A. C. McCLURG & CO.
1905

The Lakeside Press
R. R. DONNELLEY & SONS COMPANY
CHICAGO

"*A SYMPHONY orchestra shows the culture of a community, not opera. The man who does not know Skakespeare is to be pitied; and the man who does not understand Beethoven and has not been under his spell has not half lived his life. The master works of instrumental music are the language of the soul and express more than those of any other art. Light music, 'popular' so called, is the sensual side of the art and has more or less devil in it.*"

—THEODORE THOMAS

"*THROUGHOUT my life my aim has been to make good music popular, and it now appears that I have only done the public justice in believing, and acting constantly on the belief, that the people would enjoy and support the best in art when continually set before them in a clear and intelligent manner.*"

FROM LETTER OF MR. THOMAS TO THE DIRECTORS
OF THE BROOKLYN PHILHARMONIC SOCIETY, 1874.

# CONTENTS

# CONTENTS

6

8 CONTENTS

## APPENDIX

# LIST OF ILLUSTRATIONS

# THE MASTER OF MUSIC

In Memoriam
### Theodore Thomas
1905

## BY HENRY VAN DYKE

Power of architect, power of painter, and sculptor, and bard,
   Living forever in temple, and picture, and statue, and song,
Look how the world with the lights that ye lit is engirdled and
      starred!
   Brief was the flame of your life, but the lamps of your art
      burn long.

Where is the master of music, and how has he vanished away?
   Where are the works that he wrought in the air as a palace
      of dream?
Gone—all gone—like the light on the cloud at the close of the
      day!
   Darkness enfolds him and silence descends on the field and
      the stream.

Once, at the wave of his wand, all the billows of musical sound
   Followed his will, as the sea was ruled by the prophet of old:
Now that his hand is relaxed, and the rod has dropped to the
      ground,
   Lo, how mute are the shores where the mystical harmonies
      rolled!

Nay, but not still are the hearts that were filled with that
      marvelous sea;
   Purer and deeper forever the tides of their being shall roll,
Sounding with echoes of joy, and of thanks, O Master, to thee,—
   Music immortal endures in the depths of the human soul.

# EDITOR'S NOTE

The sudden death of Mr. Thomas, which occurred January 4, 1905, would have necessitated, from a strict biographical point of view, some changes in the manuscript which he furnished, and which he took such pleasure in writing last summer at Felsengarten, his New Hampshire summer home. I have preferred, however, to leave his preface and autobiography as he wrote them, feeling certain that if any incongruities appear, this explanation will account for them. Not having all his references with him, Mr. Thomas naturally touched briefly upon many events in his exceptionally long career, and in such instances I have sought to fill out his narrative with notes based upon authentic documents.

G. P. U.

THEODORE THOMAS AT FIFTEEN
(FROM A DAGUERREOTYPE)

# PREFACE

I WISH to begin with a statement, to which my friends will bear witness, that I never intended to write my autobiography, or anything else; I desired only to preserve my programmes — representing over half a century of a very important part of the history of music in America — in some permanent form, and this is the result.

I am happy to say that at my request, Mr. George P. Upton, whose interest in the cause of good music has been of such marked benefit to Chicago for fifty years, has undertaken the laborious task of compiling and editing this publication, of selecting and classifying the programmes to be printed, and of writing such explanations as they have required. But he has also shown me the necessity of adding some historical matter which no one but myself can supply, and without which these volumes would be incomplete.

What I have written will, I hope, prove interesting enough to the reader to recompense him for the time he will give to its perusal. I have written it reluctantly, and without being able to form the slightest opinion as to how much it will interest any one beyond my personal friends. In justice to myself, I must say that if some of my statements seem severe, they have been written with regret; but I have been compelled by truth, without which the whole would have been worthless, as well as by the urgent requests of earnest and truth-loving men, to clear up, for the sake of history, some matters which have been perverted, or transmitted to the present generation through unreliable sources.

*Felsengarten, September 7, 1904.*

# AUTOBIOGRAPHY

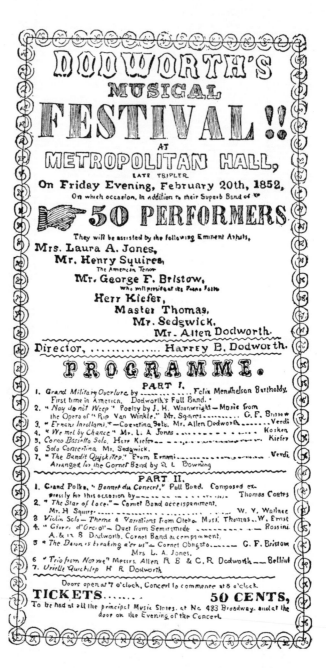

THEODORE THOMAS'S FIRST PROGRAMME

(FACSIMILE OF ORIGINAL)

# THEODORE THOMAS
## A MUSICAL AUTOBIOGRAPHY

### VOL. I.—LIFE WORK

### CHAPTER I

Birth and Parentage.— Early Life.—Comes to America in 1845.—New York.—Joins a Brass Band in the Navy.— Travelling as a Solo Artist in the South.—Plays in Theatre Orchestras in New York.—A Member of Jullien's Orchestra.—Jullien's Programmes.

ACCORDING to the records of the church in Esens, East Friesland, by the North Sea, I was born on the 11th of October, 1835. At this place my father was *Stadtpfeifer*.[1] I have no family records beyond what I learned from him in early boyhood. He was born in Erfurt, Thüringen, where his father kept a bookstore. My grandfather later emigrated to South America, whence he never returned. My mother was born in the old university town of

---

[1] *Stadtpfeifer*, or town musician. These musicians, paid by the town in which they lived, were privileged to play on all important public or private occasions. They were a close organization, admission to which could be gained only by regular apprenticeship. They were not without honor, for nearly all the Bachs belonged to them, and during the Thirty Years' War they were the conservators of music to some extent in Germany. —EDR.

Göttingen, and her father was a physician. This is the end of my knowledge of my family history. Both my parents were refined and honest people.

I have been told that I played the violin in public at the age of five. I have not, however, the slightest remembrance of when I began to play. My earliest recollection is that my father played the violin, so I played, and that I soon played the music he did. The members of his band, or orchestra, amused themselves by bringing music to me and trying to find something that I could not read off at sight. I do not remember the character of the music, except one piece — an "Air Varié" by De Bériot.

The most important event in my young life occurred when my father emigrated with his large family to America. We had the good fortune to find quarters on an American merchant vessel. The captain had his family on board, and I remember having a general good time, playing the fiddle, and blowing the fog horn by turns! We were six weeks on the ocean — this was before the days of ocean steamboats — and landed in New York on a hot July day in 1845. The metropolitan city was then a provincial town of two-story houses, and the pigs ran through Broadway and ate the refuse. For the benefit of any European who may read this, I will say that there were plenty of negroes to be seen, but no Indians.

In those days, the only resource open to an instrumentalist was to join a brass band, and play for parades or dancing. I do not remember having heard of any teaching, except of the piano and the cornet.   The orchestra, as we have it to-day, was almost an unknown quantity, although the Philharmonic Orchestra[1] had made a feeble beginning, and there were small so-called orchestras, consisting of a dozen musicians, more or less, in the theatres.   Better music was played in the theatres then, however, than at the present time.   It was in a theatre orchestra that I first made the acquaintance of Beethoven's "Coriolanus Overture," which was played before the curtain rose for Shakespeare's tragedy, with what musical results I cannot tell, but there was at least an endeavor to have the music in keeping with the drama. The theatres were few in number, and the orchestra leaders were English; as a matter of course, the orchestras were composed principally of English musicians.

It must have been difficult for my father to support his large family, for I had to help him when I could, and that meant much night work, for the theatres, even then, kept open far beyond midnight.   First came a tragedy, melodrama, or comedy, and afterwards a farce.   I remember, for instance, that I saw the elder Booth in the "Merchant of Venice" at a theatre in Spring Street, four or five blocks west of Broadway, after which he appeared in a farce.   Besides playing in the theatre orchestra, I remember I also played at a French dancing school.   Of course,

[1]The New York Philharmonic Society, to which Mr. Thomas refers, was organized in 1842, and gave its first concert on December 7 of that year. Its principal founder was Uriah C. Hill.   There was also a Philharmonic Society in New York about the middle of the eighteenth century, but its life was brief.—EDR.

all this night work made it impossible for a boy of my age to go to school during the day.

In 1848 my father enlisted in a navy band, and so did I, and I played second horn to his first in the band stationed at Portsmouth, Virginia. It was our duty to go on board the old ship "Pennsylvania" daily, and play at nine o'clock in the morning, and again at sunset, after which we left the ship and had our evenings free to follow our profession.

In 1849 my father appears to have become prosperous enough to dispense with my financial assistance, so it was not long before I obtained my discharge from the navy, and was off for the South. I do not remember taking anything with me but my fiddle, my little box of clothing, and some posters which I had had printed, announcing a concert by "Master T. T." I kept a supply of these posters in my trunk, and when I had no money I first obtained permission to use the dining hall of a hotel for a concert, and then I went around on the day before the concert took place and put up my posters with tacks. When the time for the concert arrived, I would stand at the door of the hall and take the money until I concluded that my audience was about gathered, after which I would go to the front of the hall, unpack my violin, and begin the concert! Sometimes I played with piano accompaniment, but oftener without. I have yet in my possession a set of variations on "Home, Sweet Home," which I wrote down some years later as a souvenir of those days. I did not have printed programmes.

When I had money I did not play in concerts, but vegetated, Southern fashion. In some places I met amateurs who made much of me, and there I stayed a while. Often I sent my trunk on ahead, and travelled on horseback alone — if possible at night — carrying with me plenty of cigars and a pistol, hoping to be attacked on the road by bandits! I remember one place in Mississippi where, after I had announced a concert, I was ordered by the authorities to leave town, because they believed the devil was in the fiddle! On one of these trips I carried my violin in a bag, and, lying down on the ground in the woods for a rest, suddenly jumped up and stepped on it, breaking it, of course. I then went to a carpenter shop, took off its top, pieced it, glued it on again, and played on it the next day. All this is not so easy without the help of tools made for the purpose, and how I managed to place the sounding-post I do not know — probably with a string.

In the summer of 1850 I arrived again in New York, with the intention of going to Europe. I was then fifteen years of age, and somehow had recognized the necessity of studying if I expected to accomplish anything in this world. But what? I did not know, of course, that a general education was needed, or even what it meant. My first idea was to become a virtuoso, so I began to practise and play in concerts. New York had changed immensely in the few years which had elapsed since my arrival in America. Many German musicians, singly or in bands, had come over. But probably the most important educational influence on my mind came through the establishment of a German theatre with a fair-sized orchestra, in which I was engaged as the leading violinist. Here I received my first intellectual impetus, by becoming acquainted with the plays of the great German poets. As a few years before I had learned of the existence of Shakespeare through the medium of an English theatre orchestra, so now, in the orchestra of the German theatre, I became familiar with the masters of German literature, Goethe and Schiller, and they made a strong impression upon me. Another feature of this engagement was the regular Sunday-night concerts given there, in which I often appeared as soloist. My repertoire already included Lipinski's "Concerto Militaire," Vieuxtemps's First Concerto, and the "Othello Fantaisie" of Ernst.

The next two or three years can be easily sketched together. The right influence came to me at the right time, and, musically speaking, gave me the opportunities to prepare myself for my later-day task, and shaped my future as no other influence could have done. The beginning of the fifties brought over to this country not only instrumentalists, but the most brilliant, finished, and mature vocalists of the world, such as Jenny Lind and Sontag, besides a large number of eminent Italian singers, among them Mario, Grisi, Bosio, Alboni, and others. I doubt if there were ever brought together in any part of the world a larger number of talented vocalists than were gathered in New York between

1850 and the early sixties. The pure and musical quality of their art was of great value in forming the taste of an impressionable boy, at the outset of his career. It was under this influence, also, that Adelina Patti grew up, for she attended the rehearsals of these singers daily with her parents. I played everywhere, in opera and concerts, and was very popular. The only thing against me was my youth. I was very small, and looked even younger than I really was. The orchestras, of course, were still not numerous or large, for Italian opera in those days could be well given with an orchestra of thirty-five or forty men. The concert orchestras then, towards the end of the forties, were those of Gungl, and the Germania.[1]

The season of opera and concerts was short, however, and the problem of making a living was as difficult for an orchestral player to solve then as now. I remember that when my funds ran out I used to go to my friend, Harry B. Dodworth, tell him that I was in need of money, and ask him to let me play for balls to earn the money to pay my board! This he

---

[1] Josef Gungl, of Berlin, came to New York with his band in 1849, but remained in this country only one season. Upon his return to Germany he wrote a most scathing criticism of musical conditions in New York. The Germania Orchestra, the nucleus of which was formed from Gungl's band, also came in 1849, and made a tour of the principal cities in the United States. For a time it greatly flourished, but after five years of varying fortunes it was disbanded. The Germania unquestionably exerted a most important influence upon popular musical taste, and helped to prepare the way for the great work Mr. Thomas was destined to perform.—EDR.

always did, and I still thank him for it. I played for the dancing faithfully the whole night through, and used it as a mode of practice. Once, when I was a boy, I remember, seeing no way of earning the money for my board, I took my fiddle under my coat, went to the bar-room of a hotel, and played, and soon had the money I needed, after which I left. Other well-known musicians had to beat the big drum all day in street parades. I was, fortunately, not driven to that.

Jullien,[1] the musical charlatan of all ages, who, nevertheless, exerted some useful influence upon orchestral music, made his appearance in the United States in August, 1853.

He brought over with him a number of soloists — flute, hautbois, clarinet, cornet, trombone, and ophicleide players — the last an instrument now replaced by the tuba, but much missed in works like

[1] Louis Antoine Jullien, son of a bandmaster, was born at Sisteron, Basses-Alpes, April 23, 1812. He was educated in Paris, and conducted his first concerts in London, where, during many years, he gave an annual series of concerts. He remained in this country until June 28, 1854, then returned to London, where he was in severe financial straits, and thence went to Paris. In that city he was imprisoned for debt, and finally died in a lunatic asylum in 1860. Mr. Thomas's sharp characterization of him is warranted by his many eccentricities, sensations, and extravagances, as well as by his affected deportment at the conductor's desk, which at times reached the extreme height of silliness. He was fond of prodigious effects. Upon one occasion in London he used six military bands in addition to his permanent orchestra, and in a "musical congress" announced "six grand musical fêtes, with four hundred instrumentalists, three distinct choruses, and three distinct military bands."—EDR.

the "Midsummer Night's Dream," by Mendelssohn.
He also brought Bottesini, the contra-bassist, and a
number of violinists, amongst them the Mollenhauer
brothers, and others. New York has never had,
before or since, the like of his wood-wind players.
The rest of the orchestra was made up of New York
players, and I was one of the first violinists. Jullien
was the first, as I remember, who played with a large
orchestra — I think he had, in Castle Garden, twenty
first-violinists. His programmes were all popular in
character, and some of the special features of them
were the "Katy-did Polka," the "Prima Donna
Waltz," and the "Fireman's Quadrille." As a feature of the latter, an alarm of fire was regularly
sounded, and a brigade of firemen appeared in the
hall! This created great consternation in the audience the first time it was given. He also played overtures and movements of symphonies.

# CHAPTER II

JENNY LIND, Sontag, and Patti are three prominent names in musical history. Jenny Lind
was the first to appear. She had conquered the
world on the operatic stage, and, while still young,
had retired to the concert stage. She was truly a
great singer. She had an exceptional voice, compass,
technique, and warmth, and impressed one with a
sense of grandeur.

Mme. Sontag, who left the stage early and retired to private life, returned to it again after an
absence of twenty years, during which time she had
developed into a mature artist, having, at the same
time, preserved her voice in perfect condition by
leading a quiet life. I do not remember another
singer in whom art and experience were combined
with such freshness and quality of voice. She would
appear one night as *Zerlina* in "Don Giovanni," and
the next, perhaps, in the title part of "Lucrezia
Borgia." No one who saw her in the first role
could ever be satisfied with any other impersonation
of it. As for the second, a dramatic role, if she was
surpassed by some artists of heavier voice and more

28

dramatic acting, the artistic unity of her performance, nevertheless, left nothing to be desired.

Neither of these exceptional women conquered the
world with voice and execution alone. It was the
perfection and blending of these qualities, together
with the single aim — that of truthful expression,
which gave greatness to whatever they rendered. I
have never heard their equals.

Patti's voice was of delicious quality and great
charm, easy in delivery and true, like the singing of
a bird — but it expressed no more soul than the song
of a bird.

The important musical influence of one man, who
appeared at this time, has, never to my knowledge,
been recognized. This man was Karl Eckert,[1] who
had been brought over with Mme. Sontag as leader
of her orchestra. Eckert was a man of the world,
and had moved in good society. He was an educated
man, a gentleman, a high-grade musician, violinist,
composer, and, last but not least, the only really fully
equipped and satisfactory conductor who visited this
country during that period. All of the rest were
more or less "time-beaters." What I learned from

[1] Karl Eckert was born at Potsdam, December 7, 1820.
His musical ability was displayed at a very early age, and he
at once became a favorite with Mendelssohn, with whom he
studied in 1839. In 1851 he was accompanist at the Italian
Theatre in Paris, and after his return from this country, in
1852, was conductor of the Italian Opera in the same city.
In 1854 he went to Vienna as director of the Court Opera,
in 1861 to Carlsruhe as Capellmeister, and in 1868 was appointed director at Berlin, which position he held until his
death, October 14, 1879.—EDR.

Eckert it is difficult at this time to say, but his influence probably laid the foundation of my future
career.

Eckert was not a disciplinarian, but he had been
associated with the best, and would have nothing
else. For the first time there was order in the
orchestra. I remember that at the beginning of
the season constant changes took place among the
men at every rehearsal. I was one of the first violinists, and think I sat at the second stand. One morning Eckert said to me: "I cannot procure a satisfactory leader for the second violins. Will you help us
out?" A leading violinist, or, as the English say,
"principal" of a part, is the man on whom the conductor must depend under all circumstances to bring
the attack when he gives the beat. He is also responsible, in some measure, for the other players in the
same part. Each part of the quintette has such a
leader. In opera he is often of great importance
when mistakes happen on the stage.

I accepted the offer, and at once had an independent and responsible position, which also brought me
into close contact with a thoroughly experienced
musician, perhaps a master. I must have done well,
for, in spite of my being a boy, and an American
boy at that, Eckert and I remained very good friends.
This was probably one of those important opportunities which Providence opens for one, and I had
sense enough to recognize it.

At the head of the first violins sat a man who ought
not to be overlooked here. a very good violinist and

a routined but conservative musician, named Joseph Noll. He was first violinist in the Eisfeld Quartette, and everywhere else. Noll had probably held similar positions in Germany, and had the virtues, as well as the faults, of the German school of those days, the principal aim of which was to produce a large tone, irrespective of quality. A vibrating, velvety tone was considered effeminate. In this respect the Germans have changed very much since then — and to their advantage — owing to international influences. Noll, however, produced a good tone, but always so loud that he made ensemble playing impossible. Toward the close of his career he was a loyal member of my orchestra, as viola player.

According to my recollection it was in the following year that I became the leader of the first violins — concertmeister — with Arditi as conductor. The troup included artists of the first rank, like Lagrange, Mirate, and Badiali. The voice of Lagrange did not compare in quality with that of either Jenny Lind or Sontag, but it, nevertheless, was of good quality, large compass, highly cultivated, and was used in a musicianly manner.

I have always considered Mirate[1] the greatest tenor I have heard, without exception, in voice, com-

[1] Mirate was a great favorite in Italy, and highly esteemed by Verdi. He created the part of the Duke in the latter's "Rigoletto," and received an ovation for his singing of the well-known canzone, "La donna è mobile." Mr. Thomas's panegyric is a deserved tribute to an artist whose name is not found in any of the modern dictionaries of music, not even in Grove's "Dictionary of Music," or the Century "Dictionary of Names."—EDR.

pass, method, and musicianship. He staid only a short time in this country, and then returned to Italy.

Badiali ranked with these two singers, but baritones, or high basses, according to quality of voice, were not so rare as tenors.

Arditi was an Italian, as his name indicates. He began his career as a violinist. He was a good conductor of Italian opera. He knew his music, and one could instantly perceive that he had pounded it over on the piano many times with his singers. In those days the education of the average singer was very limited, and it was the duty of the conductor, except in large European institutions, to pound on the piano with the singers until they knew their parts well enough to go to an orchestra rehearsal. There the same methods would be continued, the music being played over until it went together. I can remember singers of great renown who did not know the name of a note. Arditi, who was a small, nervous, energetic man, was in touch with his orchestra.

Many conductors do not interest themselves in the orchestra they conduct beyond expecting it to be a willing instrument. This is especially true of an opera orchestra. In the days when Italian opera was supreme, the highest accomplishment of an orchestra was to follow the singer. Furthermore, there was no permanancy in opera, orchestra, or anything pertaining to music in this country. The conductor also was never in any place long, and

HENRIETTE SONTAG

(FROM AN EARLY PRINT)

KARL ECKERT

expected to find the best orchestra talent which circumstances permitted provided for him. So it happened that the orchestra was generally engaged and formed by some man who was an inferior musician himself, but who was supposed to know the better musicians, and had some business capacity. This man would receive, besides his salary from the manager, a percentage from every man in the orchestra, and whoever was unwilling to submit to this exaction could not get an engagement. As concertmeister, I had both power and responsibility, and I dispensed with this middle man, and began by making all engagements with the members of the orchestra myself. The order I had learned under Eckert I retained, and this made a first-class orchestra possible, and gave me much influence. From that time on there was probably no good instrumentalist who did not spend his first years in America in the orchestra I formed. It had a standard thereafter which made itself quickly felt.

# CHAPTER III

The New York Philharmonic Society.—Henry C. Timm and William Scharfenberg.—Elected a Member in 1854.— Theodore Eisfeld.—Carl Bergmann.

THE concerts of the New York Philharmonic Society by this time had begun to attract some attention, probably owing to the efforts of good teachers, like Henry C. Timm[1] and William Scharfenberg.[2] These two men had great influence. They were educated musicians, good pianists, loved their art, and were highly respected. I was elected a member of the Philharmonic Society January 21, 1854. Its principal conductor at that time was Theodore Eisfeld.[3] Later, Carl Bergmann alternated with him.

[1] Henry Christian Timm was born at Hamburg, Germany, July 11, 1811, and made his *début* as a pianist in 1828. He came to this country in 1835, and for several years made concert tours. He played the organ at some New York churches, and did most efficient work as chorus master. He was one of the earliest members of the Philharmonic Society, and its president for several years. He died September 4, 1892.—EDR.

[2] William Scharfenberg was born at Cassel, Germany, February 22, 1819. He was a pupil of Hummel, and later played second violin in Spohr's quartette. He came to this country in 1838, and made his *début* as pianist. For many years he was recognized as a superior teacher, and was a great favorite in concerts. He also made valuable contributions to musical periodicals, and held various offices in the Philharmonic Society. He died August 8, 1895.—EDR.

[3] Theodore Eisfeld, who conducted the Philharmonic Society for many years, was born at Wolfenbüttel, Germany,

34

Eisfeld belonged to the class of "time-beaters," and would make corrections in the harmonies of master-works he did not understand. Bergmann was a talented musician and a fair 'cello player, who came to this country in 1850 as a member of a small orchestra, the Germania, of which he afterwards became conductor. The Germania had its headquarters in Boston early in the fifties, and made several tours. After it disbanded, in 1854, Bergmann went to Chicago.[1]  Eisfeld became sick in 1855, and

April 11, 1816. From 1839 to 1843 he was Capellmeister at the Wiesbaden Court Theatre, and the "Concerts Viviennes," Paris. He came to New York in 1848, and shortly afterwards became conductor of the Philharmonic, as well as of the Harmonic Society, when it was first organized. He also established quartet soirees in 1851, with Noll, Reyer, and Eichhorn, Otto Dresel being the pianist, and continued them for several years. He went back to Europe in 1866, and died at Wiesbaden in 1882. Mr. Eisfeld must be credited with having introduced the first regular concerts of chamber music in New York.—EDR.

[1] Carl Bergmann went to Chicago in November, 1854, and gave a concert, at which he was assisted by the Chicago Philharmonic Society, of which, at that time, Christopher Plagge was conductor. He was invited to remain and take charge of the Society, and consented. He gave his first concert December 22, 1854, at Metropolitan Hall. His season, however, was limited to two concerts. Musical jealousies arose, and at last became so bitter that Bergmann left in disgust and went back to New York. The society went to pieces, but was reconstructed in 1856 with Prof. C. W. Webster as conductor. It dragged along a sickly existence until 1860, when it was revived and placed upon a sounder footing under the direction of Hans Balatka. For several years his concerts were the fashionable rage; but fashion is fickle, and on April 3, 1868, the Society died insolvent. Mr. Balatka gave two concerts on his own account in 1868, and four in 1869. The last of the four was given November 26, 1869, and on the next

Bergmann was sent for to conduct the last Philharmonic concert of that season. At this concert he brought out the "Tannhäuser Overture," and made with it probably the greatest success of his life. I remember it well. It sounded little as we know it to-day, but it shook up the dry bones and made the dust fly, anyway! The following season (1855–56), Bergmann was engaged to conduct all the Philharmonic concerts, Eisfeld still being sick.

It has been said by those who are unfamiliar with the history of that time, that Bergmann was my model in conducting. This is incorrect. Eckert, as I have already said, was the one who influenced me, and from whom I learned. Bergmann was very reticent about his past life. He gave the impression that he never worked much, or cared to do so. He lacked most of the qualities of a first-rank conductor, but he had one great redeeming quality for those days which soon brought him into prominence. He possessed an artistic nature, and was in sympathy with the so-called "Zukunft Musik."[1] He lacked the force, however, to make an impression, and had no standard. He derived his principal inspiration from our chamber music practice. His readings of Beethoven's works showed clearly that he had no tradition, and that it was not based on study. I remember well one morning, after we had been playing

evening Theodore Thomas's orchestra played for the first time in the same hall. Mr. Balatka retired from the field. A new musical revelation had been made to Chicago.—EDR.

[1] Music of the future.

the Schumann string quartets for the first time, his saying to me: "You have lifted the veil from our eyes to-day." It was after this that he brought out hitherto unknown orchestral works by Schumann.

After I had formed my own orchestra, Bergmann and I remained good friends, and enjoyed each other's company. He always spoke appreciatively to me, but as I grew more successful his companions tried to make him jealous of my success — which he had not sufficient energy to emulate. I always felt that under favorable conditions Bergmann might have been of greater service to his adopted country. He did not play the piano well enough to be an accompanist, and had not the energy to make a position for himself as a teacher, so his income was always small. The Philharmonic societies paid little. I remember when I began to conduct the Brooklyn Philharmonic concerts, the conductor's fee, which was the same as Eisfeld and Bergmann had had, was not much more than that of any member of the orchestra. Afterwards, with the growing success of these concerts, my salary was increased until it reached several thousand dollars for the season.

A few years before his death, I offered to share the conductorship of my orchestra with Bergmann, and pay him a salary. He accepted the offer, but when the morning came for the rehearsal, at which he was to appear, he staid away.

# CHAPTER IV

Chamber Concerts.—The Mason-Thomas Quartette. — William Mason. — Joseph Mosenthal. — George Matzka.— Bergmann in Chamber Music.—Frederick Bergner.— The Quartette disbands.

DURING 1855 chamber concerts were established by William Mason, under the name "Mason and Bergmann." [1] The following year they

[1] The following is a copy of the original announcement of these famous chamber concerts:

### MUSICAL MATINEES.

"Messrs. William Mason (pianoforte) and Carl Bergmann (violoncello), assisted by Messrs. Theodore Thomas (first violin), J. Mosenthal (second violin), and G. Matzka (viola), propose a series of six monthly classical musical entertainments, to be given on the last Tuesday of each succeeding month, at 2 P. M.

"In consequence of the numerous evening engagements of the city, and to enable lady amateurs and students to be present without escort, it is proposed to give matinees in preference to soirees. This arrangement will also enable those residing in the suburbs to attend, as each performance will occupy only about an hour and a half. The novel and most important feature of these entertainments will be the presentation of such music — quartets, trios, sonatas, etc.— as opportunity is rarely afforded to listen to, except in some very select circles of Europe. The later quartets of Beethoven, rarely heard in public even abroad, the works of Schumann, Schubert, Franck, Volkmann, Brahms, Rubinstein, and Berwald will form the leading features of the programmes. Two leading compositions, quartets, or trios, will be given entire at each performance, while the programmes will be completed by compositions of a lighter character. In short, it is intended to arrange these matinees after the celebrated ones of Liszt at Weimar."—EDR.

were discontinued, but were resumed in 1857–58,
under the name, "Mason and Thomas." Bergmann being absent, his place was filled by C.
Brannes until the third matinee, when Bergmann
resumed his place. The influence of these concerts during the fourteen years of their existence is
best shown by their programmes. Of course these
did not pay, and I suppose that Mason must have
borne the losses for many years, for they never paid
more, at best, than the expenses of the hall and the
doorkeeper.

William Mason, as sincere in art as in his daily
life, had a genuine musical nature. He showed
talent at an early age, and was sent to Europe, where
he had exceptional opportunities for study, and favorable surroundings. After his return, he appeared as
a virtuoso, but soon realized the conditions of his
country in musical affairs. He gave proof of his sincerity by inaugurating chamber concerts at once,
although the Eisfeld organization was still in existence. It knew neither flood nor ebb, however,
whereas the first programmes of Mason and Bergmann sounded the war-cry of death to stale and
meaningless music, and proclaimed progress.[1] Works

[1] It is evident that Mr. Thomas, when he wrote this, had
in mind the grand trio in B major, op. 8, of Brahms, which
closed the first programme, and was performed by Mr. Mason,
Mr. Bergmann, and himself. The house was crowded upon
this occasion, but the critics did not greatly relish Brahms.
"The New York Times" said the next morning:

"The trio in B flat by Mr. Brahms is an early work
written, we believe, at the age of eighteen. With many good
points, and much sound musicianship, it possesses also the

by Schubert, Brahms, Beethoven (ops. 59, 95, and 130), Schumann, Rubinstein, and Bach were the principal features of the first season.

Of course this spirit was transmitted directly from Weimar. It is true that some programmes showed that undue influences had been brought to bear by the insertion of silly songs and solos between the quartets and trios, and that there was no standard in sight yet. But at that time everything relative to music in this country was, so to speak, in its infancy.

Mr. Mason afterwards turned his attention to teaching, and we all know how successful and influential his work has been. He decided to devote his life to this calling, and his aptitude for this field cannot be doubted. He had the best pedagogic foundation, wide experience, the highest sense for tone-quality, great patience, and was then, as now, a thorough musician.

usual defects of a young writer, among which may be enumerated length and solidarity. The motivos seldom fall on the ear freshly; they suggest something that has been heard before, and induce a skeptical frame of mind, not altogether just, for the composer evidently has ideas of his own (*sic*). In the elaboration of these ideas he is frequently original, always correct, and generally too lengthy."

"The New York Dispatch" said with philosophical resignation:

"The Brahms Trio is a composition in the ultra new school of which we may say briefly that we do not yet understand it. Whether this be due to our dullness of perception, or lack of appreciation, or the intricate character of the music, we do not pretend to say. . . Yet we feel obliged to Messrs. Mason and Bergmann for the opportunity they afforded us for hearing and becoming acquainted with this peculiar and *outré* style of music."—EDR.

Other members of the Quartette were Joseph Mosenthal and George Matzka. Mosenthal was the most conservative musician of us all. He was lovely and sincere of nature, well educated, and a good violinist and musician. He was born in Cassel, and, belonging to the Spohr school, was still, of course, enthusiastic for that composer's music.[1]

Matzka came from the Coburg orchestra, and was an able and ambitious musician.

Bergmann was only a moderate performer, but he did everything with a certain grace; his technique was limited, and his tone, of course, was not large, because he never practised. The quartette rehearsals were held at my house, from nine to twelve o'clock in the morning, about three times a week. Why Bergmann should have gone through this drudgery of early rehearsals, often being obliged to carry his instrument in all kinds of weather, may possibly be explained by the fact that these rehearsals were the only existing source of artistic food for him. It was also characteristic of him that while he was so susceptible to modern music, I never had his support in placing one of the later quartets by Beethoven on our programmes. I understood readily why Mosenthal

[1] In an interview several years ago, Mr. Mosenthal said: "I think that no men ever played together who understood each other better than did Thomas, Matzka, Bergner, and I. Theodore Thomas was a magnificent violin player, as you may have observed last summer, when he played a solo at Gilmore's Garden, the first one in a long while in public, I think. Our first concerts were given at the old Dodworth Hall, next to Grace Church."—EDR.

and Matzka were not enthusiastic about the matter, for they were still somewhat under the influence of their European training. But Bergmann and I had had no training. However, the programme making was left to me, and I fought, and did my duty as I saw it. We played the last quartets, but perhaps not so often as I wished.

Our Quartette generally played together in the orchestras of opera or concerts. Mosenthal always played at the same stand with me, and Matzka and Bergmann were also at their respective places. There were rather strong contrasts in our work at times, as, for instance, when a rehearsal of one of the last Beethoven quartets was followed by a rehearsal of "Trovatore." Again, when Brahms's Second Serenade appeared, I called a rehearsal for the orchestra to run it over an hour before a rehearsal of "Rigoletto." Bergmann was in the orchestra, and brought out the Serenade in 1862 in a Philharmonic concert. He remained in our Quartette until after the first concert in 1861. The immediate cause of his withdrawal I do not remember, but I believe one reason was that he was tired of the work. Frederick Bergner, by far the most able 'cellist of that time, took Bergmann's place, and the Quartette was, no doubt, the gainer by the change. Bergner remained with us until the Quartette disbanded.[1]

[1] Bergner once said to the late Charles D. Hamill, when asked his opinion of Mr. Thomas as a violinist: "One of the greatest violinists in the world was spoiled to become the greatest conductor."—EDR.

Each member of the organization had made his way, and gained influence. It is hardly necessary to say that our influence was thrown in favor of Bergmann as a conductor, especially of the Philharmonic concerts, as neither the programmes nor the execution suited us. We represented, in those days, the ultra-modern spirit. The Quartette was continued until April, 1868, when it died a natural death, because my time was gradually absorbed by the orchestra, and I had to travel. The other members devoted their time to teaching.

I should like to close this chapter with a tribute to Karl Klauser, a musician and a man of culture, who was at the head of the musical department in Miss Porter's school at Farmington, Connecticut, from 1855. He is mentioned here on account of the influence he has had in this country in cultivating the taste for everything that is noble in music. He created an artistic and refined atmosphere for his pupils, and the young women who studied at his famous school, and who came from all parts of the country, took away with them genuine love and respect for the art of music, and were active in promulgating this spirit all their lives. I have often met with instances of this most unexpectedly, and in widely distant localities. He inaugurated annual chamber concerts at the school for the pupils, and Mason, Thomas, Mosenthal, Matzka, Bergmann, and Bergner gave regular concerts in Farmington from 1856 until the Quartette was disbanded. He also engaged artists

like Rubinstein and Bülow to give recitals there when
they visited America.   Why have not other similar
institutions taken an example from this effective mode
of cultivating the tastes of their pupils? [1]

[1] Mr. William Mason, in his " Memories of a Musical Life,"
says: "Through Mosenthal our Quartette became acquainted
with Mr. Karl Klauser, who was an active and enthusiastic
musician of thorough education, and who has accomplished a
great deal of useful work, both as a compiler and teacher of
classic and modern composition.  Mr. Klauser is a native
of St. Petersburg, born of German parents.  He came to
New York in 1850, and was engaged as musical director in
Miss Porter's famous school for young ladies in 1855, a post
which he filled with credit and ability for many years.  He
was enthusiastically fond of chamber music, and frequently
attended the rehearsals of our quartette; and it was through
him that we were induced to give recitals in Farmington six
months after our beginning in New York." It should be
added to Mr. Mason's reference to Mr. Klauser, that he not
only selected the material used in his teaching with the utmost
care, but enriched it by rectifying corrupt texts, as well as
with correct fingerings and indications for the performance
of embellishments.  His work in this direction includes over a
thousand piano compositions from the classics critically
revised, several editions of lighter works, a volume of progressive studies, and numerous arrangements of orchestral
and chamber music for the piano.  "Dwight's Journal of
Music" in 1872, in a long sketch of this indefatigable worker,
pays him this tribute: "Only by such uninterrupted efforts
as these of Klauser can a great and truly musical public grow
up in America.  Therefore honor to the man who, one of the
first, has set out upon his artistic mission with earnestness and
decision, and who now, after some seventeen years of toil,
has already been able to send out more than one thousand
young apostles of this musical faith into all parts of North
America."—EDR.

# CHAPTER V

Musical Studies.—Ullmann's Opera Troupe in 1857.—Grand
Concerts.—Sigismund Thalberg, and Henri Vieuxtemps.—
Carl Anschütz.—End of Thomas's "Apprenticeship."

THE time had now come for me to make the
best use of my opportunities for study. I had
studied harmony, five or six years previously, with
Rudolph Schwillinger, and now took up counterpoint
and fugue with an able organist, William Meyer-
hofer. I still continued my position with Ullmann as
concertmeister of his opera company. In 1857, for
the first time in America, the proportions of grand
opera were properly balanced. There were first-
rank singers, an increased chorus, and an enlarged
orchestra, which had reached the efficiency of European grand orchestras. Ullmann used to say that I
was ruining him by engaging so large an orchestra.
My answer was, "Then discharge me!" whereupon
he would reply, "*Sein Sie doch nicht so hitzig.*"

Besides the opera troupe Ullmann had under his
management Thalberg, the pianist, Vieuxtemps, the
violinist, and plenty of material for grand concerts,
and we gave them. He also brought over Carl
Anschütz, to conduct. Anschütz belonged to the
class of conductors I have called "time-beaters,"
though he was the most intelligent and the best educated of them all. Besides a good general schooling,

45

he had a liberal musical education, but he never could be in sympathy or touch with an orchestra. He neither played any stringed instrument, nor any other used in the orchestra. He had never been in the rank and file, and accomplished only a certain kind of routine with small opera troupes. He pounded the piano for the singers, which, we have seen, was the custom of the day. His influence, for a time, however, was good. He was a hard worker and a well-meaning man; but, after all, he was a *routinier*, and succumbed gradually to his surroundings.

Those were busy days. An opera season was begun without a library, so to speak. When works like "Robert the Devil" and "The Huguenots," were given, we had the orchestral parts, but they were new, and had never been played from. To understand the situation, it is necessary for me to explain that the orchestral parts in those days were very faulty. The Italian music was mostly manuscript, and seldom corrected, and routine was necessary to know the notes and traditions. I remember one season that the last act of "Lucia di Lammermoor" (an opera much given in those days), was missing in the part of the first stand, at which Mosenthal and I sat, and we had to "revamp" it, as the saying is. In the French music the print was too small, to begin with, besides being printed from worn-out plates. The general outfit was so slovenly that the parts needed careful revising before they could be used. As an illustration, "The Huguenots" was announced by the management, and we had the parts, but the score had

JENNY LIND

(FROM A PAINTING)

## GRAND MUSICAL FESTIVAL,

under the direction of Mr. L. F. HARRISON.

### Monday June 3d.     Handel's Oratorio of the Messiah.

MADAME PAREPA-ROSA.          MRS. ZELDA HARRISON-SEGUIN.
MR. WM. CASTLE.     MR. J. R. THOMAS.     MR. E. J. CONNOLLY.

New York Harmonic Society and Orchestra,
Conductor, - - - Mr. F. L. RITTER.

### Tuesday, June 4th.     Mendelssohn's Hymn of Praise.     46th Hymn.

#### OVERTURE TO OTHELLO.

MADAME PAREPA-ROSA.          MRS. EMELINE REED.
MADAME RAYMOND RITTER.     MR. W. J. HILL.     MR. E. J. CONNOLLY.

New York Harmonic Society and Orchestra,
Conductor, - - - Mr. F. L. RITTER.

### Wednesday, June 5th—Evening.

## HAYDN'S ORATORIO OF THE CREATION.

MADAME PAREPA-ROSA.
MR. GEO. SIMPSON.     MR. J. R. THOMAS.     MR. E. J, CONNOLLY.

New York Harmonic Society and Orchestra,
Conductor, - - - Mr. F. L. RITTER.

### Wednesday Matinee, June 5th.     Miscellaneous Concert.

MISS HENRIETTA BEEBE.          MISS NETTIE STERLING.
MR. W. J. HILL.     MR. S. C. CAMPBELL.
MR. ALFRED H. PEASE.     MR. G. W. COLBY.

Orchestra,
Conductors, - - - Mr. CARL ROSA and Mr. G. MATZKA.

### Thursday, June 6th.     ORCHESTRAL CONCERT,

MADAME CARMELINA POCH.          SIGNOR BARAGLI.
SIGNOR BELLINI.     MR. WENZEL KOPTA.
MR. J. N. PATTISON.     MR. G. W. COLBY.     MR. G. W. MORGAN.

Full Orchestra,     Conductor, Mr. CARL BERGMAN,

### Friday, June 7th.

## MENDELSSOHN'S ORATORIO OF ELIJAH,

MADAME PAREPA-ROSA.          MISS CHARLOTTE V. HUTCHINGS.
MRS. EMELINE REED.     MISS ALICE HARRISON.
MR. GEO. SIMPSON.     MR. JULES LOMBARD.     MR. E. J. CONNOLLY.

New York Harmonic Society and Orchestra,
Conductor, - - - Mr. F. L. RITTER.

### Saturday, June 8th.—Evening.     Miscellaneous Concert.

MADAME PAREPA-ROSA.          MR. WILLIAM CASTLE.
MISS MARIE GILBERT.     MR. S. C. CAMPBELL.
MR. J. N. PATTISON.     MR. ALFRED H. PEASE.     MR. G. W. COLBY

Full Orchestra.  Grafulla Military Band.  Graham's Drum Corps.

Conductors: Messrs. CARL ANSCHUTZ, C. MATZKA & C. S. GRAFULLA.

### Saturday Matinee, June 8th.

## MISCELLANEOUS CONCERT.

MADAME PAREPA-ROSA.          MRS. ZELDA HARRISON-SEGUIN.
MISS MARIE GILBERT.     MR. WM. CASTLE.
MR. S. C. CAMPBELL.     MR. J. N. PATTISON.
MR. ALFRED H. PEASE.     MR. G. W. COLBY.

Orchestra,
Conductors, - - - Messrs. CARL ROSA and G. MATZKA.

### Sunday, June 9th.

## SELECTIONS from THE PROPHET and STABAT MATER.

OVERTURE TO JOHN THE BAPTIST.

MADAME PAREPA-ROSA.          MADAME CARMELINA POCH.
MADAME NATALI TESTA.     MR. CARL ROSA.
SIGNOR BARAGLI.     SIGNOR BELLINI.     SIGNOR ANTONUCCI.

Orchestra,
Conductors, Mrs. MAX MARETZEK, G. W. MORGAN and G. MATZKA.

---

PROGRAMME OF A MUSICAL FESTIVAL, 1867

(FACSIMILE OF ORIGINAL)

not arrived from Paris, or had been lost. The usual cuts had to be marked to save time in the rehearsals, and we would find, for instance, a page from the clarinet part in that of the 'cello; a flute part in the trumpet, or a trombone part among the violins, etc. Having no score to go by, clerical help could not be hired to make these corrections, and it became a work, not of love, but of nights, to straighten these matters and put the parts in fit order for use on the players' desks. Anschütz was at home in this kind of work, and I quickly became his assistant and "right-hand man" in everything on the stage and in the orchestra.[1] It is hardly necessary to say that I thus

[1] The New York correspondent of "Dwight's Journal of Music," writing under date of December 10, 1860, thus refers to Mr. Thomas as conductor of the Ullmann Opera: "Carl Anschütz appears to be involved in the fall of the Ullmann dynasty and his place as conductor of the orchestra is taken by Theodore Thomas, the young violinist, who looks 'severe in youthful beauty,' as he wields the baton, rather nervously it must be confessed, and directs the performance of venerable, spectacled, and bald-headed 'cellists and trombonists, old enough to be his great grandfathers. It is always a treat to me to see him in the orchestra. He plays the violin with such careless grace that even his elevation to the conductorship does not reconcile me to the loss of his violin performance."

Mr. Thomas has touched but lightly upon the days of his apprenticeship, but they were busy ones, like all his days to the end of his career, and of importance as they were helping to prepare him for that career. Before taking leave of this part of his life, a few leading events should be recorded to complete its story. The earliest of his collection of programmes shows that he played as "Master Thomas" at "Dodworth's Musical Festival" in Metropolitan Hall, New York, February 20, 1852, the other performers being Miss Laura A. Jones, soprano; Mr. Henry Squires, tenor; Mr. George F. Bristow, pianist; Herr Kiefer, corno bassetto player; Mr. Sedgwick,

learned much from him, for he was at his best under such circumstances.

These years I might call my "apprenticeship,"

concertina player; Mr. Allen Dodworth, cornetist, and the Dodworth Band. At this concert "Master Thomas" played Ernst's "Othello" theme and variations. On the 26th of the following April he played Lipinski's "Concerto Militaire" and Ernst's "Carnival of Venice" at a concert for the benefit of a member of Dodworth's Band. In 1856 his name appears for the first time as leader in eleven sacred concerts at the City Assembly Rooms, conducted by Carl Bergmann. At these concerts Schumann's Fourth Symphony, Manfred overture, and the "Overture, Scherzo and Finale," op. 52, Haydn's D major symphony, Berlioz's "Carnaval Romain" and "Waverly" Overtures were given for the first time in this country. April 13, 1857, at the Thalberg concert he played the Beethoven B flat trio with Thalberg and Bergmann, and also in a duo from "The Huguenots" with Thalberg. In the fall of 1858 and spring of 1859 he made a concert tour with Ole Bull in the West and South. In April and May, 1859, he conducted opera for Ullmann. October 10, 1860, he was leader to a gala performance of opera at the American Academy of Music, Philadelphia, in honor of the Prince of Wales, Max Maretzek and Sig. Muzio conducting. "Martha" and the first act of "Traviata" were given and the principal artists were Adelina Patti, Fanny Natali, Pauline Colson, Brignoli, Barili, Errani, and Carl Formes. December 8, 1860, he conducted "Stradella" with Fabbri as *Leonora*, Stigelli as *Stradella*, and Carl Formes as *Barbarino*. January 24, 1861, he conducted at an operatic entertainment at the American Academy of Music, Philadelphia, in which Mme. Bertha Johannsen, Mme. Von Berkel, Mme. Anna Bishop, Sig. Stigelli, and Herr Carl Formes took part in selections from "Martha," "Tancredi," "Der Freischütz," and "Masaniello," the whole concluding with "a grand National Tableau of Washington in which the entire company will sing 'The Star Spangled Banner.'" In this year (1861), Mr. Thomas gave up all connection with the theatre. He became animated by his great purpose of educating the public to an appreciation of music, and to this purpose he devoted the remainder of his life, resolutely, courageously, and untiringly, winning at last the laurels of success.—EDR.

as a practical musician and conductor. It was easy and pleasant to work with Anschütz, for he was a kindly, congenial, and most generous man. I was gradually drawn into the conductor's chair by his illness, though I avoided it as long as I could, for I wished all my time for study.

# CHAPTER VI

The New York Philharmonic Society.—First Series of Thomas Symphony Soirees, 1864.—Belvedere Lion Park Concerts, 1865.—Terrace Garden Summer Night Concerts, 1866.—Building of Central Park Garden Hall.—Elected Conductor of Brooklyn Philharmonic Concerts.—Inception of the Thomas Orchestra.—Plans for a Permanent Symphony Orchestra.—Summer Concerts and Winter Travelling.—In Boston, etc.—Proposals from P. T. Barnum.

IN 1862 I concluded to devote my energies to the cultivation of the public taste for instrumental music. Our chamber concerts had created a spasmodic interest, our programmes were reprinted as models of their kind, even in Europe, and our performances had reached a high standard. As a concert violinist, I was at that time popular, and played much. But what this country needed most of all to make it musical was a good orchestra, and plenty of concerts within reach of the people. The Philharmonic Society, with a body of about sixty players, and five yearly subscription concerts, was the only organized orchestra which represented orchestral literature in this large country.

It is true that the public was admitted to a number of its rehearsals, in addition to its concerts, but their influence was not salutary. The orchestra was often incomplete. If a member had an engagement, he would go to it instead of to the rehearsal. When one of the wind choir was thus absent, his place would be filled for the occasion as best it could. A clarinet or oboe part would be played on a violin, or a bassoon part on the 'cello, etc. The conductor therefore could not rehearse as he ought, and the audience talked at pleasure. Under these circumstances justice could not be done to the standard, much less to the modern and contemporary works. Such conditions debarred all progress.

I had been prominent before the public in chamber concerts, and as concertmeister (leader of the violins), of the opera since 1855, and during later years, also, as conductor of concerts and opera, and I thought the time had come to form an orchestra for concert purposes. I therefore called a meeting of the foremost orchestra musicians of New York, told them of my plans to popularize instrumental music, and asked their coöperation. I began by giving some concerts at Irving Hall,[1] and conducted some Brooklyn Philharmonic concerts, alternating with Theodore Eisfeld, and in 1864 I gave my first series of Symphony Soirees, with an orchestra of about sixty men. These concerts were at once successful artistically but only moderately so financially. During the

[1] The first of the Irving Hall concerts was given December 3, 1864. In his prospectus, Mr. Thomas says: "The desire for good music and for a prompt acquaintance with the latest works of the schools that produce it is now one of the settled conditions of New York society, and in endeavoring, year after year, to satisfy it, Mr. Thomas is always gratified to know that he appeals to an ever extending audience. He is persuaded therefore, that the present intention to lay before the public some of the most interesting works of modern and

summer of 1865 a series of concerts was given in the afternoon at Belvedere Lion Park, One Hundred and Tenth Street, with an orchestra of thirty players.

During the winter of 1865–66 more concerts were given, and in the summer of 1866 a series of one hundred Summer Night Concerts was inaugurated at Terrace Garden, with enough success to give promise for the future. An audience had been collected and educated to enjoy that form of entertainment, and I had succeeded in finding a respectable occupation during the summer months for a small orchestra. During the season of 1866–67 several concerts were given, the number of which was increased by the opening of Steinway Hall. There were concerts with many soloists and an occasional symphony,

classical composers will meet with a ready and liberal support." The programme of this memorable concert was as follows:

### PART I.

1. Symphony, No. 8, F major   .   .   .   . *Beethoven.*
   Orchestra.
2. Scena and aria, "Non più di fiori"   .   .   . *Mozart.*
   Miss Fanny Raymond.
3. Concerto in F minor, op. 21 (larghetto and finale) . *Chopin.*
   Mr. S. B. Mills.

### PART II.

4. Suite, op. 113, in D   .   .   .   .   . *Fr. Lachner.*
   Orchestra.
5. Cavatina, "Ah! S'estinto"   .   .   . *Mercadante.*
   Miss Fanny Raymond.
6. Dramatic Symphony, "Romeo and Juliet" (second
   part)   .   .   .   .   .   .   .   . *Berlioz.*
   Orchestra.

It will be seen from this that the young conductor, at this time twenty-nine years of age, was pluming his wings for an eagle's flight.—EDR.

under the management of L. F. Harrison, and a series under the management of Bateman, in which Madame Parepa was the chief attraction, as well as many others in both New York and Brooklyn. In this year also I was elected conductor of the Brooklyn Philharmonic Society for the season, which added to the income of my orchestra, an engagement of twenty performances — fifteen rehearsals and five concerts.[1]

The musical season in New York closed with a festival under the management of Mr. Harrison, in which I did not take part, having gone to Europe to learn what orchestras were doing there. It lasted a week, and the programmes are worth transcribing as typical of the times.

In 1867 a second season of Summer Night Concerts was given at Terrace Garden, which opened June 10, and continued until September 15. During my absence in Europe they were conducted by F. J. Eben and George Matzka. I returned July 1,

[1] The letter offering the directorship to Mr. Thomas was as follows:

BROOKLYN, N. Y., June 28, 1866.
MR. THEODORE THOMAS,

DEAR SIR:—At a meeting of the Executive Committee of the Philharmonic Society of Brooklyn, held this evening, you were elected conductor for the next season (1866–67) at a salary of $500, and I was authorized to inform you of such action. I was also desired to request you to meet the Music Committee at an early date so that any details affecting your acceptance or declination of the position might be thoroughly understood before your decision in the matter.

Very truly yours,
GEO. WM. WARREN,
Chairman of the Music Committee.

in time to conduct, bringing many novelties with me.
These concerts were very successful, and the programmes had improved and advanced.  It was in
this season that some business men offered to build a
hall for me, which would be suitable for summer concerts.  The Terrace Garden concerts had always
been given in the open air, the orchestra playing in
an inclosure, while the audience were seated under
the trees.  When it rained there was a scramble for
a hall in the adjacent building.  We also had many
little extravaganzas, which provoked much amusement.  On one occasion, for instance, while playing
the "Linnet Polka," I requested the piccolo players
to climb up into the trees before the piece began.
When they commenced playing from their exalted
position in the branches, it made a sensation.  I
remember another funny incident which happened
about this time.  In the "Carnival of Venice" the
tuba player had been sent, not up the trees, but back
of the audience into the shrubbery.  When he began to
play the police mistook him for a practical joker who
was disturbing the music, and tried to arrest him!  I
shall never forget the comical scene, as the poor man
fled toward the stage, pursued by the irate policeman,
and trying to get in a note here and there, as he ran.[1]

[1] The Terrace Garden concerts were given every evening
except Saturday.  On that day there was a matinee performance.  Every Friday evening in the first season the second
part of the programme contained  movements of symphony
or classical overtures.  In the second season the second part
was similarly arranged for both Tuesday and Friday evenings
and  "composers'  nights"  figured  on the  programmes — a
practice which Jullien introduced some years before this.—EDR.

The season of 1867–68 was a repetition of the previous year, but on May 25 the new hall, Central Park Garden, was opened with the first concert of the Summer Night series, which continued nightly through the entire summer and even into November.[1] The occupation of the orchestra during the summer season seemed now assured. During the winter months there were the Symphony Soirees, the Brooklyn Philharmonic concerts and public rehearsals, and numerous miscellaneous concerts besides. The thought of a permanent orchestra was natural and

[1] As the Central Park Garden concerts were one of the landmarks in Mr. Thomas's career the opening programme may prove of interest:

## CENTRAL PARK GARDEN
### Seventh Avenue, between Fifty-eighth and Fifty-ninth Streets.
*Opening Concert, May 25, 1868.*

#### Part I.
1. Opening March, "Central Park Garden" . . . . . . *Theodore Thomas.*
2. Overture, "Rienzi" . . . . . *Wagner.*
3. "On the Blue Danube" Waltz . . . *Strauss.*
4. Fantaisie, "Daughter of the Regiment" . *Donizetti.*

#### Part II.
5. Overture, "Oberon" . . . . *Von Weber.*
6. "Ave Maria" . . . . . *Bach-Gounod.*
7. Allegro vivace from "Reformation Symphony" . . . . . . *Mendelssohn.*
8. Scène de Ballet, "Robert le Diable" . . *Meyerbeer.*

#### Part III.
9. Overture, "Pique Dame" . . . . *Suppé.*
10. Polka Mazurka, "Libelle" . . }
    Polka. " 'S giebt nur ein Kaiserstadt" } . . *Strauss.*
11. "Serenade" . . . . . . . . *Titl.*
    Messrs. Siedler and Schmitz.
12. Quadrille, "La Grande Duchesse" . . *Offenbach.*

inevitable.   The support of the public was growing,
the orchestra was progressing in every way, and it
had gained in size and quality of tone.   For the Symphony Soirees, even as early as 1867, we had already
increased  the  number  of  the  orchestra  to  eighty
men.

In the season of 1868–69, I began to travel with
the orchestra.   I found, however, that although New
York and Brooklyn did not provide engagements
enough to fill the necessary time of an orchestra,  they
nevertheless offered too many to permit us to go far
from home.   After the summer of 1869, therefore, I
thought  the  orchestra  was  sufficiently  well  known
over the whole country, and I decided, as the only
means  whereby  I  could  keep  my  organization  together, to devote our entire time to travelling.   Accordingly I organized my orchestra on a permanent
basis, and for the first time (1869), went to Boston.
Our success there was instantaneous, and the people
of that city were loyal to me as long as I travelled.[1]

[1] " The visit of this famous New York orchestra has given
our music lovers a new and quick sensation.   Boston had not
heard such orchestra performances before; and Boston in the
frankest humor gave itself up to the complete enjoyment and
unstinted praise of what it heard. . . . Picked men, most of
them young, all of them artists, all looking as if thoroughly
engaged in their work, eager above all things to make the
music together and as well as possible. . . . We rejoice in the
coming of this orchestra.   It is just the kind of thing that we
for years have longed for in view of our own progress here.
We sincerely thank Mr. Thomas, first for giving us a hearing,
under the best advantage, of a number of works which were
new to us, but more we thank him for setting palpably before
us a higher ideal of orchestral execution.   We shall demand
better of our own in future.   They will demand it of themselves.

I gave a large number of concerts there every winter until I went to live in Cincinnati.

After Boston I went west as far as Chicago, touching every city on our route, and returning by way of St. Louis, Cincinnati, Pittsburg, and intermediate cities, to New York. In the latter city, however, I had abandoned my Symphony Soirees and all regular series of concerts in winter. We travelled over the whole country, giving concerts daily, and on May 9, the Central Park Garden Summer Night Concerts began again, continuing until September 24, a series of one hundred and thirty-four consecutive concerts. The season was very successful, and the size of the orchestra was now enlarged. After this travelling was resumed, and in 1870, which was the centennial anniversary of the birth of Beethoven, I gave a Beethoven programme, including a symphony, all over the country.

The next year brought again the regular Summer Night Concerts at Central Park Garden, and in the fall we travelled again. The orchestra had now become a first-rank organization, numbering sixty permanent members. Leading solo artists were sitting at all the first desks, and a high standard began to appear — higher in fact, than had ever been reached before in America, both in programmes and in

They cannot witness this example without a newly kindled desire, followed by an effort to do likewise. With the impression fresh in every mind of performances which it is not rash to say may (for the number of instruments) compare with those of the best orchestras in Europe, improvement is a necessity."—"Dwight's Journal of Music," November 6, 1869.

execution.   The public began to be interested, and
the future looked bright.

It was sometime during the seventies that an
amusing incident occurred.   I received a visit from
a man who was known over the whole civilized world
— it is even said that the French, having no equivalent in their language for the word ''humbug,''
adopted his name as a substitute!   If so, they at least
recognized him as a master, and so did I.   It is
P. T. Barnum to whom I refer.   He called upon·me
to arrange with me to ''star'' around the country
under his management.   Our interview, though
brief, was pleasant.   After he had gone, and I had
recovered from my astonishment, can anybody blame
me for feeling properly elated that the greatest manager of the greatest menagerie on earth considered
me worthy of his imperial guidance, and was willing
to place me advantageously before the public, beside
the fat woman and the elephants!   This was a high
tribute — but what had I done to deserve it?

# CHAPTER VII

The Chicago Fire.—Financial Losses.—First Programme of
Finale from "Tristan and Isolde."—Symphony Concerts
in New York.—First Wagner Programme in America,
September 17, 1872.—The Wagner Verein.—Tour to
New Orleans.—Travelling with Rubinstein and Wieniawski.
—The New York Festival.—First Cincinnati Festival.—
Appointed Musical Director of the Philadelphia Cen-
tennial Exposition.—Mrs. Gillespie and her Work.—Failure
of Philadelphia Summer Concerts.—First Season of Chicago
Summer Night Concerts, 1877.—Summer Night Concerts
in St. Louis, Cincinnati, and Cleveland.

ONE Monday morning we suddenly found ourselves facing one of the great historical fires.
It was October 9, 1871, and we were to open the
season at the Crosby Opera House that evening in
Chicago.[1] For the first time, everything, even from the
business point of view, looked very promising, but it
was an illusion. Providence evidently wished to discipline me a little more. I was still too young, too pre-
suming, and had too much vitality. But let that pass.

[1] The Crosby Opera House had been brilliantly decorated
and renovated throughout during the summer of 1871 and was
to have been dedicated anew by Mr. Thomas and his orchestra
on Monday evening, October 9. It was lit up for the first time
on Sunday evening, for the pleasure of friends of the managers,
and two or three hours later was in ashes. Mr. Thomas and
his orchestra reached the Twenty-second Street station of
the Lake Shore Railroad while the fire was at its height and
left the burning city at once, *en route* for St. Louis.—EDR.

It is sufficient that I became so involved financially
by this disaster, and the consequent interruption of
our tour, that it was many years before I recovered
from my losses, and the wearisome travelling had to
go on indefinitely.  We got away from the burning
city as best we could, and spent the time intervening
before our next engagement, which was at St. Louis,
October 21, in rehearsals.  We began by studying
the Finale of "Tristan and Isolde," and I played it
in connection with the Vorspiel (which I had brought
out in 1865), for the first time in America in my next
series of eight concerts in Boston, the following December.

In January I began the year with a series of concerts in New York, Philadelphia, Baltimore, and
Washington, and then went South.  In all the larger
cities on our route a series of concerts was given,
though in many places the people did not know what
to make of them. In one city a morning paper said,
"The concert last night was the greatest orchestral
circus the city has ever seen!"  In New Orleans,
the "Träumerei" made such a sensation that when
people met in the streets the morning after the first
concert, they greeted one another by shaking hands
and humming the tune.  I have even received, during the current year (1904), a letter from one who
heard this piece during that tour, and still enjoys the
recollection of it.  In April we reached Boston again
for another series of concerts.

Our winter season closed  May 8, and on May 13
the Summer Night season opened as usual, at Central

Park Garden, in New York. It will be remembered that for three years I had discontinued my Symphony Soirees in New York, and devoted my time to travelling during the winter months. In September, 1872, however, the following letter came to me:

NEW YORK, August, 1872.

THEODORE THOMAS, ESQ.,

DEAR SIR:—The undersigned, remembering with pleasure the Symphony Concerts with which you favored us in former years, take the liberty of requesting of you, if not inconsistent with your plans, a series of similar concerts during the coming season. They feel deeply how excellent an influence such performances exercise in informing and elevating the public taste for music, and sincerely hope that nothing will prevent you from giving us the desired repetition of them.

| | |
|---|---|
| JULIUS HALLGARTEN, | CHARLES P. DALY, |
| CHARLES C. DODGE, | DR. A. ZINSSER, |
| J. WREY MOULD, | DR. KRACKOWITZOR, |
| J. W. SELIGMAN, | MORGAN DIX, D.D., |
| J. R. G. HASSARD, | JOHN S. WILLIAMS, |
| FRED. DE BELLIER, | A. FORSTER HIGGINS, |
| HENRY DE COPPET, | WHITELAW REID, |
| DR. AUSTIN FLINT, JR., | GEORGE WILLIAM WARREN, |
| S. J. GLASSEY, | CHARLES COUTOIT, |
| S. LASAR, | CHARLES M. CONGREVE, |
| J. H. CORNELL, | CHARLES E. HARMAR, |
| DR. J. WEINER, | P. BORNER, |
| | and others. |

To this letter I sent the following reply:

Messrs. JULIUS HALLGARTEN, CHARLES P. DALY, CHARLES C. DODGE, and others,

GENTLEMEN:—Your letter, dated August, 1872, has been received. It is a satisfaction to me to know that the remembrance of those concerts is still fresh after the lapse of three years, in a country where the past is so soon forgotten. This fact speaks for the influence they have had, and prompts me to comply with your wish.

The interest manifested in your communication, together with the improved taste in the musical community within the last few years, gives me assurance that these concerts cannot fail to be successful.

Respectfully yours,

THEODORE THOMAS.

NEW YORK, September 18, 1872.

It was in response to the foregoing request that I resumed my Symphony Concerts in New York during the season of 1872–73, but this time I gave six in place of five, and called them "Concerts" instead of "Soirees." Before the close of the Summer Night season I gave, for the first time, at the one hundred and twenty-eighth concert, September 17, a Wagner programme, which met with tremendous success.[1] After the "Ritt der Walküren," which was played that night for the first time (from manuscript), the people jumped on the chairs and shouted. After the concert a grand banquet took place, given to the

[1] On that evening, September 17, 1872, Mr. Thomas laid before the members of his orchestra and other friends, assembled at his invitation, his project of founding a Richard Wagner Union, on the plan of similar societies in Europe. His purpose was realized the same evening, and he was chosen president of the Union. Its immediate object was to raise a fund by subscription for the purchase of tickets to the Baireuth Festival in the summer of 1874 for the use of members of the orchestra and also to defray their travelling expenses. The fund was still further increased by the proceeds of two concerts given by the orchestra.—EDR.

orchestra by prominent citizens of New York, and that same night the New York Wagner Verein was organized with great enthusiasm.

Our winter season, which opened as soon as that of the summer had closed, September 26, found us in Albany at the outset of our regular tour west to Chicago. We returned via St. Louis, Pittsburg, and intermediate cities, to New York in time for the first Symphony Concert, November 9. This season, 1872-73, was doubly memorable; first, because the Wagner programme, which I first gave at the Central Park Garden, I now repeated in many cities where I gave a series of concerts, thus familiarizing the public everywhere with Wagner's music, which at that time was unknown outside of New York; and, second, because of the arrival of two great instrumentalists, Rubinstein and Wieniawski, who were brought to America by Maurice Grau.

These two famous artists gave many concerts and recitals in America, and afterwards, in December, a "Grand Combination of the Rubinstein and Thomas Concert Companies," as they were advertised, was effected. The attraction was sufficient to justify me for the first time in my life in making programmes without making allowance for ignorance or prejudice. Before the season closed, we had given many concerts in all the larger cities of the Eastern and Middle states. Programmes of works of the highest standard, rendered by such artists and such an orchestra, were a revelation everywhere, and made a lasting impression. They gave this country the great artistic impetus for which it seemed at last to be ripe.

Our season closed with two Festivals, one at the end of April, in New York, to which the famous Handel and Haydn Society of Boston accepted my invitation, and by its assistance enabled me to give the Ninth Symphony of Beethoven. It also gave a number of choral works under its own conductor, the well-known Carl Zerrahn.[1] The other was the first Cincinnati Festival, which took place in May, 1873. On my return from the latter, the Central Park Garden Concerts began, May 14, continuing daily until September 23, when they closed with a Beethoven-Wagner programme.

An agitation was now started in New York for a hall, suitable for our concerts, for both the summer and winter seasons, and this prospect of a home for my orchestra encouraged us to announce our next travelling season as "the last." I little thought that my last season of travelling was still *thirty years* in the future! We began the tour in Troy in September,

[1] This Festival began April 22 and closed April 26. The soloists were Mrs. J. H. West and Mrs. H. M. Smith, sopranos; Miss Annie Louise Cary, alto; Mr. Nelson Varley, tenor; Mr. Myron W. Whitney and Mr. J. F. Rudolphsen, bassos. The instrumentalists were Rubinstein, Mills, and Mason, pianists; Wieniawski, violinist; B. J. Lang, organist. Mr. Zerrahn led his own society and Mr. Thomas conducted the remainder of the works. The principal works performed were "Israel in Egypt," Handel; "Hymn of Praise," Mendelssohn; "Elijah," Mendelssohn; Concerto in D minor for three pianos and string orchestra, Bach; "Im Walde" Symphony, Raff; Suite, No. 3, in D, Bach; "Unfinished" Symphony, Schubert; and Ninth Symphony, Beethoven.—EDR.

LUIGI ARDITI

THE THOMAS ORCHESTRA IN STEINWAY HALL, NEW YORK

and took our usual route, going westward as far as Chicago, returning through the more Southern cities, and getting back in time for the first Philharmonic Concert in Brooklyn. Both the Brooklyn Philharmonic and my New York Symphony Concerts were successful, but nevertheless the travelling had to be continued to fill out the rest of the time of the orchestra, for I had no subsidy from others to help to meet the expenses of the organization, but was personally responsible for the salaries of my musicians, and my only source of income was the box-office.

In 1874 and 1875 the conditions of the previous year remained unchanged. The usual Summer Night Concerts were given, and, as the prospect of a hall had evaporated, the travelling had to be continued. The only difference was in the programmes, which became better and better, and in the public, which began to show more appreciation. An audience had been obtained with a taste for intellectual music, and a fair artistic standard had been reached all over the country. Boston and its surrounding towns and cities continued to remain loyal, and Philadelphia, Baltimore, and Washington likewise gave their support to our organization, but the necessity of returning constantly to New York for the public rehearsals and concerts of the New York and Brooklyn Philharmonic Societies, and of my own Symphony Series of concerts, prevented us from making extended tours, and was, also, because of our large troupe, so expensive that I found myself, in 1876, again in the same position as in 1869, with only this difference — that at that time I had to travel to obtain a first-rank orchestra; now I had to do it to maintain one.

The Summer Night Concerts at Central Park Garden had been given for seven years, every night, from May until October, with varied success. Musically these concerts exerted a greater educational influence than any institution in America; for the first time, the people enjoyed a good orchestra and good music. Their popularity, of course, induced others to try something similar. Band concerts were given at more convenient locations, where talking and encores could be indulged in without restraint, and these took away from us the average amusement seekers, and with them our pecuniary profits.

Meanwhile, I had been appointed musical director of the opening ceremonies of the Philadelphia Centennial Celebration, in the spring of 1876, and a company was also organized in that city to provide a suitable building for Summer Night Concerts during the continuance of the Exposition. These concerts were to be given under the auspices of the Women's Centennial Committee, the president of which was Mrs. E. D. Gillespie, one of the noblest women whose friendship I have had the good fortune to enjoy. She was as patriotic in art as for her country — a true descendant of Benjamin Franklin. The prospectus of these concerts sets forth the proposed scheme, mainly as follows:

"The appointment by the Commissioners of the Centennial Exposition of Theodore Thomas as Di-

rector of Music for the inaugural ceremonies of the
Exposition, the highest possible recognition of his
labors in the cause of art, engendered a widely expressed desire that Mr. Thomas should give a series
of concerts in Philadelphia during the entire period of
the Exposition, for the purpose of illustrating the
musical progress of America. To carry out this idea
pràctically, the Women's Committee, under the
efficient presidency of Mrs. E. D. Gillespie, and representing the wealth and culture of Philadelphia,
with one accord united in inviting Theodore Thomas
to give concerts in Philadelphia during the Centennial
season of six months, and offering to do everything in
their power requisite for the accomplishment of the
object in view."

Notwithstanding the efforts of Mrs. Gillespie and
her committees, the undertaking was a dismal failure,
and the orchestra had to be disbanded at the end of
July. It proved then — as it has since — that people
go to a World's Fair to see and not to hear, to be
amused, not to be educated. At the end of September, however, a successful series of Festival Concerts
at the Academy of Music in Philadelphia was arranged by Mrs. Gillespie and her ladies, which
brought my orchestra together again.[1]

[1] While the musical scheme for the Centennial Exposition
was under discussion, the gentleman who had purchased the
mansion and grounds formerly belonging to Edwin Forrest,
tendered them to the Women's Centennial Commission. Mr.
Thomas inspected and approved them and the outcome was
the Women's Centennial Music Hall and Garden, which were
opened to the public on the evening of May 11. A hall capable

On October 4 the first of a series of concerts was
given in New York, and the first Symphony Concert
of our tenth season took place October 26, with the
following remarkable programme:

Beethoven—Symphony No. 8.
Schubert—Fantaisie, for piano and orchestra.
Berlioz—Dramatic Symphony, "Romeo and Juliet," com-
plete.

Some more Festival performances were given in
Philadelphia, and on November 10, 1876, the closing
ceremonies of the Centennial Exposition took place.

Concert tours now had to be resumed, and as in
former years, Boston was our first place of refuge.
In the spring I continued travelling in the West, and
in the summer of 1877 I gave my first series of Summer Night Concerts in Chicago, beginning Monday,
June 18, in the old Exposition Building, under the

of accommodating 4,000 persons had been erected and the mansion was used as a restaurant.  The programme of the first
concert included Beethoven's overture, "Consecration of the
House"; Weber's "Invitation to the Dance"; the aria, "In diesen
heil'gen Hallen," from Mozart's "Magic Flute," sung by Myron
W. Whitney; Liszt's "Fourteenth Rhapsody"; Strauss's "Blue
Danube Waltz"; Schubert's "Serenade"; overture to Auber's
"Masaniello," and a repetition of the inaugural ceremonial
music, as follows: "Grand Centennial Inauguration March"
(written for the occasion) by Wagner; J. K. Paine's "Centennial Hymn"; Dudley Buck's Cantata, "Centennial Meditations
of Columbia"; and Handel's "Hallelujah Chorus."  Sixty-
three Summer Night Concerts were given, and then ensued the
failure which Mr. Thomas mentions.  The Festival concerts,
ten in number, beginning September 20 and closing November 4,
were given in the Academy of Music in Philadelphia, and are
noteworthy for the splendid composers' and international programmes which Mr. Thomas arranged for these occasions.—EDR.

management of Carpenter and Sheldon. The building in which these concerts were given had been erected for exposition purposes, and was an immense structure, two Chicago blocks long, and proportionally wide, and innocent of either partitions or interior finish. One end only was used for concert purposes, and was converted into a sort of German garden by evergreen trees planted in tubs, and tables for refreshments in the rear part of the building. Common wooden chairs were placed in rows upon the rough flooring of the front part for seats, and the passing of many railroad trains outside at times completely drowned out the music. In short, it was the last place in the world in which one would have expected orchestral concerts to succeed. Nevertheless, there was something in the very size and informality of the building which made these concerts always delightful, notwithstanding its unsuitability for musical purposes, and the programmes, though popular in character, were always filled with good standard music, besides many novelties, and each week we gave one Symphony and one Composer's programme. The season, though not very successful financially, owing to a great railroad strike, which had affected general business, nevertheless extended through fifty concerts, and gave promise for the future which was amply redeemed in many subsequent years, first under the management of Mrs. Geo. B. Carpenter and Mr. Milward Adams, and later under Mr. Adams alone. At the close of the engagement I received the following letter:

CHICAGO, July 27, 1877.

MR. THEODORE THOMAS,

DEAR SIR:—We believe it to be the universal sentiment of our citizens that in the way of pleasure and musical instruction there has been nothing in Chicago comparable with your summer garden concerts. We regret that unlooked for occurrences have in some degree broken the attendance.

While your efforts in every way deserved success, we had hoped that the result of this season would justify your return next summer. In this expectation we trust our people may not be disappointed.

Permit us to request you to name an evening for a concert when our citizens, by their presence, may confer a compliment personal to yourself.

Very respectfully,

WIRT DEXTER,                    ROBERT T. LINCOLN,
EDWARD S. ISHAM,                HENRY W. BISHOP,
E. B. McCAGG,                   J. M. WALKER,
HENRY W. KING,                  N. H. FAIRBANK,
J. D. HARVEY,                   A. A. MUNGER,
MARSHALL FIELD,                 C. E. DUNCAN,
JOHN G. SHORTALL,               CHARLES D. HAMILL,
JAMES S. HAMILTON,                    and others.

I answered this as follows:

CHICAGO, July 28, 1877.

MR. WIRT DEXTER and others,

GENTLEMEN:—In accepting the compliment extended to me in your letter of the 27th, permit me to say that the cordial welcome I have met with in public and private, during my stay this summer has greatly attached me to your city.

When, eleven years ago, I inaugurated nightly summer concerts in New York, I did it with a view of elevating my profession and the public taste for music. In a few years these concerts have become a recognized institution of the country. However, as my repertoire extended, my orchestra had to be increased to meet the enlarged demands of modern composers. In order to sustain so large an organization I was obliged to travel a portion of the year, and it was this necessity which first introduced me to the West. Still it was New York, Boston and Philadelphia that enjoyed the fruits of all this labor, in the shape of Symphony Concerts which could never have reached the high standard attained, had not the whole country contributed to the support of the organization.

After eleven consecutive years of Summer Night Concerts I have been obliged to leave New York for want of a suitable hall in which to give them. *What New York offered I refused, and what I wanted I could not have.* That metropolis not having supplied my needs, I was induced to try the West, and I gladly confess I do not regret the experiment. I find the people here open-hearted, generous, and enthusiastic, and in thanking them through you for their kind appreciation of the labor my colleagues and myself have done here during the last few months, it would give me pleasure, circumstances permitting, to return here next summer.

The support we have received justifies me in saying that Chicago is the only city on the continent, next to New York, where there is sufficient musical culture to enable me to give a series of fifty successive concerts.

Thanking you again for your kindness, I will, with your permission, name next Wednesday, August 1, as the evening most convenient for the complimentary concert,[1] and will, with your consent, combine with it a request programme.

Very respectfully yours,

THEODORE THOMAS.

Summer Night Concerts were continued after the close of the Chicago engagement, in St. Louis two weeks, Cincinnati two weeks, and Cleveland one

[1] The programme on this occasion contained the Prelude, Chorale, and Fugue of Bach, adapted for orchestra by Abert; Handel's concerto for string orchestra, two solo violins and

week, the summer season finally closing September
14, 1877.

violoncello, (Messrs. Jacobsohn, F. Hemman, and C. Hemman);
the andantino and March tempo from Spohr's "Consecration
of Tones" Symphony; the Overture, Scherzo and Finale of
Schumann; Liszt's symphonic poem, "Tasso"; Vieuxtemps's
"Fantaisie Caprice"; and ballet music to Wagner's "Rienzi."
Mr. H. A. Bischoff sang Schubert's "Erl King" and Lachner's
"Ueberall Du" with violin obligato by Mr. C. Hemman.   It
was a jubilee week for the summer-nighters.   The next evening
there was a Berlioz, Liszt, and Wagner programme; August 3,
a request programme, the principal features of which were
Haydn's "Military Symphony," Brahms's "Hungarian Dances,"
the "Pastorale" from Bach's "Christmas Oratorio," and the
ballet music and wedding procession from Rubinstein's "Fer-
amors"; and August 4 the season closed with programmes
which included all the most successful features of the summer's
work.—EDR.

# CHAPTER VIII

The New York Philharmonic Society.—Malicious Statements Corrected.—Elected Conductor of the New York Philharmonic.—Abandons Symphony Concerts in New York for the Benefit of the Philharmonic Society.—More Travelling.—Third Cincinnati Festival.—Summer Night Concerts at Gilmore's Garden, Madison Square. — Offers from Europe Refused.—Leaves New York to Live in Cincinnati.

THE New York Philharmonic Society is the oldest orchestral organization in America, and has the great merit that it gave good music and an opportunity to hear the great master-works when no other society did so. Its endeavors were always for a noble cause — for art. Many misstatements and perversions of fact have been made, some with a sinister purpose and others ignorantly, with reference to the history of this society. It has been charged, for instance, that it was forced to elect me its conductor on account of my rivalry, and because I took away its best men for my orchestra. Except for these untruthful statements, I should not have alluded to the following facts, but I think I owe it to myself to give them to the public, and show that the reverse was the case.

My first instrumentalists were mostly brought over from Europe, and as long as I travelled I could offer them the inducement of a good engagement.

I had the pick of the men, and had absolute control. I could make changes in my orchestra when I thought it necessary without consulting any one.   The Philharmonic Society could not.   This was, of course, to my advantage, but it was also for the benefit of the public, for it resulted in progress.   Previous to Carl Bergmann's death, consultations had taken place between prominent members of the Philharmonic Society and myself for the purpose of effecting a combination which would enable me to become its conductor.   We could not come to an understanding, however, because they desired me to give up my Symphony Concerts.   I refused to accept any conditions.   In 1876, Bergmann died, and I was approached again, but as the same conditions were insisted upon, I again refused.   Leopold Damrosch was thereupon elected conductor, and the season was financially disastrous.   The following year I was elected conductor without any conditions, but later I voluntarily showed my respect for the society by discontinuing my Symphony Concerts, against the wishes and advice of my personal friends, because I thought it better for the cause of art that a society rather than an individual should be in authority. Besides this, during all the years that I was its conductor, I never drew the full amount of salary to which I was entitled by my contract.

The Philharmonic and Thomas orchestras were now united, and all my principal men became members of the society.   The situation, however, only grew more aggravating for me.   The house was sold

WILLIAM MASON AND THEODORE
THOMAS, IN 1855

THE MASON–THOMAS QUARTETTE IN 1856

G MATZKA    T. MOSENTHAL    F. BERGNER    THEODORE THOMAS    WILLIAM MASON

out for the Philharmonic Concerts, and in the case of my Symphony Concerts, which were not yet given up, I had to add a second series of public rehearsals, to satisfy the demands of the patrons. The result of this was that the intervals between the various performances in New York and Brooklyn were too short to allow me to make any extended tours with my orchestra. I would not have been sorry for this had New York and its vicinity yielded sufficient engagements to support the orchestra. Hence we were obliged to travel when we could, and these "forced marches" meant great hardship for the orchestra and myself, and left no time at home for rehearsals. It also involved great and constant financial risks for me. For instance, during the previous winter we had made a week's tour to Buffalo and return. A storm came up on the way out, and we were snowbound, with the result that when we returned to New York for the Symphony Concert, we had spent most of the time in the ordinary day cars, had given but two concerts on the trip, instead of six or seven, and I had become indebted for salaries, etc., about three thousand dollars. I confess I felt that I ought to be relieved of this financial responsibility. As time went on, I became still more involved, and recovery was more and more difficult. The so-called "benefit concerts" tendered to me at the end of the seasons by prominent citizens became very irksome. Popular taste had developed, artistic rendering had become a necessity, and I felt that the time had arrived when a permanent orchestra ought to be established by the people, and that New York had means enough to support easily both the Philharmonic Society, with its six afternoon and evening concerts, and a permanent, subsidized orchestra.

There could be no greater educational charity, in an art centre like New York City, than to give its people one or two weekly performances of orchestral master-works in music free, or at low prices, following the example of the picture galleries and museums, which are free on certain days to the public. Justice cannot be done to the present musical literature, either in quality or quantity, except by a permanent orchestra which rehearses together constantly. To make such an orchestra earn its own maintenance by playing every night — which means anywhere and everywhere — and travelling all day, does not allow time for proper rehearsals, nor for any high purpose, and makes artistic performance impossible. I saw no way of keeping together what I had built up during so many years of hard labor.

When I travelled all over the country with about sixty men, and returned to New York only at given times for my Symphony Concerts, rehearsals would go on continually while travelling, and portions of the New York programmes would be given in our concerts. Then, on my return to New York, I would rehearse with the twenty or thirty string players who strengthened the orchestra for the New York performance, separately, and previous to uniting the forces. In this way New York City had the benefit of an organization which the country at large supported, and which the hardships of incessant travelling and playing every night in a different city made possible. I could not have carried this on for so many years without the aid of my friend, Jacob Gosche, who looked after the business side and sacrificed himself — and me also — for the cause.

The season of 1877–78 ended May 21, with the third Cincinnati Festival, and a series of concerts in Cleveland, and on Saturday, May 25, we began the Summer Night Concerts in the Gilmore Garden, Madison Square, New York City. The Cincinnati Festival had been a tremendous success, both artistically and financially, and its citizens were ready for higher musical efforts. During the summer the Cincinnati possibilities were discussed with some of its leading men, whom I saw in New York, and I began to look around for another centre large enough to support an orchestra. I refused to leave this country and go to Europe, which had made me some offers. I knew this field, saw my opportunities, and preferred to grow up with this country. So I accepted an engagement in Cincinnati.

The Summer Night Concerts in Gilmore's Garden were continued daily until the end of September, and after another of those well-meant but irksome "benefit concerts," I left New York for Cincinnati, October 3, 1878, with many regrets expressed by my professional friends, my orchestra, and the Philharmonic Society.

# CHAPTER IX

Cincinnati in 1869.—Founding of the Cincinnati Festival Association.—Director of the Cincinnati Festivals.—Musical Director of the College of Music.—Disagreement with its President.—Resignation from the College.—The Cincinnati Festivals and their Board of Directors.—The Chorus.—Arthur Mees's and Edwin W. Glover's Services.—The Festival Orchestra.—Return to New York in 1880.

CINCINNATI, one of the oldest settlements in the West, not only possesses wealth and culture, but it also has sincere and capable musicians, who by their influence as teachers developed a genuine love and understanding of music in that community. About one-fourth of its population, thirty-five years ago, was German, or of German descent, and while I, for one, do not believe that the German in America is necessarily musical, he nevertheless has a high respect for art. For many years music has been a large part of the daily life of the Cincinnati people, and the city at that time ranked second only to New York, Boston, or Philadelphia, in musical achievement. When I made my first visit to Cincinnati with my orchestra, in 1869, even at that early time I found excellent choral societies there, and an orchestra superior to that of any city west of New York. On my next visit, in 1871, a young married lady, who was a member of one of the leading families of the city, laid before me a plan for a large

78

CARTOON OF A CENTRAL PARK GARDEN CONCERT

(FROM A CONTEMPORARY PRINT)

THE THOMAS ORCHESTRA AT GILMORE'S GARDEN, NEW YORK

(FROM A GILMORE'S GARDEN PROGRAMME)

Musical Festival. She proposed that I should be the conductor of it, saying that if I would be responsible for the artistic side, she would find the men who would take charge of the business details. I soon found out that this lady was not only very talented herself in many ways, but that her taste was not amateurish in anything, and I readily consented to undertake the work she wished me to do. Some of the programmes were sketched at her house, and the Festival took place, as planned, in May, 1873, and was a great success. Its directors decided to give a second of similar scope in 1875.

The programmes of the second Festival show at once a high standard for the evening performances — in fact, fully up to that of the present day — while those for the afternoon concerts correctly reflect the standard and taste of that time.

For the third Festival, which took place in 1878,[1]

[1] The third Festival was one of the most memorable in the whole series, for, during that week in May (1878), the new hall and the great organ were dedicated, the programmes were in keeping with the dignity of the occasion, and the financial result was unprecedented. Mme. Eugenie Pappenheim, Mrs. E. Aline Osgood, Miss Annie Louise Cary, Miss Emma Cranch, and Messrs. Adams, Fritsch, Whitney, and Remmertz were the soloists, and Mr. George E. Whitney was the organist. For this occasion Mr. Thomas had an orchestra of 106 men and a chorus of 700. The principal works performed were scenes from Gluck's "Alceste," Mr. Otto Singer's "Festival Ode," Handel's "Messiah," selections from Wagner's "Götterdämmerung," Liszt's "Missa Solennis," Beethoven's "Eroica" and Ninth Symphonies, and Berlioz's "Romeo and Juliet" symphony. The financial showing was most gratifying. The receipts were $72,000 and after all expenses were settled the association found itself with $32,000 in its treasury, which

a large and handsome building was erected, which is unlike any structure devoted to festival uses in America. It was the direct outcome of the Festivals, and built only for festival purposes.

A school of music had already been established there in the same year, known as the Cincinnati College of Music, the musical directorship of which was offered to me. This was the situation as I found it in 1878, and it was the high expectations raised by the possibilites of the school and the Festivals that induced me to try my fortunes in that Western city.

The Festivals always maintained the high standard which characterized their inauguration, but unfortunately this was not the case with the school. Two fundamental conditions which are necessary for a successful school of music were not recognized by its leading official — first, talent in its pupils, and second, a musical course of sufficient duration for their education. Instead of this, the spirit which governed the institution was financial. It was insisted that "it must pay," and all kinds of pupils were accepted, for any desired period of study, so that no high standard of scholarship was possible. Of course, under these circumstances my connection with the school was short, for it was impossible for me to work in harmony with the president and guiding spirit of the institution. In the spring of the second year I made conditions which brought mat-

placed it upon a secure financial footing. Its future was assured.—EDR.

ters to a crisis, resulting in my resignation. The directors of the school made a statement to the public, trying to explain from their point of view the reasons for all this trouble. I do not know whether they succeeded or not, for I did not care to read it. After my retirement from the directorship, the school went on, although I understand that it has passed through many vicissitudes, and many changes have taken place in its government. So much for the school.

My experience with the Festival Association was very different, and my relations with the gentlemen who were responsible and active in giving these Festivals — with the exception of the first President of the Board, who was also the president of the school before alluded to — have been of the most pleasant and harmonious character during the thirty-one years we have worked together. Some of these gentlemen have, of course, a better understanding of music than others, but all have an appreciation of high aims, and all love their city. So long as a community has men like these to foster and promote its interests, it need have no concern about its future.

It is not my province to write the history of the Cincinnati Festivals, and, besides, I have always been too closely identified with them for that. But the work of the association has been too imporant to be passed by without mention. I will also take this opportunity to express my opinion on some points in which improvement and progress are desirable, and to show some of the disadvantages under which the Festivals have been carried on for more than thirty years

With a single exception the Cincinnati Festivals have been given biennially from 1873 to the present year, 1904. A comparison of our programmes with those of similar festivals in Europe would be in our favor, and the fact of rehearsing the world's masterworks for so many years would alone stamp Cincinnati as a musical community. The chorus was composed of local singers, and the programme book of 1904 states that since its inception it has included more than ten thousand persons.

Here we note at once the first deficiency in the organization, and one which is characteristic of America; for while a constant change in the personnel of the chorus may be an advantage to the community, it is not so to the association, for it prevents the chorus from having a repertoire, and consequently at every Festival the old works require as much time for preparation as the new, instead of requiring only to be re-polished, as would be the case if they were in the repertoire of the chorus. The percentage of members who remain for a number of years in the organization, and those who are changing constantly I do not know, but I believe the time has come when the same system can be carried out with the chorus as has already been done with the orchestra, and a higher standard can be reached with a smaller body of singers.

Another difficulty has been the lack of a suitable hall in which the chorus rehearsals could be held. A rehearsal hall for chorus work should not be too small, nor should it have too much vibration, for the

THEODORE THOMAS IN 1857

ANTON RUBINSTEIN

singers must be able to hear all the other parts easily, and learn that the blending of voices is the same as the blending of colors. Shouting is not singing, and without shading expression is impossible. In 1880 I was able, owing to my residence in Cincinnati, to superintend the work of the chorus and rehearse with it a great deal. I treated its members like intelligent beings, taught them to think, and compelled them to distinguish the intervals mentally instead of merely singing "by ear." As a result, such rapid progress was made that the chorus of that year was pronounced by the Eastern musicians who attended the Festival the best in the country.

When I left Cincinnati I placed the chorus under the direction of Mr. Arthur Mees, who had been my accompanist, and who conscientiously continued the work and further developed the chorus as long as he remained in that city. After his departure it deteriorated, owing to several causes, the principal one of which I will mention. Amateur musicians, of whom American choruses are, of course, always composed, need encouragement, and their work is good only when their enthusiasm is aroused. But, instead of encouragement, a singular hostility was shown toward our chorus by the daily press of Cincinnati. To such an extent was this carried, that the confidence of our singers was destroyed, and, indeed, at one time it was even quite heroic for one to be a member of the Festival Chorus. The reason for this antagonism was probably that it gave more satisfaction to a few musical reporters to create a

sensation in the community than to help a noble
cause or advance art.   Knowing the effect these adverse press notices had upon the chorus, I used to ask,
after a performance, "How is the press?"   The
answer was always, "The same."   Owing to this
cause, as I have said, the chorus lacked confidence,
and the slightest untoward event during a performance would create confusion.   So we had our "ups
and downs," but notwithstanding this drawback,
good performances were given, and some were even
memorable.

In 1898 Mr. Edwin W. Glover, a former member
of the chorus, became its director, and since then it
has not only regained its former standard, but even
surpassed all previous efforts.   I cannot say too
much in praise of the members of the chorus.   Both
the ladies and gentlemen challenge the respect of
every music-lover, for the loyalty and enthusiasm
they have shown in making the Festivals a success,
and it is a hopeful sign that great works, some containing almost insurmountable difficulties, appeal
more to the chorus than those of lighter calibre, or
those written by less intellectual composers.   Public
sympathy and interest have been regained, and a
more friendly attitude is manifested by the press, and
I believe the Festivals have now such a hold on the
people that they will not allow them to be discontinued.   I trust that this may prove to be the case,
for while Festivals may not be necessary for the advancement in art of large world-centres — because
everything in them is done upon a large scale — they

are of vital importance in the smaller centres, in enabling them to keep abreast of the times. This is especially true in the art of music of the present day.

The orchestra employed at the Cincinnati Festivals was, for many years, composed of my own, increased to Festival proportions by the addition of the better players of the Cincinnati Orchestra. But of late years, owing to the higher standard of our choral performances, the orchestra and I had to devote the whole of our time in Cincinnati to the rehearsal of the choral works, preparing those for orchestra alone in Chicago before leaving home, and playing them in the Festival without further rehearsal. As the Cincinnati musicians could not, of course, come to Chicago for the rehearsals, this naturally made it impossible to engage them for any but the choral works. In earlier years we could not have secured satisfactory results without an orchestra of large dimensions, but as the Chicago Orchestra progressed, and its general standard became higher, we were able to replace quantity by quality, and produce better artistic results.

The soloists of the Festivals have always been artists of the highest distinction obtainable in the musical world. Nevertheless, it was one of the most difficult problems to find soloists who were familiar with the great choral works and could do them justice. The opera singer has not the time to learn them, and only very few have had the training and opportunity necessary to know the difference in style between the operatic and the concert stage. As for taking part in concerted music, and subordinating themselves to others, that would be a new idea for stars! Here, however, I must except Mme. Lilli Lehmann and Mme. Sembrich, and in former years Miss Annie Louise Cary and Mr. Myron W. Whitney. In England there is a demand for choral works, and consequently singers are trained for that music. So our best results have been with English singers — who also have an advantage in the matter of language. American singers are at a great disadvantage. Choral works are not in demand in this country, and the public taste does not admit of their reaching the high standard required for this class of music.

During the first winter of my stay in Cincinnati, the Brooklyn Philharmonic Society had made arrangements with the directors of the school which permitted me to go to Brooklyn once a month to conduct the Philharmonic Concerts — the school receiving in return a certain percentage of my fee. The second winter the New York Philharmonic Society combined with the Brooklyn in the arrangement, and the latter even changed its days to enable me to conduct the concerts of both societies on my monthly visits. By the time I had decided to leave Cincinnati, both societies had made me offers, and, these being taken as a basis, the future again looked hopeful in New York, and I once more returned there in the fall of 1880.

# CHAPTER X

A FTER a short vacation in Europe, I returned to
New York in 1880. The Brooklyn Philharmonic Society resumed concerts on its customary
days, Fridays and Saturdays, and both the Brooklyn and New York Societies began work with
renewed vigor, which was rewarded with financial
success for many years.

I did not resume my own Symphony Concerts in
New York, preferring to throw all my influence into
the scale of the Philharmonic Society. The Philharmonic Orchestra was then composed of all the best
players in the city. It was the largest, and, take it
for all in all, the best orchestral organization this
country had had. The men were quick in response
to the conductor, and certainly developed a good
quality of tone. We gave many concerts, and some
of them were great performances. But, as in former
years, we had to travel, and were soon overworked.
One sign of progress, however, was the formation of

choruses in New York and Brooklyn of which I was the conductor, and which gave variety to our programmes.[1] The work of these choruses culminated in a gigantic musical Festival, given in the Seventh Regiment Armory of New York, May 2–6, 1882.

[1] Immediately after his return from Cincinnati, September 8, 1880, Mr. Thomas issued a prospectus announcing his desire "of forming a chorus worthy to coöperate with his orchestra. The immediate object of this organization will be the performance of choral works in connection with the Philharmonic Society of New York. The requirements necessary for entrance are (1) good voices with ability to read music of moderate difficulty fairly well at sight; and (2), regular and punctual attendance at all rehearsals." The result was the formation of the New York Chorus Society with Mr. Thomas as conductor and Hon. Carl Schurz as president, which gave regular seasons of concerts for five years. In this connection the following statement of Mr. Thomas in an interview will be of interest:

"It has been an old habit to treat the chorus like a body of children, telling them simply to do so and so, to repeat a phrase as directed, as though they were a lot of bullfinches to whom a tune was whistled. What can you expect? Treat them like bullfinches and they are little else than a body of those musical imitators of airs; appeal to their intelligence, force them to read their music, to think it out, promptly correct but intelligently explain their errors, and you have at last a thoughtful, accomplished body of singers who comprehend what they are undertaking and thoroughly succeed in its accomplishment. Treat them like musicians, and they become musicians. It is really ridiculous how some choral bodies are taught. Music should be to the vocalist what painting is to the artist. The score should be his brush and pigments. The first should be only the rough materials and his intelligence should so dispose them that the picture should be the masterpiece of his own work and imagination, not the single result of direction or accidental combination of colors. Let these vocal artists once understand that you expect them to think out their musical picture and they will astonish you with the breadth and truth of their imagination."—EDR.

For this Festival the choral forces numbered three thousand singers, and included the following eminent societies:

The New York Chorus Society, 600 singers.

The Brooklyn Philharmonic Chorus, 600 singers.

The Boston Handel and Haydn Society, 550 singers.

The Philadelphia Cecilian Society, 350 singers.

The Worcester County (Mass.) Musical Association, 450 singers.

The Baltimore Oratorio Association, 550 singers.

The Reading (Pa.) Choral Society, 100 singers.

The orchestra numbered nearly three hundred players, and was composed wholly of musicians who at one time or another had been members of my orchestra in previous years. It was a great reunion, and there was much excitement and enthusiasm displayed at times. An incident happened in one of the rehearsals which has been related in so many ways and usually so incorrectly, that I will correct it here. In "Wotan's Abschied," from "Die Walküre," a passage for the violoncellos occurs which begins in the bass clef and continues with the tenor clef. 'Cellists, unless very familiar with the music, are apt to make a mistake and read this passage in the bass clef all the way through. On this occasion there were thirty-six 'cello players, and the last stand was about eighty feet away from me. When we came to this place, I heard the mistake in the passage, and remembering how it was written, suspected the cause at once. I knew the mistake was made at the last

stand of the 'cellos, and glancing at the players I saw
that one of them had his hand on his instrument in
the position where it would be if he had played in the
bass clef.   I stepped quickly to the stand and pointed
out to the man his mistake, and returning to my
place, continued with the rehearsal.   This took less
time than if I had made the correction from the conductor's desk at that distance, but the orchestra was
aghast that I had been able to single out the man
who had made the mistake from amongst so many
players.   The incident only illustrates that the conductor sometimes hears with his eyes as well as his
ears!

I had placed the players on the stage so as to form
a triple orchestra, similar to an organ with three
manuals, which could be played on either singly or
in combination, at the pleasure of the conductor.   Of
course the parts were all marked, and rehearsals had
been held accordingly, but in such an immense
auditorium as that in which the Festival was given,
the difference in the acoustics when it was empty and
when it was full of people was so great that I had to
be prepared for any emergency.   I made use of my
combinations with good effect in the concerts, and
accomplished some unusual shading by manipulating
my triple orchestra, even in such works as Mozart's
"Jupiter Symphony."   Some of the works given were
overpowering, but others again, such as the Beethoven Mass, for instance, were disappointing, for
reasons easy to understand.   Neither the chorus nor
the orchestra escaped encores entirely.   The greatest

and most enduring effect was produced by the Wagner programme, especially the excerpts from "Die Götterdämmerung," for which Madame Materna had been brought over from Vienna. This performance created the greatest excitement I have ever witnessed, and made many converts to the Wagner music dramas. Considered from every point of view, this Festival was one of those great and unusual occasions which rarely occur twice in a lifetime; it will long be remembered in the musical annals of New York.[1]

[1] The New York Festival of 1882, like the Festival in Chicago given the same year, was the outcome of the Cincinnati Festival. In an interview at that time Mr. Thomas said: "The matter of a great musical Festival under my direction was broached to me by a number of gentlemen who were present at the Cincinnati Biennial Festival and they were desirous to have similar musical efforts undertaken here." The promoters, 163 of the leading citizens of New York and Brooklyn, organized under the name of the "Musical Festival Association," with Mr. Thomas for conductor and the following officers: President, George William Curtis; Vice-Presidents, Cyrus W. Field and Henry G. Marquand; Secretary, Daniel Lord, Jr.; Treasurer, Joseph W. Drexel. The Festival was given May 2–6, and included four evening and three afternoon concerts. The list of solo artists was an imposing one: Sopranos, Frau Materna, Mrs. E. Aline Osgood, Miss Hattie Schell, Miss Amalia Wurmb and Mme. Etelka Gerster; contraltos, Miss Annie Louise Cary, Miss Emily Winant, Miss Antonia Henne; tenors, Italo Campanini, William J. Candidus, Theodore J. Toedt; bassos, A. F. Galassi, George Henschel, Franz Remmertz, Oscar Steins, and Myron W. Whitney; organist, Dudley Buck. The principal vocal works performed were Bach's cantata, "A Stronghold Sure," Handel's "Utrecht Jubilate," Beethoven's "Missa Solennis" in D major, Handel's "Israel in Egypt," Berlioz's "Fall of Troy" and selections from Wagner's "Nibelung Trilogy"; instrumental, Mozart's symphony in C major (Köchel, 551), Schubert's symphony in C major, No. 9 and Beethoven's symphony in C minor, No. 5,

During the same month of May, 1882, the fourth Cincinnati Festival, as well as the first of the Chicago Festivals, took place, in a style commensurate with that of New York. The Summer Night Concerts that year began in Cleveland, and continued during the customary five weeks in Chicago, followed by short seasons in Milwaukee, St. Louis, and Cincinnati.

During the winter I introduced the low pitch into this country, a difficult but important matter to accomplish. Two years previously I had held a consultation with my orchestra on the subject, and had given them two years in order that the wind choir might have time enough to procure new instruments of lower pitch from Europe, and also to allow the string players to prepare their instruments for the change. On a given date one morning the low pitch became a settled fact, and it was at once a success, in spite of intrigues and coarse assaults by certain instrument makers.

During the winter of 1883–84, many concerts were given in New York besides those of the Philharmonic Society, among which may be mentioned the first series of Young People's Concerts, and also a series on Sunday afternoons for the working people.

and Liszt's "Divina Commedia" symphony. It was contemplated to make the association permanent and by-laws were printed, setting forth as its object: "The promotion of musical art by musical Festivals, or in such other manner as it shall determine." Unforeseen changes, however, in Mr. Thomas's plans made regular Festivals in New York impracticable.—EDR.

A tour through the South also was made, and subscription concerts were given in Boston, Philadelphia, Jersey City, and Orange.

In the spring a Festival tour was made from ocean
to ocean [1]— starting in New York and continuing to
San Francisco, and returning to Chicago, where it
ended in the Summer Night Season. The following
season, 1884–85, was only a repetition of former
ones, but it culminated, in the spring, in a series of
Wagner concerts, managed by Charles E. Locke,
and planned on a very large scale. Besides Mme.
Materna, Herr Winkelmann and Herr Scaria were
brought over, which enabled me to give all the
excerpts from Wagner's operas that were suitable for
the concert stage. We also had the assistance of the
New York and Brooklyn choruses, as well as that of
the New York Liederkranz, which did admirable
work in the third act of "Die Meistersinger." Our
orchestra was increased to one hundred and fifty
players, and in the New York concerts the chorus
numbered six hundred. After this I gave similar
Wagner concerts in all the principal cities, and every-

---

[1] On the "March to the Sea" sixty-five concerts were given.
There were concerts at Baltimore, Bradford, Pa., Buffalo,
Erie, Cleveland, Columbus, Louisville, Memphis, Nashville,
Chicago, St. Louis, Kansas City, Keokuk, Cedar Rapids, St.
Paul, Minneapolis, Waterloo, Ia., and a week's Festival in
San Francisco. Returning, concerts were given in Salt Lake
City, Denver, Topeka, Leavenworth, St. Joseph, Lincoln,
Omaha, Fort Dodge, Des Moines, Rock Island, and Burling-
ton. The soloists who made the tour with Mr. Thomas
were Mrs. E. Humphrey Allen, Mrs. Anne Hartdegen, Mrs.
Belle Cole, Frederick Harvey, Franz Remmertz, and Julia
Rivé-King, pianist.—EDR.

where they made a deep impression.[1]   The season of
German opera, which was inaugurated the following
year in the Metropolitan Opera House, was due to the
success of these concerts.   Before the organization of
the Metropolitan Company, offers were made to me
to take the conductorship of a company which should
include the famous Baireuth singers, Materna, Winkelmann, and Scaria, in the leading roles, and give
the Wagner music-dramas for the first time in America.   At first I refused, as the promoters of the project wished to. put it into effect immediately.   After
consultation, however, they agreed to my conditions,
and I consented.   These conditions were that the
plan should not be carried out until 1885–86, and
that I should spend the intermediate year in Europe,
studying and familiarizing myself with the German
opera, and especially with the Wagner music-dramas
as given in Germany.   The three singers also agreed
to this arrangement, and Winkelmann and Scaria
kept faith with us in the matter.   Materna did not.
She accepted an engagement with the Metropolitan
Opera Company, which was formed the next season,
and our enterprise, consequently, was abandoned.

Meanwhile, I had spent the summer in Germany
with my family, and I returned to New York as

[1] The Wagner Festival tour began the first week in April,
1884, and ended in Montreal, June 28.   The sixth biennial
festival in Cincinnati, May 20-24, was part of the scheme.
In addition to the Vienna artists mentioned by Mr. Thomas,
Christine Nilsson, Emma Juch, Emil Winant, Theodore
Toedt, and Fanny Remmertz sang in many of the concerts,
which numbered seventy in all.—EDR.

usual in the fall for the customary Philharmonic Concerts, and incessant travelling. The New York Chorus was disbanded in 1886, because the travelling and orchestral duties did not allow me the necessary time for chorus rehearsals.

During this season a company was formed to give grand opera in English, called the American Opera Company, and it aroused such popular interest that under ordinary circumstances it would have been successful. The conductorship was offered to me, and I accepted it, for I believed in the idea, and I knew it would also give my orchestra a permanent engagement, and relieve me from the responsibility of paying salaries. My hopes, however, were doomed to disappointment, for it soon became evident that there were peculiarities of management which neither art nor business could long endure. Financially the case was soon hopeless, and the only question left for me was how to get out of the toils in which I had been cunningly ensnared. The management refused to allow the much-abused and at last fatally stricken organization to die a natural death or have decent burial, and so it came about that toward the close it was either a disgrace or a calamity to every one connected with it. Even after it finally was dead and buried, its apparition haunted different cities all over the country for a time. My official connection with it had been limited to that of musical director. I had no business interest in it whatever, but I was for years afterwards involved in lawsuits brought against me by its victims.

# CHAPTER XI

The End of the Thomas Orchestra, 1888.—Why I Left New York.—Founding of the Boston Symphony Orchestra in 1880.—Founding of the Chicago Orchestra in 1901.—Accepts Directorship of the Chicago Orchestra.—The Difficulty of Maintaining a First-rank Orchestra in Chicago.—Henry L. Higginson and his Influence.—Chicago Raises an Endowment Fund for the Orchestra by Popular Subscription.—The Building of a Home for the Orchestra in 1904.—The Work of the Chicago Board of Directors.—Coda.

AFTER my disastrous experiences with the American Opera Company came to an end, in 1888, I found myself in a very discouraging position, for I was no nearer to the permanent orchestra for which I had worked so long than I was in 1878, when I left New York for Cincinnati. Nor was there any prospect of a change in the situation. To maintain my orchestra I must continue to follow in the same weary and unsatisfactory round of travelling and overwork, which precluded progress. The only other alternative was to disband the orchestra and retire from the field. I had now been travelling with my orchestra almost continuously for twenty years, and the situation, instead of being better, was even worse for us than at the start, because all these years of educational work were beginning to bear their legitimate fruit. The people all over the country

96

were acquiring a taste for orchestral music, but were
not yet sufficiently cultivated to be very discrimina-
tive, and this opened a field for inferior orchestras
and military bands. As they interfered with our
pecuniary success, I preferred to stop. At the close
of our Summer Night Season in Chicago in 1888, I
made the following address to my orchestra at our
last rehearsal:

*Gentlemen:*—The time has come to communicate to you
what I can offer for next season. This, however, is more easily
said than done owing to the peculiar circumstances in which
affairs in New York have placed me. I pray you, therefore,
to listen attentively in order that you may understand and
appreciate them.

You will remember that last spring, after the close of our
winter season, I said to you our future prospects were encouraging. What caused me to believe this was, first that the
building of a large and well-appointed music hall in New York
seemed assured. I was shown the detailed plans and understood from the architect and other interested persons that its
construction would begin May 1, and consequently that it
would be in readiness for our concerts next winter. But for
these assurances I should have told you then that our prospects
were bad and that we had better stop. In the second place,
my friends gave me the assurance that they would raise a
guarantee fund which would guard us against losses and insure
our position during the winter months in New York. Thus
encouraged I looked at a theatre (the Broadway), which was
suitable for matinees, and hoped to get through without serious
loss until the hall was built. So far as the hall is concerned,
however, I only know that it was not begun May 1, and that
there are no signs any hall will be built, so we are left without
one. So far as the guarantee fund is concerned, it is in better
shape and has already been started, but it is accompanied by

the condition that our concerts shall be given in some place up-town more favorably located than that to which we have been accustomed.   All that is left to us is the theatre, which, as you will see, would confine us to matinees.   We have no hall.   Even if we should take the Metropolitan Opera House it is question-able whether we could make dates that would be advantageous to us.   From a business point of view I should have no fears of non-success, but for regular concerts we should have to have an orchestra of eighty or ninety men and give our concerts with a single rehearsal.   Such concerts are not desirable and can lead to no good results.

To retain a permanent organization there is apparently only one thing we can do, and that is to travel during the whole year.   You, however, would not be willing, even if I were, to lead such a life, which is wearisome and not conducive to the retention of a high musical standard.   So long, therefore, as New York gives us no hold upon success in the shape of a hall and declines to build one where the public can be pleasantly and conveniently accommodated, a permanent orchestra seems to me impossible.

It was only last week that I wrote the committee of the guarantee fund that I could not say whether we would give matinees or not, as that would depend upon the orchestra at my disposal.   I can tell you this: that I have been requested to give winter concerts in Chicago, and that offers have been made to guarantee them, but the number of concerts would depend upon those we could give in other cities, in one at least from New York here and in another on the return, to make it practicable.   This, even if it could be accomplished, would take a long time to arrange.   I hope you will under-stand, therefore, that I cannot say how much work I can promise you.   It would seem that there might be several con-certs, but the standard of such desultory work would be doubt-ful.   It is only lately that I have been able to come to a decision and to know just what is best and right to do.   It goes without saying that I cannot keep you or prevent you from making other engagements, signing other contracts, or giving lessons, but I shall expect that you will notify me if you make any engagements that will hinder you at any time from appearing in concerts in or out of New York, and meanwhile will ascertain as expeditiously as possible how many concerts will be at my disposal.

The members of the orchestra could not believe that this was the final disbanding of the Thomas Orchestra, to which many of them had belonged for years, and which they all loved and took pride in. After our return to New York, many of them refused to take engagements which would prevent their returning to me, for they thought that New York would not allow our organization to be abandoned after so many years of service, but would raise an endowment fund and make it a permanent institution. New York, however, was now absorbed in its new operatic venture, and did nothing at all.

I now ceased to make any further effort, and merely conducted the various series of Philharmonic Concerts in New York, Brooklyn, and Philadelphia, and some Popular Sunday Night Concerts. I made an occasional tour when I was engaged by others, and had no financial risk, but I had no longer an orchestra, nor any hall for rehearsals. I simply engaged the men from concert to concert, and for the first time in my life, "went on my reputation"— as the saying is — to make my living.

I made a plain statement to my friends and the Philharmonic Society, that I should wait two years to see if any thing would be done in New York toward a permanent orchestra, and if nothing were done, I should then leave. So I waited, but beyond personal offers made to me by friends, of from three thousand to ten thousand dollars, nothing came of it. These personal offers I of course refused. I needed no assistance for myself, as I could always earn my own living. What I wished was a large orchestra, sufficiently subsidized to enable it to hold the rehearsals necessary for artistic performances, its object and aim to be to attain the highest artistic performance of master-works, and to set a standard for the whole country, and give New York one of the greatest orchestras of the world. This would have been progress, and the time was ripe for it.

In the meantime, Boston did what I had worked for in vain in New York. A permanent orchestra had been established there in 1880, and was experiencing the customary vicissitudes of infancy. Encouraged by its inspiring example, Chicago, newly awakened to educational interests of all kinds, in 1890 became ambitious to do the same. What could I do then, when Chicago offered me the conductorship of its projected orchestra, but ''go West,'' like Mr. Greeley's young man, and make a new start? What New York had denied, Chicago provided. I should add, however, that while the maintenance of a permanent orchestra would have been comparatively easy in New York, it was nearly impossible in Chicago, for reasons some of which I shall presently enumerate.

Modern musical literature requires an orchestra

of about ninety men. I took with me from New York an orchestra of sixty, which included only half a dozen of the members of the old Thomas Orchestra, and completed the new orchestra by the addition of about thirty Chicago men. The sixty whom I brought with me from New York made a complete travelling orchestra, for we expected to travel more or less in the vicinity of Chicago, in order to help defray the expenses of the Association. The result of our concert tours, however, was very disappointing, for nearly all the towns and cities which were large enough to support orchestral concerts were so far from Chicago that the expenses of transportation more than consumed the profits. The general public of these places also preferred band concerts, with double and triple encores, to our programmes. So our travelling resulted in loss instead of profit, and besides, the time required by these long journeys left us insufficient time at home for the rehearsals of our own concerts.

In Chicago the conditions at that time were very unfavorable to success. Thus difficulties confronted the Association on every hand. Chicago is a city of nearly two million inhabitants, but the great majority of them belong to the class employed in mills, factories, and at all kinds of manual labor, while the cultivated class is comparatively small. This gives only a limited field of activity for a musician, and offers him little opportunity to add to his income by teaching or private engagements. The consequence is that there is little inducement outside of the orchestra for men of the ability required for a first-rank orchestra to settle there, and this makes it very difficult to procure them. The modern repertoire does not permit any curtailment in the size of the orchestra, and as Chicago could not furnish our leading players, they had to be brought from other parts of the world. In many cases the men thus imported were unused to such a rigorous climate as that of Chicago, and were driven away again by sickness, and had to be replaced.

Another obstacle the Association had to contend against was the lack of a building suitable for orchestral purposes. The only hall in which our concerts could be given was the Auditorium — an immense theatre, with a seating capacity of four or five thousand, which had been erected a few years previously for opera festivals, political conventions, and other large popular gatherings. The great size of this theatre called for the largest possible orchestra, but even then it was often ineffective, notwithstanding the remarkable acoustic properties of the building. It also contained so many seats that people felt under no obligation to buy season tickets to our concerts, knowing full well they could always find good places at the box-office at the last minute, whenever they desired to attend a performance. Thus our audience, instead of being regular, fluctuated from concert to concert, according to the weather or any other distracting cause. Our season was also interrupted several times a year by the other engagements for which the building was rented, such as the opera

HENRI  WIENIAWSKI

THEODORE THOMAS, JULIUS FUCHS, ADOLPH W. DOHN,
IN 1875

season, flower show, balls, and the like. This had the effect each time of scattering our audience and preventing people from forming the habit of regular attendance, as well as of interfering with our rehearsals, while the preparations for these events were in progress. In other ways the Auditorium was not suited to our use.

A building which is properly equipped for the work of a large permanent concert orchestra should contain, in addition to its stage, audience chamber, and foyers, a large room in which the musicians can tune and prepare their instruments before performances, and a cloak room for the use of the orchestra. It should also have a suitable storage room with lockers in which the instruments can be kept without danger of injury from heat, cold, or dampness, and where they will be safe from handling by meddlesome or careless persons. It should have a commodious library, furnished with clean, closed cases for storing the music, and long, well-lighted tables at which copyists and librarians can bind, repair, copy, and sort it for daily use. Finally, it should have rooms for part-rehearsals, offices for the manager and his staff, and a private office for the conductor, in which he can transact his business undisturbed. Nearly all of these conveniences were lacking in the Auditorium, and therefore, while it may have been well enough adapted for travelling opera troupes and the festivals and public meetings for which it was built, it was very unsuitable for our purposes.

A greater obstacle than any yet mentioned, how-

ever, was the indifference of the mass of the people to the higher forms of music. The Summer Night Concerts had done valuable service by awakening a general love of music, but it was chiefly music of a lighter character, with symphonies administered in very small doses. The people expected the same class of music at the orchestral concerts as that to which they were accustomed at the Summer Night Concerts, and found much fault with my programmes, which they thought were too severe.

It was a very discouraging time for us, for while Wagner had to some extent interested the people, he had also accustomed them to strong doses of excitement, and contrast, and everything without these tonic properties was regarded with indifference. Indeed, the announcement of a symphony was enough to keep many persons from going to a concert. The situation at last became serious; and when it seemed as if there were no immediate relief, the example of the Boston Orchestra came to our rescue and helped me to maintain the standard of our programmes. When fault was found with their severity, I would say, "Do you wish our programmes to be inferior in standard to those of the Boston Orchestra?" "No," was the answer. "Well, we give every year a number of programmes without a symphony. The Boston Orchestra does not." That helped! I was able to keep up the standard of my programmes, notwithstanding all opposition, until finally the intelligent and influential minority were ready to give up their musical trifles for broader forms, carrying with them

the rest of our musical world, and at last I risked
arranging programmes for a cultivated audience,
though with many fears as to the result. But behold! it was said that I had never made such good
programmes! That was true enough, but had I
offered them a few years previously, it would have
been our ruin. It never occurred to our concert
goers that it was they who had progressed.

The service which Mr. Henry L. Higginson has
rendered to art in this country can hardly be fully
estimated at present. A man of broad intellectual
culture, and a lover of music, he felt the need of that
art in his city which only an orchestra could interpret.
He also estimated its beneficial influence upon
humanity. He was not only a philanthropist in his
undertaking, but also an experienced business man.
His first step was to secure a home for his orchestra
— a suitable hall, where rehearsals and concerts
could be held at regular times without interference.
Natural causes and circumstances soon led him to
develop the organization he had formed into a first-
rank orchestra. His cultivated taste would not allow
him to make concessions to the ignorant, as he knew
perfectly well that a first-rank orchestra can be maintained only by preserving the highest standard, and
that the public ultimately would accept it. Other
cities soon had the benefit of his generosity, and the
influence of his organization spread; for New York
had now gone backwards, and the musical standard of
the East was set by the Boston Orchestra. He came
at the right time to help every sincere conductor

throughout the land, and he certainly saved the ship on which I was sailing, and which carried symphonies. The influence of his work insured the permanency of the symphony orchestras of Chicago, Pittsburg, and Philadelphia.

The foregoing pages have set forth only a few of the many difficulties which the Chicago Orchestral Association encountered during the thirteen years through which we struggled to establish the institution, and will give some idea of the complex nature of the problem, both from the business and the artistic standpoint. But although often disheartened and at times almost discouraged, the men and women who had founded it did not falter, but year after year personally paid its large deficit without complaint. Nor was I ever asked by our directors to lower its artistic standard in order to gain the patronage of the multitude. Some of our guarantors supported the orchestra from love of art, others from a broad spirit of humanity which sought through this agency to establish an elevating influence in the community. So they carried the heavy financial burden of it as long as they saw any hope that the plant they were protecting would take root and live.

At last the time arrived, however, when all agreed that the institution must now stand on its own feet, or else be abandoned. It was decided to test the public and find out whether or not the work had really taken hold of the community. A general appeal was made to every music lover in Chicago to come forward and do his share in raising an endowment fund to be invested in a suitable building or home for the orchestra, which would enable it to carry on its work to advantage and serve as a nucleus for the musical life of the city.

It was with many anxious doubts and fears that this course was finally adopted. But the result more than justified it, and there were some unlooked-for and extremely gratifying manifestations of popular interest. In less than a year, more than six-sevenths of the great fund of $750,000 was given by *eight thousand subscribers*, of all classes, rich and poor. It was a wonderful example of the influence of art in a community. I know of no similar instance in which so large a sum has been given absolutely without conditions by the general public of a city for an institution dedicated to the highest form of musical art.

When I left New York in 1901, it was prophesied that my sojourn in the West would not be longer than it had been when I went to Cincinnati in 1878. But we are now in the fourteenth season of the Chicago Orchestra. Its permanency is secure, its home is built, and the object for which I have worked all my life is accomplished. The old saying, "Better late than never," comes to mind as I see in my seventieth year the realization of the dreams of my youth. But I trust I may still live long enough to show my gratitude to the men and women who have made this possible, and to leave behind me a young and vigorous institution to crown their achievement with a long future.

[Sad as these last words seem which he wrote so hopefully, so thankfully, so happily, it is better they should remain, that the men and women of all classes in Chicago who saved his orchestra and gave it a permanent home may know his love for them, his gratitude for their splendid achievement, and the lofty purposes he contemplated before he should lay down his baton and give over the position he held so long, so honorably, so masterfully, to his successor.  The dream of more than fifty years was at last a reality, and he saw that the reality was all and more than he had hoped for, and he knew that his reward had come from the grateful hearts of the people. He lived to consecrate the house, to direct the immortal harmony of the symphony which he greatly loved, and then the Master of Music passed from our sight.  His fame was secure, his work was finished, and "the end crowns the work." —Edr.]

# THE
# LAST DAYS OF THEODORE THOMAS

[The following account of the last days of Theodore Thomas was written by Mrs. Thomas at my request.—EDR.]

THEODORE THOMAS died at daybreak, on Wednesday, January 4, 1905, in his city home, No. 43 Bellevue Place, Chicago, Illinois. For several years the magnificent health which had always been his had been failing, little by little, but so stealthy was the hand of time in its destruction of the earthly tenement which held this great and pure soul, that only those who lived under his roof were able to note its remorseless progress. To the world at large, Theodore Thomas retained to the very last his vigor, freshness, and magnetic personality. His eye was seemingly as bright, his ear as true, and his capacity for work as inexhaustible as ever. But those who watched him anxiously at home knew that this outward appearance of health and strength was no longer a reality, and that the overwrought and high-strung nerves were now strained by public life to the breaking point. He himself realized all this, but he hoped that the peace and freedom from anxiety which he anticipated would be his when the orchestra should at last be permanently installed in its new home, would permit him—by a careful husbandry of his powers—to continue his work with the Chicago

Association until he had carried the orchestra safely through the transition period, and could pass it on to his successor a completed institution.

No doubt this would have been the case had not untoward circumstances changed the natural course of events. The first of these was an unavoidable delay in the completion of the new hall. Every one connected with its construction, from its famous architect-in-chief down to its humblest hod-carrier, worked with love and pride upon the noble structure, and strained every nerve to have it finished at the appointed time. But in spite of their almost super-human efforts, when the Dedication Concert took place on December 14, 1904, it was still far from complete; to hold rehearsals and concerts in it was a serious risk to the musicians, for the plaster was not fully dry, the air was charged with lime dust from recently removed scaffolds, and through the still unfitted doors and windows strong draughts flowed into the hall, bringing colds and influenza in their wake. Many of the musicians were made quite ill in consequence, and among them was Dr.[1] Thomas himself, who contracted a severe attack of grippe. Even then it is probable that had he re-mained at home a few days, under his doctor's care, he would have recovered without difficulty. But unfortunately an adverse criticism of the new hall appeared, which he feared would injure its reputation

[1] The title Doctor of Music was conferred on Theodore Thomas by Yale University in 1880; also by Hamilton College in 1881.—EDR.

unless immediately counteracted, and this made him feel, all too keenly, the necessity of adjusting the orchestra to its new surroundings in the shortest possible time, in order that the fine acoustics which he knew the hall possessed, *and with which he was perfectly satisfied*, might be made apparent to the world also without delay.

When art or duty called he never considered himself, and so, in spite of the fever and lassitude of the disease, he arose from his sick bed every day, with his old indomitable will, and conducted concerts and rehearsals for ten days. But outraged nature revenged herself at last, and on Christmas Eve, 1904, at the close of the concert, he laid down the baton for the last time. Christmas Day he was very ill, nevertheless the next morning he insisted on dressing, and came down-stairs with the intention of going as usual to the rehearsal. But even his heroic will was no longer equal to the effort, and after sitting at the breakfast-table for a few minutes, like one dazed, he yielded to the solicitations of his family physician, Dr. C. F. Ely, whose anxiety had prompted him to call at this early hour, and returned to bed.

The sad details of the ten days which followed need not be recounted. By Friday grippe had developed into pneumonia, and from then on it was a losing battle, fought, inch by inch, by doctors, nurses, family, and friends, armed with all the facilities of modern science, reinforced by the tenderest love and by the public and private prayers of the whole nation. During Sunday and Monday it seemed as if his splendid constitution would triumph over the disease, for he made such steady improvement each day that by Tuesday morning every one was jubilant with hope. All through his illness, speaking had been very difficult for him, and although he was not at any time unconscious or delirious, he had hardly noticed the various members of the family as they came and went at his bedside, and had seemed anxious only to make as little trouble as possible for his kind nurses. But on this morning he observed everybody—made little jokes with the doctors and his sons, and talked to his wife about their White Mountain home, "Felsengarten," which was always much in his thoughts. About twelve o'clock the effort of even these broken sentences seemed to tire him; he paused a while, and then said to her in a dreamy, almost ecstatic voice, "I have had a beautiful vision . . . a beautiful vision," and then drifted off into silence. She little thought that these were to be his last words, but fearing he was tired she left him to rest, and went down-stairs to luncheon. He had given her at Christmas a little chime of silver bells, to be used to summon the family to meals. As he had been ill ever since Christmas Day these bells had not been used, for fear of disturbing him. To-day, however, he had seemed so much better that she thought perhaps he might like to hear his bells for once. So she stopped as she passed them, and played a little bugle-call which came into her head. Hardly had she finished when one of the family said, "Do you know that you have just played 'taps'—the call

that is sounded over the graves of dead soldiers?"
Struck with consternation at the sinister omen which
she had unconsciously wrought, she rushed back
to the bells and played another call which was
engraved upon a metal plate above them. Afterwards she noticed that it was *"reveillé"*—the soldier's
signal to arise. And thus it chanced that the last
music heard by Theodore Thomas on earth was sym-
bolical of death and the resurrection. Like the true
soldier he was he obeyed the command. Within an
hour came the change which placed him beyond all
human help, and at daybreak the next morning he
passed quietly and painlessly into the presence of the
God he had served so faithfully and well.

REMINISCENCE AND APPRECIATION

THEODORE THOMAS

*From a photograph taken in 1890*

# REMINISCENCE AND APPRE-
# CIATION

## BY GEORGE P. UPTON

### MY FIRST MEETING WITH MR. THOMAS

I FIRST made the acquaintance of Theodore Thomas November 27, 1869. He arrived in Chicago on the morning of that day, a stormy Saturday, with his Central Park Garden travelling orchestra of forty members, and announced three concerts at Farwell Hall. Being musical editor of "The Chicago Tribune" at that time, I was invited by Mr. Adolph W. Dohn, a mutual friend, to call upon the young conductor who had already made such a strong impression on musical taste in the East. Mr. Dohn, who had been the conductor of the Mendelssohn Society, and who was elected first conductor of the Apollo Musical Club in 1872, was a man of great influence in the musical affairs of Chicago by reason of his comprehensive scholarship, his thorough training in music, and his intimate knowledge of both vocal and instrumental work. He was also of much service to Mr. Thomas from that time to the end of his life[1] in many matters pertaining to the orchestra, and several times assisted him in score-making and preparation of vocal texts. An introduction by an

[1] Mr. Dohn died in February, 1901.

117

intimate friend, for Mr. Thomas held most persons at arm's length until they had been tried and tested, was an open sesame to a gracious reception. He greeted me most cordially, with a strong grip of that powerful hand, and then with that peculiar smile of his, which had so many different meanings, said in a brusque way:

"I am glad to meet any friend of Mr. Dohn's, and will be pleased to have you come and see me while I am here. You must not expect me to call upon you, for I am too busy, and besides, I never go into newspaper offices. I have no need to cultivate the critics, for I know my work. I do not care to read what they write, and would not have time if I did care."

I replied in effect that this was a new experience. I had been so persistently visited by advance agents, business agents, artists, and even impresarios of concert and opera troupes, that it was refreshing to meet a musician who did not care to see the interior of a newspaper office.

Such was my first meeting with Theodore Thomas, the man.

The first concert was given that evening to a small audience. Musicians and connoisseurs attended. The great public stayed away. Eight of the twelve numbers on the programme, Stigelli's "Tear," which Letsch, the trombonist, sentimentalized so pleasantly, Schumann's "Träumerei," the overture to "William Tell," Strauss's "Blue Danube Waltz," and his polkas "Lob der Frauen" and "Jocus," Meyerbeer's first "Fackeltanz," and the Titl "Serenade" for flute and French horn, are now rarely taken from the shelf. There were three numbers, however, which had staying qualities — Mendelssohn's "Midsummer Night's Dream" music, the overture to "Tannhäuser," and the allegretto to Beethoven's Eighth Symphony, the last two belonging to his programme "pillar" work, of which he speaks elsewhere. It was the little reverie of Schumann's, however, with its Matzka romanza, and the Thomas string setting, that proved to be the musical revelation. The "Träumerei" had been played the evening before upon the same stage by a local orchestra under the direction of Hans Balatka. The difference in setting and reading, the precision, shading, and tonal beauty, and particularly the "pianisissimo," as Mr. Thomas calls it, of the close, all proclaimed a new musical departure for Chicago. It would never again be content with the old musical performances. The "Träumerei" was the dawn of a new musical day for the West.

Such was my first meeting with Theodore Thomas, the musician.

This was Mr. Thomas's first visit to Chicago as a conductor. He came here for festivals, hall, and summer night concerts, almost every year afterwards until 1891, when he made Chicago his home, organized the Chicago Orchestra, and subsequently realized the dream of his life in the dedication of its permanent home. In one of our numerous conversations touching upon the preparation of the work with which he honored me, he said, after long persuasion on my part: "I will write my autobiography as part of our work. It will be only a general sketch of my life, and you must fill in the details, for which

I have not time." At that time I expected his judgment upon what I should write, but fate ordered otherwise. I will strive, however, to carry out his request in "our book" to the best of my ability, touching upon some matters which it is proper to attend to now, avoiding any invasion of his personal affairs, which would have been repugnant to him, but seeking to give him his just meed of praise, to which he would have offered objection in life, but which is due to him now that his great service for music is ended, save in its enduring influence.

## II

### APPRENTICESHIP

M̲R. THOMAS has told the story of his early years with a certain reserve, due to his often expressed belief that the public cared little for his personal affairs, as well as to his aversion to personal publicity. A few details may be added, however, making the account of his apprenticeship more complete.

The period between 1845 and 1850 may be called his "wander years," and their story he has told with sufficient detail. Then came his years of violin playing in concerts and operatic performances which, uncertain and desultory as they were, nevertheless, as he often has said, were of great importance to him in developing his style, cultivating his tone, and, indeed, helping to shape his career; for from a player in the ranks he was soon leader or "concertmeister," and at last operatic conductor. It is curious to note

in these early days the outcropping of those characteristics which so sharply differentiated him from
other conductors.   The boy, in his way, was as much
the musical autocrat as the man.   During Madame
La Grange's concert tour he was not only leader of
the orchestra which accompanied her, but had the
sole power of hiring or discharging players.   The
prima donna requested him to place her valet, who
was a musician, among the violins.   He courteously
declined.   She insisted.   He still refused, whereupon
she testily said, "Have I got to get down on my knees
and beg you?"

"I do not care whether you kneel or not, Madame.
I should think it would be more convenient to stand
upright.   But your man can't play, and that is the
end of it."

Mr. Thomas played an obligato to one of her
numbers that evening.   Afterwards the Madame
said to him: "You were real mean to me, but you
played like a god."

Mr. Thomas has related one story in his autobiography relating to Ullmann, the impresario.   Upon
another occasion Frezzolini, the prima donna, who
was notorious for her tardiness, was an hour late at
rehearsal, and sent no word.   She arrived just in
time to see the last of the orchestra leaving the stage.
There was no rehearsal, consequently no performance.   Ullmann, in a towering rage, sought Mr.
Thomas, and declared that some one must be dis-
charged.   "Certainly," replied the conductor.   "Discharge me.   I am the only one responsible.   If you

don't, and Signora Frezzolini continues coming late to rehearsals, I will discharge myself." Frezzolini was not late after that.

He even had the temerity to disagree with Adelina Patti once about the tempo of an aria. She claimed she ought to have her way because she was the prima donna. "I beg your pardon, Madame," he replied, "here, I am prima donna."

Of his ability as a violinist I shall speak further on. The earliest programme in his half-century collection, February 20, 1852, is reproduced elsewhere in fac-simile. About two months later his name appears again upon a programme of a benefit concert, in a style at which he laughed heartily in his later years. The programme is as follows:

M. CONKLIN
of
Dodworth's Band
begs leave to announce to his friends and the public that his
Benefit Concert
will take place at the
Apollo Saloon
on Monday evening, April 26, 1852
when he will be assisted by the following eminent talent, who
have most kindly volunteered their valuable services:
DODWORTH FAMILY
MASTER THEODORE THOMAS
probably the most extraordinary violinist in the world of his age,
DODWORTH'S BAND
MASTER MARSH
the infant drummer, and
MR. DANIEL DAVIES.

## Part I

1. Introduction from "Lucrezia Borgia"   .   *Donizetti.*
Dodworth's Parading Band.

2. Serenade, "Star of Love".   .   .   .   *Wallace.*
Dodworth's Serenade Band.

3. "Concerto Militaire," for violin   .   .   *Lipinski.*
Master T. Thomas.

4. "Glendon Polka"   .   .   .   .   *A. Dodworth.*
Dodworth's Parading Band.

5. Cavatina, "Still so gently," for ebor cornet, from
"Sonnambula"   .   .   .   .   .   .   *Bellini.*
Mr. Charles P. Dodworth.

6. Infant Drummer's extraordinary performance.

## Part II

7. Grand Quartet from "Bianca e Faliero"   .   *Rossini.*
Dodworth's Serenade Band.

8. Violin Solo, "Carnival of Venice".   .   .   *Ernst.*
Master T. Thomas.

9. Serenade from "Don Pasquale".   .   .   *Donizetti.*
Dodworth's Serenade Band.

10. Cavatina, "Son vergin vezzose," from "I Puritani,"
for cornet   .   .   .   .   .   .   .   *Bellini.*
Mr. Allen Dodworth.

11. Quadrille, "Grove Songsters"   .   .*H. B. Dodworth.*
Dodworth's Quadrille Band.

12. Trio from "Norma," "A di qual se"   .   .   *Bellini.*
Messrs. Allen, Harvey B., and Charles R. Dodworth.

13. "Trip by Railroad".   .   .   .   *H. B. Dodworth.*
Dodworth's Quadrille Band.

14. Reveille   .   .   .   .   .   *H. B. Dodworth.*
Messrs. M. Conklin and D. Davies.

The confidence which the young musician had in himself at this period of his career is shown in the following incident, related by William Mason in his "Memories of a Musical Life":

"One evening, as Thomas came home, tired out from his work, and after dinner had settled himself in a comfortable place for a good rest, a message came to him from the Academy of Music, about two blocks away from his home in East Twelfth Street. An opera season was in progress there. The orchestra was in its place, and the audience seated, when word was received that Anschütz, the conductor, was ill. The management had not provided against that contingency, and was in a position of much embarrassment. Would Thomas come to the rescue? He had never conducted opera, and the work for the evening performance was an opera with which he was unfamiliar. Here was a life's opportunity, and Thomas was equal to the occasion. He thought for a moment, then said, 'I will.' He rose quickly, got himself into his dress suit, hurried to the Academy of Music, and conducted the opera as if it were a common experience. He was not a man to say 'Give me time until next week.' He was always ready for every opportunity."

Mr. Mason's version of this incident is not historically complete. The first opera conducted by Mr. Thomas was Halévy's "Jewess." It was first given under the management of Max Maretzek, in 1859, and was revived by Ullmann in 1860, with Carl Formes and Mme. Fabbri in the principal roles. Notwithstanding its musical success it did not pay, and after five performances Ullmann withdrew it and also retired from the management of the Academy of Music. This was in December, 1860. "The Musical Review and World," of December 8, 1860, says in this connection:   "We hear that Mr. Anschütz will not conduct under the new management, but that Mr. Theodore Thomas will take his place.   Considering what this young, talented leader achieved during the last performances of 'The Jewess,' when he took the baton at a moment's notice [1] and brought the performance to a very satisfactory close, we should think that the change is a highly acceptable one."

## III

### LIFE WORK BEGINS

THE year 1854 may be called the close of Mr. Thomas's apprenticeship.   In 1855, as first violinist of the Mason-Bergmann Chamber Concerts, a year later known as the "Mason-Thomas," he was the master-musician — master in every sense, for he dominated that organization in its methods, its music, its programmes, and its progress.   Mr. Thomas in his autobiography dwells at some length upon the personnel of its members and the work they accomplished.   Mr. Mason, in his Memories, from which I already have quoted, supplies the information as to the part Mr. Thomas took in this work: [2]

"The organization as originally formed would probably have remained intact during all the years the concerts lasted had it not become apparent almost from the start that Theo-

[1] This evidently refers to the incident mentioned by Mr. Mason.—EDR.

[2] Mr. Thomas at this time was in his twentieth year.—EDR.

dore Thomas had in him the genius of conductorship.  He possessed by nature a thoroughly musical organization, and was a born conductor and leader.

"Before we had been long together, it became apparent that there was more or less friction between Thomas and Bergmann, who, being the conductor of the Germania and afterward of the Philharmonic Orchestra, also a player of long experience, and the organizer of the quartette, naturally assumed the leadership in the beginning.  The result was that Bergmann withdrew after the first year, and Bergner, a fine violoncellist and active member of the Philharmonic Society, took his place.  The organization was then called the 'Mason and Thomas Quartette,' and so styled, it won a wide reputation throughout the country.  I should say in passing that Bergmann was an excellent, though not a great, conductor.

"From the time that Thomas took the leadership, free and untrammeled, the quartette improved rapidly.  His dominating influence was felt and acknowledged by us all.  Moreover, he rapidly developed a talent for making programmes by putting pieces into the right order of sequence, thus avoiding incongruities.  He brought this art to perfection in the arrangement of his symphony concert programmes."

Mr. Thomas was now fairly launched upon his life work.  To understand the nature and the difficulty of that work, it should be borne in mind that up to 1855, and, indeed, for a few years after, music had been only a source of amusement to New York. There had been a few chamber concerts given by the Eisfeld Quartette, but they were only sparsely attended, and were without any important results. As for an orchestra, the Philharmonic Society had been in existence for about ten years, but its existence was precarious, and it had little vitality at best until Mr. Thomas saved it from financial collapse and

THEODORE THOMAS IN 1875

THEODORE THOMAS IN HIS WORK-ROOM

elevated its standard of performance several years later.  Opera was the musical staple, and was then, even more than now, simply an occasion for social, fashionable, and musical entertainment.  The young conductor conceived the noble purpose of elevating the musical standard, introducing the higher music, and making people not only acquainted with it, but desirous of hearing it.  Thus he was the musical pioneer, and he always had faith that he could accomplish his mission.  Some years afterwards, in 1874, when the directors of the Brooklyn Philharmonic Society tendered him a complimentary benefit, he said in his reply to them:

"Throughout my life my aim has been to make good music popular, and it now appears that I have only done the public justice in believing and acting constantly on the belief that the people would enjoy and support the best in art when continually set before them in a clear, intelligent manner."

This extract sufficiently explains the musical purpose of his life.  His courage and determination to accomplish that purpose are still further illustrated by a statement made at the time when he was striving to secure support for his orchestra:

"I was hungry last night, but no fox gnawing at my side, as in the Spartan story, can make me abandon the course of life I have laid out for myself.  I have gone without food longer than I should, I have walked when I could not afford to ride, I have even played when my hands were cold, but I shall succeed, for I shall never give up my belief that at last the people will come to me, and my concerts will be crowded. I have undying faith in the latent musical appreciation of the American public."

Without money, without backers, having no capital but his indomitable will, untiring energy, sublime
faith in himself, and confidence in the people, he set
about the task of securing an orchestra, and a hall
which should be suitable for his concert purposes, as
well as the elevation of the popular taste.  His ideal
of an orchestra is contained in a letter which he
wrote me many years ago:

"Musicians playing together year after year rehearse together.  This co-working is not disturbed by playing in theatres
and  concert  combinations.  Nothing  impairs  the  artistic
morale.  By thus offering permanent engagements, the conductor can induce the best artists to join him.  That is a
permanent orchestra in the true sense.  With such an orchestra
its first charm is the purity and vitality of the intonation, and
besides the good  tone-quality and color of each instrument,
the mutual subordination and blending of them all.  Next,
careful, admirable phrasing, and gradation of light and
shade."

As for the hall, in a letter dated in 1887, he writes:

" Give me a proper concert-hall, where the beautiful works
of the great masters of symphony and purely orchestral compositions can be properly given and properly heard, and I will
banish opera and musical drama excerpts from my performances.  My life work has been for the concert-hall, and year
after year, but never more than at the present time, have I
deplored the absence in New York of a large hall suitable
for producing large works."

He once said to me, speaking of a musician who
was reported to have died broken-hearted, ''He had
no Chicago to go to."   It was Chicago which gave
him his permanent orchestra in its permanent home

and the opportunity to do his best work, after fifty years of herculean labor.

I have spoken of opera as the main source of entertainment for the musical New York of that day, but how little operatic managers appreciated or understood the real work Mr. Thomas had in view, even after his orchestra had become established, is shown by the following incident. During the Nilsson season in New York, Max Strakosch, the impresario, came to one of the orchestra rehearsals with Vieux-temps, the violinist, and Mr. Jarrett, Nilsson's agent, who desired to make Mr. Thomas's acquaintance. The latter had long known Vieuxtemps. Strakosch introduced Jarrett with his customary beaming smile, saying, "Mr. Jarrett, allow me to present Mr. Thomas, our American Strauss." Vieuxtemps re-garded Strakosch with mingled surprise and indig-nation, perceiving which, Strakosch recognized the mistake he had made, and jumped from the frying-pan into the fire with the ludicrous amendment, "Strauss in the Beethoven style!"

I should except one manager, however, from this criticism. Col. J. H. Mapleson, in the second vol-ume of his entertaining Memoirs, says:

"Better even than the orchestra of M. Lamoreux is that of M. Colonne. But I have no hesitation in saying that M. Colonne's orchestra is surpassed in fineness and fullness of tone and delicacy of expression by the American orchestra con-ducted by Mr. Thomas. The members of this orchestra are for the most part Germans, and the eminent conductor is him-self, by race, at least, a German. Putting aside, however, all question of nationality, I simply say that the orchestra directed by Mr. Theodore Thomas is the best I am acquainted with; and its high merit is due, in a great measure, to the permanence of the body. Its members work together habitually and constantly; they take rehearsals as part of their regular work; and they look to their occupation as players in the Theodore Thomas Orchestra as their sole source of income. As for substitutes, Mr. Thomas would no more accept one than a military commander would accept substitutes among his officers.

"There has, from time to time, been some talk of the Theodore Thomas unrivalled orchestra paying a visit to London, where its presence, apart from all questions of the musical delight it would afford, would show our public what a good orchestra is, and our musical societies how a good orchestra ought to be formed and maintained."[1]

## IV

### GARDEN MUSIC

MR. THOMAS began his real life work in 1862, when he gave his first orchestral concert. That was the seed from which grew his symphony concerts, inaugurated in 1864, followed up by his concerts at Terrace Garden (1866) and Central Park Garden (1868), the latter being maintained for several years, so that his players should be kept together summer and winter. Just before a concert in Chicago, in 1872, he said to me, "I am going to play the 'Liebestod' from 'Tristan and Isolde' to-night. I want to give the audience something to chew on." A few years later there was no number on his programmes more eagerly anticipated, more gladly welcomed.

[1] The above tribute was written in 1882, just after the great New York Festival, which Mr. Thomas conducted.

This was what he was doing with the New Yorkers in that period, and what he did in the tours which began in 1869. He was giving them something to "chew on." It made no difference how much they protested, what wry faces they made, or how much they complained that they could not understand symphonies, classical overtures, and startling excerpts from the so-called "music of the future." He put them in the first or second part of the programme, and filled the third with the delicacies they liked, so that they could not get away from the better music without giving up the tinkling tunes. He played the better music until it was soon understood. If unusual protest were made against a certain number, like the "Liebestod," for instance, he kept people "chewing" upon it until it was digested and they grew to like it, and became discontented with the syllabubs.

A glance over those remarkable Central Park Garden programmes, which had such incalculable influence upon the musical taste of New York, and indirectly upon that of the whole country, will disclose how patiently and resolutely he led the people, and how surely and steadily they followed him. He began with a classical overture sandwiched in between Offenbach, Strauss, Lanner, Gungl, Bilse, and many another composer now utterly forgotten. Then he would add to his classical overture some fragment from a Wagner music-drama, and the two would appear in a setting of light and popular melodies. Presently there appeared a symphony movement, something by Raff, Spohr, Schumann, Schubert, or Beethoven, repeated over and over in connection with the light stuff also repeated over and over, until people found the latter did not stand repetition like the former, in which they discovered new beauties at each performance. At last he ventured upon an entire symphony, and soon regular symphony programmes were performed to large houses.

In his announcement of the second season in Central Park Garden he says:

"The repertoire has been largely increased year by year, and is now one of the most extensive and varied to be found in any country. It will be further augmented, from time to time, by the introduction of the latest European and American successes. The programmes will be composed with the same care and discrimination as heretofore, and will, while consulting every taste, leave nothing to be desired, even by the strictest musical purist."

He inaugurated the Garden Concerts with an orchestra of forty, Matzka being his concertmeister, Grupe leading the second violins, Schwartz the violas, Bergner the 'cellos, and Pfeifenschneider the double basses; Liedler was first flute, Eller first oboe, Wendelschaefer first clarinet, Hochstein bassoon, Schmitz horn, Dietz trumpet, Letsch trombone, Listmann tuba, Loewe drums, Klugescheid bass drum, and Benedict zither and triangle. Loewe was the only one of this orchestra who took part in the concerts of the Chicago Orchestra. In 1872 the orchestra was increased to fifty members, and June 20 of that year Mr. Thomas had a benefit concert for which the number of players was increased to sixty. The following description of him at this concert, by a contemporary, shows that he set his face against encores at an early period:

"The conductor was evidently in the best of moods. In front of his desk hung a beautiful garland of lilies. Above him the crystal chandelier chimed gaily, swayed by the river breeze. From his cheerful demeanor one would not have guessed that three sonnets had recently been written to him, yet there they were, printed on the second leaf of the programme, for every one to read. He seems somehow to be *en rapport* with hearers as well as with orchestra. Even when his audience relapses into barbarism on the subject of encores, he quietly but firmly controls them. I have seen him—under circumstances almost as trying as the famous charivari at the Cirque Napoléon, when Pasdeloup nearly broke his baton in frantic rage—leave the stand and quietly take a seat in a corner of the orchestra, remaining there until he had carried his point."

He never lost his temper in the Garden Concerts. Upon one occasion a youth on the front seat had been talking almost incessantly in a low tone of voice to the young lady with him, while the allegretto to Beethoven's Eighth Symphony was being played, and at last began scratching explosive matches to light his cigar. After two or three had snapped and gone out, Mr. Thomas gave the signal to his orchestra to stop, laid down his baton, turned to the young man, and said with one of his sweetest and most cynical smiles, in a voice audible to all around him, "Go on, sir! Don't mind us! We can all wait until you light your cigar." The cigar was not lit, and the couple were quiet through the rest of the concert. Upon

another occasion he applied a more drastic remedy.
The orchestra was playing the "Midsummer Night's
Dream" music of Mendelssohn, and Mr. Thomas
was much annoyed by the talking of a couple near by
him.   Suddenly he gave a signal to the drum player,
and a long roll went rattling through the fairy music
which startled every one.   The conductor quietly
turned round and fixed a significant look upon the
talkers, which informed them they were responsible
for the liberty which had been taken with the score.
There was no further talking.

At the opening of the Garden in 1873, the orchestra had grown steadily in excellence.   These concerts
had also made Mr. Thomas's more ambitious symphony concerts possible, for without this preparation
it would have been impossible to have given them.
These Garden Concerts also made it possible for him
to produce in that season ten symphonic works, four
of them novelties, as well as overtures representing
the development of music from  Bach to Berlioz and
they also paved the way for the Rubinstein concerts,
and gave that composer the opportunity to present his
"Ocean" Symphony.   At last the symphony became
the regular Thursday evening feature of the Garden
Concerts, and every Thursday evening the audience
was the largest of the week, and this notwithstanding
an increase in the price of admission, to meet the
expense of an increased orchestra.   The programmes
of that season would hardly have been listened to
with patience in the opening season at Terrace Garden in 1866.   During that season, besides the Garden

THE CINCINNATI MUSIC HALL

MAY FESTIVAL AT CINCINNATI, 1894

Concerts, he had given thirty-two strictly symphonic concerts.   The effect of the winter and summer concerts was such as to make each more complete, and Mr. Thomas now thought he was on the road to the organization of a permanent orchestra.   He also had visions of a permanent hall, for a movement was begun in New York to erect one.   But for both he was yet to wait more than thirty years.   The story of this period was so well told by "The New York Evening Post," in 1873, that it is worth preserving as musical history.   The "Post" said:

"With the expiration of the season of 1873-74 the series of concerts given by Thomas's orchestra, which will have extended through a period of six years, will come to an end. The announcement will be made in due form at the proper time, but knowing that the cessation is inevitable, it may not be inopportune, even in advance of it, to ask how far the organization has succeeded in the accomplishment of the task it has set itself to perform.   To do this fairly, it is impossible to regard its labors with the spirit of one who has been simply entertained, though at the same time it is allowed that the record of pleasures received from this fine band of musicians would be an unexampled one.   It has done much more than to amuse; it has earned for itself a character as an educator.

"Its labors were commenced at Terrace Garden; after two seasons they were transferred to Central Park Garden, with which it has since been identified.   Like all enterprises in which are germs of good, it encountered at the outset a heavy counter-current of disasters and cold sympathies.   Financial troubles blocked the way; doubters in newspapers, in society, in musical circles, looked askance, and the attempt of one man, with two score of players at his back, to gain the ears of a raw public by interpreting the best works of the best composers was thought to be a very pattern of temerity.

"One cannot sufficiently applaud the energy and faith that supported Mr. Thomas through the difficulties which for three long years environed him and his orchestra. It is told of him that he never once doubted that he should ultimately succeed in winning regard among the people who at first had regarded him so coldly. He knew us better than we did ourselves. We were inert. We were told that he was an experimenting innovator; that he was a closet enthusiast; that he was a fierce specialist, who intended to ply us with what he called music; that we should finally be forced to receive it by tolerance. Therefore we stayed away. His benches remained empty. It was said in the lower town that somewhere in the upper town there was a fine orchestra perpetually engaged in playing fine music. But we did not listen until the persistent story was heard one year after another.

"Curiosity and the appeals of a few believers began to work a change. Those who had been abroad and had heard the orchestras which are supported by royal subsidies, told us that we had at our doors an organization that was equal to the best. Then people began to visit the place where this wonder was. The venture which had been so hazardous and so profitless began to be strengthened. It commenced to acquire a fame commensurate with its deserts.

"Mr. Thomas had collected fifty men from all parts of the world where the science of music was understood and practised. From that foreign city he brought a violin virtuoso, from this, one celebrated for his mastery of the cornet; from here, another famous as a performer on the oboe; from there, a great harper, and so on, picking out the best and selecting the specialists, until he had under his control a true galaxy. It was only such a one as would fill his desire. He was not content to amass a quantity of mediocre talent, and to bedizen it here and there with a light, but the spirit of his endeavor required that all the portions should have equal radiance. These materials he bound together by arduous drill, intelligent direction, and supreme tact, until he produced an harmonious entirety, a toned

and symphonic whole.  Each ingredient had its value, each
function its influence, each proportion its true and exact weight,
and made a unity with that sympathy and accord that long
communion alone could give; the true orchestra was at length
produced.  It began its work.  The character of that task has
been described.  It entailed upon the laborers losses, disappointments, ridicule — everything but discouragements.  There
were no rebuffs that they did not encounter, and no disasters
that did not fall to their lot; but their leader, full of his purpose
and with a definite goal before him, carried his enterprise
through, and attained, and more than attained, the result he
wished.  That result was to imbue his hearers, wherever he
found them, with a sincere love for good music; not a transient
and fallible desire, susceptible to various prettinesses and
fashions, but a deep and earnest regard for the works of the
masters.

"What are the evidences that he has done this ?  In what
does it appear that this process of induction has been successful ?
First, in the improved character of his auditors.  That must be
a powerful magnet that draws a congregation of cultivated
Americans two miles from their homes to gain pleasure under
circumstances which are new to them.  At first the listeners
were of a poor quality of people.  They gained for the Garden
a name that was indifferently good.  But in spite of this prejudice, in spite of the fact that Americans do not appreciate popular pleasures, in spite of the distance, of the crowded convey-
ances, of the time wasted in travelling, the people whose ears
Mr. Thomas wanted to reach at length began to throng upon
him.  Second, in his periodic journeys with his orchestra into
New England and the West and the South, he has been welcomed with an ardor never accorded to others who have paid
visits for like purposes.  He carried with him the power to
render the finest music in the finest way.  He was received
with open arms.  The third witness is himself.  He is more
than satisfied, and nothing could have greater significance than
this admission.  That he who has assumed the task of teaching

the uneducated in that in which he is so perfectly educated himself is willing to assert that he has surpassed his expectations, and has found the public to be warmer and more ardent than he hoped, is an indication of great, not possibilities, but probabilities.

"Mr. Thomas found, as soon as his work and intention became clearly understood, and rose above the strata of spasmodic adventures and dishonest enterprises with which the people had long been deceived, that he was welcome. Now, then, these two great things appear to have been achieved: First, there has been produced in New York an orchestra inferior to none of its size in the great world. It is perfectly trained, perfectly attuned, perfectly combined, and is an excellent as well as a prodigious power. Second, a comprehension of the works of the great composers has been animated all over the country. Where in former days an orchestra would, in stirring abroad, pass into a chilling atmosphere, it now encounters applause and warmth. The change has been great, it might almost be said marvellous."

# V

## SYMPHONIC SOIREES

IT WAS in December, 1864, that Mr. Thomas organized an orchestra and began his famous series of symphonic "soirees" which closed in 1869. In his reference to these he disclaims any intention to compete with the Philharmonic Society, much less to injure it. Undoubtedly he felt that the latter society was not doing as effective work as it should in the cause of good music, and therefore that his new project was justifiable. Nor can it be questioned that the effect upon the Philharmonic was healthy, for at once its managers increased the

number of players, raised the standard of performance, and began looking about for new works. In
this way the Thomas Symphony Orchestra was a
much-needed stimulus for the Philharmonic. In these
soirees Bach, Haydn, Mozart, Beethoven, Schubert,
and Schumann were his foundations, as they were
ever afterwards, but he made many an incursion into
the field of the modern romanticists as well as that of
the "music of the future." As Mendelssohn revived
Bach in Europe, Mr. Thomas revived the father of
modern music in this country, and brought out in
rich profusion the works of the modern school of
Berlioz, Liszt, Wagner, Brahms, Rubinstein, Raff,
and Saint-Saëns, besides some of the lesser lights.
The second season was made memorable by the first
production (December 3, 1866) of Beethoven's Ninth
Symphony. Of this concert, the second in the season, Professor Ritter wrote at the time:

"The second symphonic soiree of Mr. Thomas was one of
the finest concerts ever given in New York, perhaps the best as
regards the works which formed the programme, for these
were Mozart's 'Figaro' overture, a Schumann pianoforte concerto, and Beethoven's Ninth Symphony entire. . . . . In
the name of the highest interests of art, Mr. Thomas deserves
our thanks for bringing out this symphony; with energy and
industry he overcame the impediments that lie in the way of
such a performance, and the call he received at the end of the
evening was certainly only a well-merited recognition."

The third season of the soirees is particularly
noteworthy by reason of Mr. Thomas's efforts to reinforce the orchestra with a chorus, the beginning of
a work which he made still more effective with the

Philharmonic Societies of New York and Brooklyn. His words in the announcement for the season are significant:

"No well-directed effort has yet been made to accomplish the union of the vocal and instrumental forces necessary to success in this important and unlimited branch of art. We have had and still have well-trained choral societies and orchestras, but owing partly to local relations and partly to the great cost of an orchestra, a union of these forces has seldom or never been effected. Until this result shall have been permanently secured, we have no right to claim for New York an advanced position with regard to music, nor can we hope to interest the people generally and develop properly their natural taste for the art."

The soirees were discontinued in 1869, and the concert tours began. Mr. Thomas makes frequent reference to them in his part of this work, and they need no further mention, except in connection with a few incidents which illustrate the crude ideas of music and orchestral playing which existed thirty or more years ago in various parts of the country.

When his manager was canvassing the prospects for a concert in a New York town he was informed by a leading citizen that the "show" wouldn't pay much unless "Thomas had a good end man." In Utah it was gravely suggested that the more wedding marches he had on his programmes the better. At a concert in an Iowa city the Boccherini Minuet was played, as usual, pianissimo and con sordini. After the concert, Mr. Thomas was entertained at dinner. When the conversation turned upon the Minuet, the mayor said, with considerable emphasis: "You should have played it louder." "But," said Mr. Thomas, "it is marked *pp*." "No matter if it is," replied the municipal critic, "such a pretty tune deserves to be played louder." Upon one of the tours the orchestra was engaged to dedicate a Coliseum in an Illinois city. One of the promoters, in closing arrangements with the orchestra manager, suggested that after the concert the floor should be cleared and the orchestra should play dances for the crowd. When informed that it did not do that kind of work, the promoter seemed greatly surprised, and asked, "Why not? Can't they play dances well enough?" It was in Keokuk, Iowa, that Mr. Thomas met with one of the few criticisms which he cared to read, and which he carefully preserved, and once showed to me as a specimen of honest criticism. The programme for the concert contained in succession the overture to "Tannhäuser," the andante movement from Beethoven's Fifth Symphony, and Weber's "Invitation to the Dance." Under the latter was inscribed "Adapted for orchestra by Hector Berlioz." The critic, evidently supposing that the inscription included all three numbers, wrote:

"The first piece was that fine trilogy which Hector Berlioz, with exquisite art, made from Wagner, Beethoven, and Weber. The thought of Hector Berlioz evidently, in arranging the trilogy, was to put after the passionate action of the one the ocean-like, star-like, measureless calm and harmony of the symphony. After you have bathed in that luxury and languor long enough, there comes Von Weber's 'Invitation to the Dance.' Oh! there has been nothing heard in Keokuk like that trilogy as Thomas's Orchestra gives it."

Mr. Thomas was frequently entertained after his concerts by prominent people, and on one such occasion he asked a gentleman who had been at the concert how he enjoyed it. "Well," said the gentleman, "I don't know much about music. But, I tell you what, Mr. Thomas, the way those violinists turned over the leaves all at once is one of the most remarkable things I've ever seen."

The reader must not infer from these incidents that the Thomas Orchestra was not appreciated. In many places there was unusual eagerness to hear its concerts. This was the case at Jackson, Michigan. The citizens of that city hailed the announcement of a concert with enthusiasm. The city government also was on the alert, as will be apparent from the following official note sent by the Committee on Licenses to the City Clerk:

CAPT. GEORGE W. STEVENSON:

In virtue of the authority given to us by the Common Council of the City of Jackson, the license of the Theodore Thomas Orchestra troupe is hereby revoked unless arrangements can be made for eighteen tickets for the Common Council of the city.

> GEO. A. FOSTER, Chairman.
> BENJ. PORTER,
> J. D. BROWN.

When Captain Stevenson presented this "hold-up" note to the suave Gosche, Mr. Thomas's business manager, he was received with the blandest courtesy. The eighteen tickets were handed him with the compliments of the management. The concert was

given in the Court House. The court-room was
crowded with Jackson's "beauty and chivalry." Just
as the orchestra was in place, and Mr. Thomas had
come to his desk, there was a stir in the rear of the
hall. The Common Councilmen had arrived. They
were escorted by Mr. Gosche himself to the seats
their tickets called for, and the only seats left in the
house — those in the jury box and the prisoner's pen,
where they were seen conspicuously by the audience,
and made uncomfortable by its unconcealed enjoyment of their situation.

The symphony soirees were resumed in 1872,
under the name of symphony concerts. In reply to
the invitation of a large number of music lovers Mr.
Thomas wrote: "It is a satisfaction to know that the
remembrance of these concerts is still fresh after the
lapse of three years, in a country where the past is so
soon forgotten. This fact speaks for the influence
they have had, and prompts me to comply with your
wish." He announced six concerts, and the first of
these, at which the overture to Gluck's "Iphigenia in
Aulis," Beethoven's Seventh Symphony, "Wotan's
Farewell," from "Die Walküre," and Liszt's "Mephisto Waltz," besides songs by Mr. George L. Osgood, were given, is particularly noteworthy because
for the first time Mr. Thomas used regularly anno-
tated programmes. The symphony concerts, however, were not long continued. They did not receive
a support which justified the expectation of making
the orchestra permanent, much less of securing a
permanent home for it. It was apparent to him that

his work must proceed upon other lines. One of these was the Brooklyn Philharmonic Society, with which he had been associated as conductor, directly and alternately, for several years.

## VI

### THE BROOKLYN PHILHARMONIC SOCIETY

THE Brooklyn Philharmonic Society was organized in 1857, and Theodore Eisfeld was its first conductor. Mr. Thomas always referred to its concerts with great pleasure. While engaged in selecting and editing his programmes, it seemed to me that the Brooklyn Philharmonic programmes were among the most important in the collection, and I asked him whether it would not be well to print them complete. He replied that the Brooklyn concerts were always a satisfaction to him, and he would be pleased if all the programmes were included. He added that the Brooklyn people were always very friendly and appreciative, and that without their patronage it would have been difficult to keep up his New York concerts.

From 1862 to 1865 Mr. Thomas alternated with Eisfeld and other conductors. A letter in "Dwight's Journal of Music," November 8, 1862, written by a Brooklyn man, says:

"In your paper of last Saturday you make Mr. Theodore Thomas our conductor *in toto*, which is not exactly correct. It is the intention of the directors (as far as I can learn) to choose a conductor for each concert, not for the whole season, as heretofore. Mr. Eisfeld was elected by acclamation for the concert of Saturday, and never did he acquit himself more brilliantly or carefully. For the second concert, conducted by Theodore Thomas, the talented violinist of the classical firm of Mason and Thomas, and a very skilful and able director, although young, ardent, and progressive (good faults such are), we are to have the following orchestral pieces: Symphony No. 1, C major (first time), Beethoven; overture, 'Struensee,' with chorus, Meyerbeer; overture, 'Dreams on Christmas Eve,' Hiller."

Mr. Thomas was conductor for the season of 1866–67, and at the close of the season the Society passed the following resolution:

"*Resolved*, That the thanks of this Society are eminently due Mr. Theodore Thomas for the great ability and untiring energy displayed by him the past season in conducting to a most successful issue the rehearsals and concerts of this Society."

The directors sent him the resolution and with it a handsome baton.

As this was Mr. Thomas's first regular season with the Brooklyn Philharmonic, the programme of his first concert, October 27, 1866, is appended:

1. Symphony No. 1, D major, op. 31, "Columbus".*J.J.Abert.*
   [First time in America.]
2. Cavatina, "Una donna," from "The Huguenots"   .   .   .   .   .   .   . *Meyerbeer.*
   Miss Adelaide Phillipps.
3. Solo for oboe, "Scène et Ballet"   .   . *De Bériot.*
   Mr. Eller.
4. Overture, "Leonora," No. 3   .   .   . *Beethoven.*
5. Fantasia for harp, "Un Ballo in Maschera"   . *Toulmin.*
   Mr. Toulmin.
6. Cuban Song, "Maria Dolores"   .   .   . *Yradier.*
   Miss Phillipps.
7. "Ritter March"   .   .   .   .   .   . *Schubert.*
   [First time in America.]

At the close of the sixteenth season (1874), the directors tendered Mr. Thomas a complimentary concert.

In 1878 Mr. Thomas's conductorship was interrupted for a time by his removal to Cincinnati to assume the duties of conductor of the College of Music in that city.  On the eve of his departure, prominent citizens of New York and Brooklyn tendered him a farewell concert, for which he made a programme which was ever afterwards a favorite with him.   Its chief interest lies in the fact that upon this occasion he gave Brahms's Second Symphony its first performance in this country.   The programme was as follows:

1.   Overture, "Coriolanus," op. 62   .     .     .   *Beethoven.*
2.   "Der Doppelgänger"     .     .     .     .   *Schubert.*
                Mr. Franz Remmertz.
3.   Symphony No. 2, D minor, op. 73 [first time]   .   *Brahms.*
4.   Fantaisie on Hungarian Airs     .     .     .   *Liszt.*
                Mr. Max Pinner.
5.   "Wotan's Farewell" } "Walküre"   .     .     .   *Wagner.*
     "Magic Fire Scene"  }

Mr. Thomas soon left Cincinnati, for reasons explained elsewhere, and returned to the East, though during the time spent in that city he was permitted to go to New York and conduct the Philharmonic concerts.  Among the important features of the remaining concerts with the Brooklyn Philharmonic were the performance of Beethoven's Fifth Symphony, scenes from "Rheingold," and "Siegfried's Death," with an orchestra of one hundred and twenty pieces, at the close of the twenty-fourth season; "The Messiah," and Gounod's "Redemption" in the twenty-fifth season; Bach's "Christmas Oratorio," Mozart's "Requiem," and Liszt's "Saint Elizabeth" in the twenty-seventh; and Gounod's "Mors et Vita," and Dvorak's "Spectre's Bride" in the twenty-eighth.

Season after season brought its splendid array of programmes, but at a concert given April 18, 1891, the programme contained the following announcement:

"The engagement of Mr. Theodore Thomas as Musical Director of the Philharmonic Society of Brooklyn terminates with this concert, in consequence of his departure to Chicago. The directors make this announcement with sincere regret. Mr. Thomas has served the Society as its conductor for more than twenty years. Its most brilliant and most prosperous seasons have been given under his management. The Society thanks him for his generous devotion to its highest interests. It wishes for him the greatest success in his new field of duty, and it bids him an affectionate farewell."

There can be no doubt as to the sincerity of this expression, or of Mr. Thomas's hearty appreciation of it. He always cherished the memories of his Brooklyn Philharmonic period, and in our consultations always spoke of it in a manner which showed he looked back to it with the same affectionate regard which his Brooklyn friends entertained for him.

## VII

### THE NEW YORK PHILHARMONIC SOCIETY

MR. THOMAS has said that he accepted the conductorship of the New York Philharmonic Society because he thought the musical interests of that city would be better cared for by a society than by an individual. That readers who are unfamiliar with the venerable New York Philharmonic may understand this more clearly, some of the details of the peculiar system or organization should be stated. Again, as his connection with that Society was one of the leading events of his long career, a brief sketch of its history may not be out of place.[1]

The Society was founded in April, 1842; its first concert was given December 7 of that year, but it was not incorporated until 1853. Its first officers were: U. C. Hill, president; A. Reiff, vice-president; F. C. Rosier, secretary; A. Dodworth, treasurer, and W. Wood, librarian. The governing body also includes the conductor, who is elected by the members. The conductors for the first season were U. C. Hill, H. C. Timm, and Mr. Etienne. How the finances of the Society are administered is explained by the first section of its constitution:

"SEC. 1. After the last regular concert of each season the Board of Directors shall, after defraying or providing for all expenses of the Society, divide among the actual performing members of the season thus passed, the funds remaining in the

[1] For many of these facts I am indebted to the History of the Philharmonic Society, published a few years ago.—EDR.

hands of the treasurer with the exception of a small balance that is to be carried over to the next season; each performing member shall receive his full dividend or part of the same according to the time of attendance."

It will be seen from this that the Society is on a coöperative basis, and is probably the oldest coöperative organization in the country. During the first ten seasons, ending in 1853, the Society had two, and sometimes three, conductors in a single concert. From the tenth to the thirty-sixth season, when Mr. Thomas was elected, the list of conductors was as follows:

Eleventh season, 1852–53, Theodore Eisfeld.
Twelfth season, 1853–54, Theodore Eisfeld.
Thirteenth season, 1854–55, Eisfeld and Timm.
Fourteenth season, 1855–56, Carl Bergmann.
Fifteenth season, 1856–57, Theodore Eisfeld.
Sixteenth season, 1857–58, Theodore Eisfeld.
Seventeenth season, 1858–59, Carl Bergmann.
Eighteenth season, 1859–60, Bergmann and Eisfeld.
Nineteenth season, 1860–61, Bergmann and Eisfeld.
Twentieth season, 1861–62, Bergmann and Eisfeld.
Twenty-first season, 1862–63, Bergmann and Eisfeld.
Twenty-second season, 1864–65, Bergmann and Eisfeld.
Twenty-third to thirty-fourth, 1865–76, Bergmann.
Thirty-fifth season, 1876–77, Leopold Damrosch.

At the close of the thirty-fifth season the Society was in a critical situation. Musically and financially its affairs were at a low ebb, while Mr. Thomas's symphony concerts were flourishing. As Mr. Thomas says, there was no rivalry between the two organizations. There could be none. It was pretty certain,

however, that unless there should come a change, one
of the two must go under, and there was little doubt
which of the two it would be. In this emergency the
Philharmonic people invited Mr. Thomas to take the
conductorship. After giving the invitation careful
consideration, he promptly and magnanimously decided to give up his flourishing symphony concerts,
and rescue the old-established Philharmonic institution from its low estate and make it again a power
for music in New York. He at once increased the
orchestra by reinforcements from his old symphony
players, and gave his first concert November 24, 1877,
the programme including the overture to Cherubini's
"Les Deux Journées," Beethoven's "Pastoral" Symphony, selections from Schumann's "Manfred," and
Liszt's symphonic poem, "Mazeppa." S. B. Mills,
the pianist, played the Raff suite, op. 200, for the first
time in this country. The next year found Mr.
Thomas in Cincinnati, and Adolph Neuendorff was
conductor, but in the thirty-eighth season he came
to New York for each concert, and in the thirty-ninth
returned for residence, and was conductor until the
close of the forty-ninth season, in 1891, when he came
to Chicago, and Anton Seidl took his place. What
had he done in the meantime for the finances of the
Society? The treasurer's evidence on this point is
convincing. Here is his statement of receipts and
dividends from the twenty-fourth season to the forty-
ninth, Mr. Thomas's last:

| | | | Receipts | Divi- dends |
|---|---|---|---|---|
| 24th season | 1865–66 | Carl Bergmann | $ 6,441 | $ 95 |
| 25th season | 1866–67 | Carl Bergmann | 3,923 | 70 |
| 26th season | 1867–68 | Carl Bergmann | 6,163 | 70 |
| 27th season | 1868–69 | Carl Bergmann | 14,255 | 156 |
| 28th season | 1869–70 | Carl Bergmann | 12,750 | 150 |
| 29th season | 1870–71 | Carl Bergmann | 15,085 | 203 |
| 30th season | 1871–72 | Carl Bergmann | 15,480 | 216 |
| 31st season | 1872–73 | Carl Bergmann | 13,830 | 180 |
| 32d season | 1873–74 | Carl Bergmann | 9,450 | 126 |
| 33d season | 1874–75 | Carl Bergmann | 3,212 | 75 |
| 34th season | 1875–76 | Carl Bergmann | 1,641 | 30 |
| 35th season | 1876–77 | Leopold Damrosch | 841 | 18 |
| 36th season | 1877–78 | Theodore Thomas | 6,402 | 82 |
| 37th season | 1878–79 | Adolph Neuendorff | 1,493 | 25 |
| 38th season | 1879–80 | Theodore Thomas | 8,714 | 123 |
| 39th season | 1880–81 | Theodore Thomas | 10,730 | 132 |
| 40th season | 1881–82 | Theodore Thomas | 12,913 | 154 |
| 41st season | 1882–83 | Theodore Thomas | 15,933 | 195 |
| 42d season | 1883–84 | Theodore Thomas | 16,022 | 195 |
| 43d season | 1884–85 | Theodore Thomas | 17,914 | 223 |
| 44th season | 1885–86 | Theodore Thomas | 16,066 | 200 |
| 45th season | 1886–87 | Theodore Thomas | 15,562 | 225 |
| 46th season | 1887–88 | Theodore Thomas | 14,168 | 168 |
| 47th season | 1888–89 | Theodore Thomas | 14,962 | 189 |
| 48th season | 1889–90 | Theodore Thomas | 15,145 | 195 |
| 49th season | 1890–91 | Theodore Thomas | 15,500 | 200 |

Mr. Thomas rehabilitated the finances of the Society, but, what is far more important than this, he restored its prestige, infused management and members with something of his own energy and spirit, and raised its standard.   It is curious to read now, when Mr. Thomas's method of rehearsing by choirs, sections, and even individuals is so well known, this statement in "Harper's Weekly," written about this period:

"During the season after Mr. Thomas's return from Cincinnati, the Philharmonic gave a performance of Beethoven's Eighth Symphony, which was remarkable for the delicacy and absolute precision of the violins in the scherzo. After the concert a member of the orchestra told me that during the intermission the conductor had called the violinists into the greenroom and made them play over their part of the scherzo several times."

In an interview in 1882 Mr. Thomas gave expression to what he called the "Philharmonic Creed," though all the musical work of his life was planned and executed in accordance with the tenets of this creed. It contains the very core of his musical belief — the principles which he held sacred — the Alpha and Omega of his life work. It reads:

"To endeavor always to form a refined musical taste among the people by the intelligent selection of music; to give, in order to accomplish the desired result, only standard works, both of the new and old masters, and to be thus conservative and not given to experimenting with the new musical sensations of the hour. I may exemplify this further by saying that while Berlioz, Liszt, Rubinstein, Brahms, and others may be, and will be, given, such masters are never allowed representation to the exclusion, even in a degree, of Beethoven and Mozart. Nor would the first mentioned be permitted on the programme if the great symphonies were not thoroughly understood by the public."

It may be interesting here to note some of the significant events growing out of Mr. Thomas's relations, active and otherwise, with this Philharmonic

THEODORE THOMAS IN 1880

THE CHICAGO ORCHESTRA IN THE AUDITORIUM, CHICAGO

Society.  He was elected an active member in 1853, being then in his eighteenth year, and played in the ranks until 1858, when he resigned his membership. Thereafter he occasionally played as soloist at its concerts.  At the first concert of the twenty-third season, November 5, 1864, for instance, he played the Mendelssohn Concerto, op. 64.  In 1866 "Dwight's Journal of Music" contains a hint of incipient rivalry between the Thomas Orchestra and the Philharmonic.  It says (October 13):

"The Philharmonic, with Bergmann for conductor, has made up its programmes for the five subscription concerts. The first public rehearsal takes place October 20, the same day on which Theodore Thomas gives his first symphonic soiree. The 'Neue New Yorker Musik Zeitung' intimates that the success of this enterprising young rival has prompted the symptoms of progress shown by the older society in the Liszt, Wagner, Berlioz selections above named.  Certainly the programmes of both parties have many novelties in common.  But Thomas is the bolder of the two, and has undertaken to do in five concerts work that might well tax the energy of an orchestra for a couple of years.  He makes the production of great orchestral works with chorus the special mark of his ambition this year."

In 1868 Mr. Thomas played at the last concert of the season (April 18) the Beethoven Concerto, op. 61. In 1871 there was great need of Mr. Thomas's discipline and mastery in the Philharmonic ranks.  Bergmann was then the conductor, but he was already in his decadence.  A critic says of one of its concerts:

"In the 'Overture, Scherzo, and Finale' by Schumann, there was some unusually crude and slovenly playing.  There

were times when belated instruments were heard coming in
after each other at a pause, and there was also a general lack
of finish in much that was done.   This was the more notice-
able by contrast with the recent concerts given by Theodore
Thomas's orchestra, which were, in every respect, superior to
those of the Philharmonic Society."

The troubles of the Philharmonic, however,
began to disappear in 1879.   In May of that year
"The New York Tribune" contained the following
statement:

"The New York Philharmonic Society is to be congratu-
lated.   At the annual election, held yesterday, Mr. Theodore
Thomas was unanimously elected conductor.   On the first
ballot the vote stood fifty-four for Thomas, nine for Damrosch,
and six for Neuendorff.   The minority subsequently changed
their votes so that Mr. Thomas became the choice of the whole
Society.   Mr. Julius Hallgarten was elected president; Mr.
Boehn retains the vice-presidency, and the Board of Directors,
we understand, is not changed except that Messrs. Brandt and
Arnold replace two of the older members.   The directors will
soon have a conference with Mr. Thomas, and it will then be
determined whether arrangements can be made to permit of
his accepting the conductorship."

The conference was held, the symphonic concerts
were given up, and Mr. Thomas became conductor
of the New York Philharmonic Society, a position
he held for thirteen seasons, resigning it when a call
came from Chicago, which he could not resist.
Those thirteen seasons were the golden days of the
Philharmonic.   They include seventy-eight concerts
and the same number of public rehearsals.   The following list of symphonies, with the number of times

performed, shows the rich profusion of music in his programmes:

*Beethoven* — Second, 1; third, 5; fourth, 5; fifth, 4; sixth, 5; seventh, 4; eighth, 4; ninth, 3.

*Mozart* — D, 2; G minor, 4; C, 2; E flat, 1.

*Brahms* — First, 2; second, 2; third, 1; fourth, 1.

*Schubert* — Eighth, 3; ninth, 4.

*Schumann* — First, 4; second, 4; third, 3; fourth, 3.

*Haydn* — B flat, 1; D major, 1; E flat, 2; G major, 1.

*Raff* — "Im Walde," 3; "Lenore," 1.

*Rubinstein* — "Ocean," 3; "Dramatic," 3; fifth, 1.

*Cowen* — "Scandinavian," 1; "Welsh," 1.

*Dvorak* — D, 2; D minor, 1.

*Tschaikowsky* — "Manfred," 1; fifth, 2.

Berlioz's "Harold in Italy," Liszt's "Faust," Huber's "Tell," Strauss's F minor, Scharwenka's C minor, Scholtz's B flat, Bruckner's seventh, Saint-Saëns's third, Mendelssohn's fourth, Franchetti's E minor, Goldmark's second, and Spohr's "Consecration of Tones," 1 each.

The works produced for the first time in this country were:

Suite for piano and orchestra, op. 200, Raff; "Tragic Overture," Brahms; overture, "Demetrius," Rheinberger; Second piano concerto, Tschaikowsky; Fifth symphony, Rubinstein; "Tell" symphony, Hubert; "Scandinavian," symphony, Cowen; vorspiel to "Parsifal," Wagner; Symphony in D, Dvorak; Serenade in G, Villiers-Stanford; "Husitzka Overture," Dvorak; F minor Symphony, Strauss; symphonic variations, Nicodé; "Welsh" symphony, Cowen; prologue to "Othello," Krug; "Scherzo Capriccioso," Dvorak; C minor symphony, Scharwenka; D minor symphony, Dvorak; B flat symphony, Scholtz; Seventh, Bruckner; "Manfred" symphony, Tschaikowsky; Third and fourth symphonies, Brahms; Third symphony, Saint-Saëns; E minor symphony, Franchetti; E flat symphony, Goldmark; overture, "Twelfth Night," Mackenzie; Suite No. 2, Moszkowski; "Prometheus Bound," Goldmark; "Antony and Cleopatra," overture, Rubinstein; fantaisie overture, "Hamlet," Tschaikowsky.

The solo artists who appeared during these thirteen seasons were:

*Pianists,* S. B. Mills, Franz Rummel, Hermann Rietzel, Rafael Joseffy, Madeline Schiller, Carl Baermann, Richard Hoffman, Carl Faelten, Adele Aus der Ohe, and Fanny Bloomfield-Zeisler.

*Violinists* — John F. Rhodes, Maud Powell, Camilla Urso, and Leopold Lichtenberg.

*Violoncellists* — F. Bergner and F. Giese.

*Sopranos* — Mathilde Wilde, Eugenie Pappenheim, Alwina Valleria, E. Aline Osgood, Emma Thursby, Agnes B. Huntington, Mme. Fursch-Madi, Louise Pyk, Helene Hastreiter, Emma Juch, Lilli Lehmann, Laura Moore, Miss Griswold, Frau Schroeder-Hanfstängl, Clementine de Vere, Frau Ritter-Goetze.

*Altos* — Emily Winant, Antonia Henne, Helen D. Campbell.

*Tenors* — Italo Campanini, W. C. Tower, William Candidus, William H. Rieger.

*Baritones* — Antonio Galassi, George Henschel, Emil Scaria, Alonzo E. Stoddard, Theodore Reichmann.

*Bassos* — Franz Remmertz, William Ludwig, Emil Fischer.

Great as was this work, and fine as were these programmes, greater work and finer programmes were to come in Chicago and Cincinnati during the next thirteen years.

## VIII

### A NATIONAL TESTIMONIAL

IN 1889 a series of testimonial concerts was tendered Mr. Thomas. He had made tours through the country for twenty years, with varying success financially, but with musical results of a solid and enduring character. The seed which he had sown so carefully and so hopefully had already reached its blossom, and in many places its fruitage. His great musical skill was everywhere recognized. His educational work was prospering. His concerts were no longer looked upon as mere amusements. Personally he was everywhere respected for his courageous and honest devotion to the cause of good music. Even those who did not thoroughly understand his work were proud of it when they saw that European artists were eager to appear at his concerts, and European composers were equally eager that he should perform their new works. When, therefore, a series of testimonial concerts was proposed, the suggestion met with a quick and cordial response. In this connection it is significant to note that the proposition was first made by a gentleman in Minneapolis, who wrote to "The New York Tribune," April 22, 1889, as follows:

"Understand that no benefit scheme is contemplated by this suggestion. Mr. Thomas would be the first to turn his back upon such a proposition. Let him simply take his orchestra and give, in the various cities, as he always does, a *quid pro quo* and more, for all he receives, but let the tour be understood to be a distinctive opportunity for the people to testify the high estimation they place upon Mr. Thomas's life-work in behalf of the music of his country. If Mr. Thomas doubts there is a deep feeling of regard for him among the musicians and people of America, and that, whatever may be said of the sharp points of his character, they are ready to testify it, let him give them the opportunity in the way I suggest."

The first response to this suggestion came two weeks later from the Brooklyn Philharmonic Society, which was always to the fore in everything pertaining to its leader. It heartily seconded the Minneapolis suggestion, and hoped the tour would be made in October, and that Brooklyn would be included. These hopes were fully realized, and the Brooklyn Philharmonic Society's programme was one of the most noteworthy of the tour. New York City spoke next. Boston and other leading cities fell in line, and even many of the smaller towns expressed a desire to participate in the testimonial. In the light of what occurred two years later, the following utterance of "The Chicago Tribune," May 19, foreshadows Mr. Thomas's important change: "Should it eventuate in securing Mr. Thomas as our orchestra leader in the near future, it will be a consummation devoutly to be wished, and it will place Chicago on a secure and prosperous musical footing." In this case, at least, the old saying, "a prophet is not without honor save in his own country," was reversed. George William Curtis, the distinguished editor and scholar, and a staunch friend and supporter of Mr. Thomas, wrote the invitation, for the New York Testimonial Concert, which I append, because the dignity and high character of its signers make it one of the most valuable tributes Mr. Thomas ever received:

THEODORE THOMAS, ESQ.,

DEAR SIR:—Learning that you have been invited to undertake a series of concerts in various parts of the country during the next autumn, we desire to express to you our sincere interest in the enterprise proposed, to assure you of our heartiest good wishes for its complete success, and to ask that New York, which is your home and the scene of your most arduous labors, may be included among the cities which are to share the opportunity of showing their appreciation of your work.    In this centennial year of national pride and joy, not the least pleasant reason of general congratulation is the growth and development of a taste for the higher forms of art, because this taste is one of the powerful forces to which we must look for the necessary chastening of the material and commercial spirit, which has thus far largely dominated American progress. Among these forces none is more popular or more effective than music; and in the education and elevation of musical taste in this country, no individual influence is more universally acknowledged, and none is more distinctive, constant, intelligent, and effective, than yours.

Your public service of this kind has been so signal that to call attention to it on the eve of a tour such as is contemplated, is but to refresh the grateful memory of lovers and students of music throughout the country, and to secure their cordial cooperation in earnestly promoting the success of the projected series of popular concerts which will be peculiarly significant among our centennial commemorations as illustrating in themselves the character and degree of the advance of the public taste, knowledge, and skill in music.

With sincere regards, we are, dear sir,

Respectfully yours,

| | |
|---|---|
| LEVI P. MORTON, | C. VANDERBILT, |
| CARL SCHURZ, | CYRUS W. FIELD, |
| WM. M. EVARTS, | HENRY VILLARD, |
| HORACE WHITE, | R. G. INGERSOLL, |
| THEODORE ROOSEVELT, | CALVIN S. BRICE, |
| HENRY HOLT, | GROVER CLEVELAND, |
| EDMUND C. STEDMAN, | C. A. DANA, |
| C. L. TIFFANY, | W. R. GRACE, |
| W. D. HOWELLS, | PARKE GODWIN, |
| R. W. GILDER, | F. R. COUDERT, |
| R. M. HUNT, | HOWARD CROSBY, |
| GEORGE WILLIAM CURTIS, | ROBERT COLLYER, |
| CHAUNCEY M. DEPEW, | AUGUSTUS ST. GAUDENS, |
| WARNER MILLER, | BRANDER MATTHEWS, |
| JOSEPH H. CHOATE, | MONCURE D. CONWAY, |
| J. PIERPONT MORGAN, | C. P. HUNTINGTON, |
| D. HUNTINGTON, | ANDREW CARNEGIE, |
| JOHN BIGELOW, | WILLIAM STEINWAY, |
| HJALMAR H. BOYESEN, | and many others. |

The tour began October 9, 1889, in Brooklyn, Joseffy, the pianist, accompanying the orchestra as soloist, and concerts were given at the following places, in the order named: Brooklyn, Poughkeepsie, Albany (the concert in Albany occurred on his birthday, which was made all the more pleasant to him by the receipt of telegraphic congratulations from all parts of the country), Utica, Buffalo, Erie, Cleveland, Toledo, Detroit, Saginaw, Grand Rapids, Jackson, Indianapolis, Chicago, Decatur, Louisville, Columbus, Pittsburg, Philadelphia, Wilkesbarre, and

New York.  The concert in New York was given November 6, and its programme will be found elsewhere.  For this concert Mr. Thomas prepared two programmes and submitted them to the committee of invitation for their choice.  To complete the history of the testimonial tour I present both:

### No. 1.

Overture, "The Flying Dutchman"   .   .   . *Wagner.*
Adagio, "Prometheus"   .   .   .   .   . *Beethoven.*
[Violoncello Obligato by Mr. Victor Herbert.]
Invitation to the Dance   .   .   .   . *Weber-Berlioz.*
Concerto, E minor   .   .   .   .   . *Chopin-Tausig.*
Mr. Rafael Joseffy.
a. Fugue in A Minor .   .   .   .   .   . *Bach.*
b. Theme and variations .   .   .   .   . *Brahms.*
String Orchestra.
Symphonic Poem, "Les Préludes"   .   .   . *Liszt.*

### No. 2.

Overture, "Rienzi".   .   .   .   .   . *Wagner.*
First and second parts of Symphony, "Lenore"   . *Raff.*
Fantasia on Hungarian airs .   .   .   .   . *Liszt.*
Mr. Rafael Joseffy.
Overture, "William Tell"   .   .   .   . *Rossini.*
Träumerei .   .   .   .   .   .   . *Schumann.*
String Orchestra.
Piano Solo { a. Berceuse .   .   .   .   . *Chopin.*
b. Valse Impromptu (new)   .   *Joseffy.*
c. Marche Militaire .   . *Schubert-Tausig.*
Mr. Rafael Joseffy.
Waltz, "Hochzeits Klänge"   .   .   .   .   . *Strauss.*
"Damnation of Faust"   .   .   .   .   . *Berlioz.*
a. Invocation—Minuet of the Will-of-the-Wisps.
b. Dance of the Sylphs.
c. Rakoczy March.

## IX
### FAREWELL TO THE EAST.

THE year 1891 was a memorable one in Mr. Thomas's life, for it was his farewell year in the East. Before it closed he was at home in Chicago, where his life-dream was destined to be realized fourteen years later. That he had been considering the possibility of this change for a long time is evident from a letter written to me under date of November 28, 1888, in which he says:

"I shall soon be ready to spend most of my time in Chicago. It is the old story — what New York offers, I refuse; what I demand, she refuses." Three years later he made the change, but even twelve years after that, wearied with much labor he sometimes doubted whether his dreams were to be realized. On December 9, 1903, at the very verge of their fulfilment, he met me and said that he had almost given up hope of success in the struggle to secure a permanent home for the orchestra, and that he might yet have to discontinue his work and retire from the field, although Chicago was then rousing herself to secure the memorable gift she soon made to the man whom she loved, and to his men, whom she admired. Is it unnatural that after fifty years of colossal labor, of many discouragements, and defeated hopes, at a time when his strength was failing, though his intellectual powers were as strong as ever, he should occasionally have given way almost to despair?

To return to 1891. It was a busy year. He was

THE WOMEN'S CENTENNIAL MUSIC HALL, PHILADELPHIA

THE INTERSTATE INDUSTRIAL EXPOSITION BUILDING, CHICAGO

making his farewell calls.  Between March 31 and April 17 his orchestra played at five concerts given by Arthur Friedheim, the pianist, at the Metropolitan Opera House.  April 11 he bade good-bye to the New York Philharmonic Society with a programme including Mendelssohn's overture, "Fingal's Cave," Tschaikowsky's overture-fantasia, "Hamlet," and Beethoven's "Eroica" Symphony.  Adele Aus der Ohe, the pianist, played the Schumann concerto, A minor, op. 54.  Philadelphia came next in order, April 14, and the programme, chosen by vote, included Beethoven's Seventh Symphony; the "Song of the Rhine Daughters," and "Siegfried's Death and Funeral March."  Mlle. De Vere was the vocalist, and Mr. Bendix played the first movement of the "Emperor" Concerto of Beethoven.  April 18 he gave his Brooklyn patrons the following noble good-bye programme: Schubert's "Unfinished" Symphony; Beethoven's Seventh Symphony; Wagner's "Faust Overture," and his own fine setting of the Chopin "Funeral March."  The next evening he took leave of the Lenox Lyceum with Grieg's "Peer Gynt" Suite, Beethoven's Fifth  Symphony, and Liszt's Second Rhapsody.  There were five soloists at this concert, Mlle. De Vere, Miss Maud Powell, Miss Adele Aus der Ohe, Sig. Del Puente, and Sig. Campanini, the concert being in the popular series.

Then he came to Chicago and gave six concerts at the Auditorium, which, for thirteen years, was to be his big concert-hall.  During May he gave scattering concerts here and there, and in the latter part of that month directed the third annual festival at Indianapolis. From that time until the middle of June he made a concert tour, playing at Kansas City, Omaha, Minneapolis, Milwaukee, Detroit, Toronto, Ottawa, Montreal, and Burlington, Vt., in the order named. July 6, 1891, he began his farewell series of New York concerts at Madison Square Garden. They were forty-two in number, and their characterization upon his programmes as "Symphony," "Request," "Ballroom," "Popular," and "Composers'," recalls the never-to-be-forgotten summer night concerts in Chicago. The last of the forty-two concerts was given August 16, 1891, the "Request" programme being as follows:

1. Prelude and fugue .    .    .    .    .    .    *Bach.*
2. Ballet air, "Paris and Helen"    .    .    .    .    *Gluck.*
3. Andante and finale from Fifth Symphony    . *Beethoven.*
4. Song, "Les Rameaux"    .    .    .    .    .    *Faure.*
    Mr. Leo Stormont.
5. Hungarian Rhapsody, No. 12    .    .    .    *Liszt.*
6. "Marche Funèbre"    .    .    .    .    *Chopin-Thomas.*
7. Polacca from "I Puritani"    .    .    .    .    *Rossini.*
    Miss Louise Natali.
8. March movement, "Lenore Symphony"    .    .    *Raff.*
9. "Largo"    .    .    .    .    .    .    .    *Handel.*
    [Violin obligato, Mr. Bendix.]
10. "Spring Song" .    .    .    .    .    *Mendelssohn.*
11. Duet from "Il Trovatore"    .    .    .    .    *Verdi.*
    Miss Natali and Mr. Stormont.
12. "Tannhäuser Overture"    .    .    .    .    *Wagner.*

His last word to New York was the "Tannhäuser Overture," always a favorite with him, and then he

turned his face to the West, there to continue his
great work, for which there was no longer need in the
East, and to remain working with heroic will and
sublime patience until death laid its pitiless hand
upon him — and he rested from his labors.

## X

### IN CHICAGO

MR. THOMAS made the acquaintance of Chicago in 1869.   For twenty-two years he was
an honored visitor; for fourteen years afterwards it
was his home.   I have already made reference to the
three opening concerts in November, 1869.   Mr.
Thomas did not leave Chicago in very good humor
at that time, but he found some stanch friends who
guaranteed him an audience if he would make another visit.   He did so, on the 7th of November,
1870, and gave seven concerts,— six at Farwell Hall,
and a sacred concert at Crosby's Opera House, with
large audiences in attendance.   Miss Mehlig, the
eminent pianist, assisted and, in addition to some
minor pieces, played concertos by Weber, Liszt,
Schumann, Chopin, and Hummel, which were new
to Chicago.   His most memorable concert of that
season was on the 14th, in which the programme
was devoted to Beethoven, including the "Pastoral"
Symphony, the "Leonora" overture, No. 3, the
Septet, op. 20, and the "Choral Fantaisie," op. 80,
for which Mr. Dohn, the leader of the Apollo Club,
drilled a select chorus.   Mr. Thomas went away

happier.    He had found his way to the Chicago people, and they had found their way to him.

In April, 1871, he came again, and gave seven more concerts. The programmes were light, the most important work being the Beethoven concerto in G, No. 4, played by Anna Mehlig. The next season was to have commenced at Crosby's Opera House, on the fatal night of October 9, 1871. Among the fire losses which were not enumerated at the time were Beethoven's Third and Fifth Symphonies, Schubert's Ninth and Schumann's First and Fourth, besides seven piano concertos which were to have been played by Marie Krebs. Mr. Thomas did not come again until the 7th of October, 1872, when he opened the new Aiken's Theatre with a series of concerts, assisted by Mr. George L. Osgood, the tenor singer. The most important works in that season were Schumann's First Symphony, op. 38, and Beethoven's Seventh; but in addition to these works he brought out Liszt's "Préludes," the Beethoven Quartet, op. 18, for string orchestra, two movements of Rubinstein's "Ocean" Symphony, Liszt's "Mephisto Waltz," and several works by Raff, Berlioz, Liszt, and Wagner, which were new to Chicago.

In 1873, under engagement with Messrs. Carpenter and Sheldon, Mr. Thomas gave five concerts, commencing February 17, at the Michigan Avenue Baptist and Union Park Congregational churches, which were, at that time, the only available concert places. Both Miss Mehlig and Mr. Osgood assisted him,

and the concerts were unusually brilliant and successful.   A week later, under the same management,
he gave two more concerts, the second of which was
devoted exclusively to Wagner's music.   The audiences were smaller and much more select than those
which a little later "crowded the house" on "Wagner
nights," and continued to do so until Wagner was
permanently displaced by Beethoven.   On the 17th
of March, under the same management, and in combination with Rubinstein and Wieniawski, two memorable concerts were given, in which Rubinstein
played his own concerto in D minor, No. 4, Handel's
air and variations in E major, a Mozart rondo, and
a Bach gigue, Scarlatti's "Katzenfuge," Beethoven's
concerto in E flat, No. 5, and Schumann's "Carnival."   Wieniawski's numbers were the Mendelssohn
concerto, Ernst's "Othello" fantaisie, and his own
concerto, No. 2.   Mr. Thomas did not come again
until October 6 of the same year, when he dedicated
Kingsbury Hall with a series of eight concerts,
assisted by Myron W. Whitney, the basso.   The
programmes were unusually brilliant.   The first four
were popular.   At the fifth concert, Beethoven's
Eighth Symphony and the four overtures to "Fidelio" were performed.   Mr. Whitney sang Mozart
and Beethoven arias, and Mr. Listemann, the violinist, played Joachim's "Hungarian Concerto."   The
last concert was given with the assistance of the
Apollo Club in selections from "Frithjof " and
"Lohengrin," and the soloists, Mr. M. W. Whitney,
Mr. S. E. Jacobsohn, violinist, Mr. Julius Fuchs,

pianist, and the local singers, Mrs. Clara Huck, Mrs. O. K. Johnson, and Mr. Fritz Foltz. The orchestral numbers were selections from Wagner's "Meistersinger," Beethoven's overture, "Coriolanus," and Liszt's Second Hungarian Rhapsody.

In February, 1874, four concerts were given with the assistance of the Apollo Club and Germania Männerchor, at the last of which (February 18), Schumann's "Paradise and the Peri" was produced for the first time in this country. Upon this occasion, Miss Clara Doria, of Boston, was the "Peri." The remaining parts were sung by Mrs. O. K. Johnson, Mrs. O. L. Fox, Mrs. T. E. Stacey, Miss Ella A. White, Messrs. M. W. Whitney, Fritz Foltz, E. W. Reuling, and L. A. Phelps. In September, 1874, four more concerts were given, Miss Emma Cranch, soloist.

On the 25th of September of the same year, many lovers of music tendered Mr. Thomas a testimonial concert, in connection with which the following correspondence is of interest:

CHICAGO, Sept. 25, 1874.

THEODORE THOMAS, ESQ.,

DEAR SIR:—After having at times in the last five years, listened with almost infinite delight to the music you have brought us, and feeling that your visits to our city may become less frequent hereafter as your duties increase, we would desire to express to you our thanks for happiness, pure and lasting; and, knowing of no method of giving the public an opportunity of expressing this gratitude other than by a Complimentary Benefit Concert, we would, on behalf of the community, ask you to

accept of such a tribute of esteem from your friends here; and
fearing this approaching visit may be your last for a time, we
would ask respectfully if you cannot add this complimentary
evening to the series of concerts you are about to give in this
city.

| | |
|---|---|
| LEVI Z. LEITER, | W. F. COOLBAUGH, |
| WM. SPRAGUE, | P. H. SHERIDAN, U. S. A., |
| HENRY FIELD, | ANSON STAGER, |
| HENRY W. KING, | A. C. HESING, |
| DAVID SWING, | FRANKLIN MAC VEAGH, |
| HENRY GREENEBAUM, | JAMES B. RUNNION, |
| POTTER PALMER, | WIRT DEXTER, |
| HORACE WHITE, | LOUIS WAHL, |
| N. K. FAIRBANK, | W. S. WALKER, |
| ROBERT GOLDBECK, | EDWIN LEE BROWN, |
| GEO. P. UPTON, | JOHN B. DRAKE, |
| JOHN L. PECK, | GEO. H. LAFLIN, |
| GEO. A. FORSYTH, | N. S. BOUTON, |
| J. D. WEBSTER, | CARL WOLFSOHN, |
| W. E. DOGGETT, | J. McG. ADAMS, |
| F. W. PALMER, | WM. BROSS, |
| L. D. BOONE, | A. H. DOHN, |
| JOHN G. SHORTALL, | DR. ISHAM. |
| J. IRVING PEARCE, | |

To this Mr. Thomas replied:

PALMER HOUSE, CHICAGO, Sept. 28.

To MESSRS. LEVI Z. LEITER, WILLIAM SPRAGUE, HENRY
FIELD, AND OTHERS:

GENTLEMEN:—In accepting your generous invitation, received by telegraph in Syracuse, I desire to express my sincere
thanks for the kindly expressions of esteem shown in your letter
toward me personally.   But I desire to place on record more
fully an expression of my grateful feelings for the tribute you,

through me, have paid to the art to which my life has been exclusively devoted.

I assure you that this evidence of appreciation, coming, as it does, from the representative city of the West, is an additional encouragement for me to continue the work of elevating the standard of musical art. In naming Saturday, October 3, for the concert, I am very respectfully yours,

THEODORE THOMAS.

In the latter part of April, 1875, while *en route* to the Cincinnati Festival, Mr. Thomas gave four festival concerts and a matinee in McCormick Hall, the Germania Männerchor, a mixed chorus of two hundred voices, Miss Cranch, and Messrs. Bischoff and Remmertz, soloists, assisting. The principal instrumental works were Beethoven's "Pastoral" Symphony, Mendelssohn's "Scotch" Symphony, and Schubert's "Unfinished" Symphony. The choral numbers were selections from Gluck's "Orpheus," Mendelssohn's "An die Künstler," Rietz's "Morgenlied," and the "Armorers'" chorus from Wagner's "Rienzi."

Eighteen hundred and seventy-seven will always be a memorable year in the history of music in Chicago. After a brilliant series of festival concerts, given early in June by the Apollo Club, in which Mr. Thomas's orchestra participated, he began that remarkable series of summer night concerts in the Exposition Building, upon the Lake Front, which were not discontinued until the summer of 1890. The opening concert was given June 18, with the following popular programme:

Overture, "La Gazza Ladra" . . . . *Rossini.*
Waltz, "Die Vorstädter" . . . . . *Lanner.*
Ballet Music, "Reine de Saba" . . . *Gounod.*
Rhapsodie Hongroise, No. 2 . . . . *Liszt.*
Overture, "Egmont" . . . . . *Beethoven.*
Larghetto
March Tempo } Symphony "Lenore" . . . *Raff.*
Selections, 1st act "Lohengrin" . . . *Wagner.*
Overture, "Martha" . . . . . . *Flotow.*
"Serenade" (adapted for orchestra), by Theodore
Thomas . . . . . . . *Schubert.*
Waltz, "Illustrationen" . . . . . . *Strauss.*
"Coronation March" . . . . . . *Farbach.*

I have Mr. Thomas's authority for the statement that Mr. George B. Carpenter, the manager of these concerts in 1877, first suggested to him the idea of the "request" programme, which explains the following announcement in the programme of July 12:

"For Monday evening, July 16, Mr. Thomas has in preparation a novel programme, in which he will endeavor to satisfy the expressed wishes of his audiences, as shown in the letters daily received, urging repetition of certain selections. This will be the 'Request' programme. It will contain only those numbers, repetition of which has been urged, making a programme representing the popular taste of the lighter programme music, reserving for another time the pieces of the more serious composers, repetition of which has been requested."

In conversation with Mr. Thomas about a year before his death, I asked him why he had discontinued making "request" programmes. He replied: "Because it is no longer necessary. My audiences no longer request. They are satisfied with what satisfies me." In this statement he referred to the regular patrons. "Transients" sometimes sent in requests, but he paid no attention to them.

The first summer night season, notwithstanding labor strikes and riots, was a great success. As it drew to a close concert goers bestirred themselves to secure another season in 1878. The agitation at last resulted in a letter signed by many prominent citizens asking Mr. Thomas to return the next summer, and tendering him a complimentary concert.

He came the next summer, and every summer but two, until 1891. In a general sense these thirteen seasons of summer night concerts are noteworthy. Their popular success, and the appreciation and encouragement extended to him when his prospects seemed darkest, and it appeared as if the longer existence of his famous orchestra were hopeless, greatly influenced him in his decision to make Chicago his home. Again, these thirteen seasons of garden music judiciously combined with higher music gradually elevated the popular taste, and prepared his audiences for his fourteen seasons of more dignified and more purely intellectual music which were to follow them in the concert-room. From the narrower and more purely personal point of view, who that had the pleasure of attending those Exposition summer night concerts will ever forget the brilliancy of the programmes, their consistency with the surroundings, the familiarity, as it were, between the conductor and orchestra on the one hand and the audience on the other, the freedom of intercourse, the Bohemian informality, and the absence

CROSBY'S OPERA HOUSE, CHICAGO, IN 1871

Toronto, Friday March 22$\underline{^{nd}}$

Symphony, "From the new World," — — Dvorak

   Adagio — Allegro molto

     Largo

      Scherzo

       Allegro con fuoco.


Prelude and Glorification, "Parsifal"     Wagner

       Intermission


Theme & variations } op. 55, — — — Tschaikowsky
Finale,

    Violin obligato M. Max Bendix

Indian Bell Song, Lackme, — — Delibes

     Miss Electa Gifford

Serenade, — — — — — Goldmark


Symphonic Poem, "The Moldau" — Smetana.

FACSIMILE OF ORIGINAL OF ONE OF MR. THOMAS'S CONCERT
TOUR PROGRAMMES

of the concert-room's etiquette of dress and demeanor?

Meanwhile, Chicago had its two festivals, the first
in 1882, the second in 1884.  The first was the result
of Mr. Thomas's years of educational effort, which
led steadily forward to such a culmination.  The
1882 festival was associated with the New York and
Cincinnati May festivals, all under the same leader,
employing the same solo artists, and utilizing the
same orchestral material; but, as I have previously
said, the biennial feature of the scheme was dropped.
New York had one and Chicago two festivals.  Cincinnati alone was able to continue them, and since
Mr. Thomas's death has pledged itself to keep up
festival work, and, so far as it is able, to maintain his
high standard.

For the 1882 festival there was the following
brilliant array of artists: Sopranos, Mme. Friedrich-
Materna and Mrs. E. Aline Osgood; contraltos, Miss
Annie Louise Cary and Miss Emily Winant; tenors,
Sig. Italo Campanini, Mr. William Candidus, and
Mr. Theodore J. Toedt; bassos, Mr. George Henschel,
Mr. Franz Remmertz, and Mr. Myron W. Whitney.
The principal vocal numbers were Handel's "Utrecht
Jubilate," scenes from "Lohengrin," Handel's "Mes-
siah," Bach's cantata, "Festo Ascensionis Christi,"
selections from the Nibelungen trilogy, Schumann's
Mass in C minor, and "The Fall of Troy," from
Berlioz's "Les Troyens."  The principal works per-
formed by the orchestra were Beethoven's Fifth
and Ninth Symphonies, Mozart's Symphony in C

("Jupiter"), the supplementary movement to Rubinstein's "Ocean" Symphony, and Brahms's "Tragic"
overture.

For the festival of 1884, the foundation of which
was a chorus of nine hundred and an orchestra of one
hundred and seventy, the soloists were Mme. Fried-
rich-Materna, Herr Emil Scaria, barytone; Herr
Hermann Winkelmann, tenor, all from the Imperial
Opera House, Vienna; Christine Nilsson, Emma
Juch, Emily Winant, Theodore J. Toedt, and Franz
Remmertz.   The principal vocal works were Haydn's
"Creation," selections from "Tannhäuser," "Die
Walküre," "Lohengrin," "Die Götterdämmerung,"
"Parsifal," and "Die Meistersinger," Berlioz's "Messe
des Morts," Handel's "Dettingen Te Deum," and
Gounod's "Redemption."   The symphonies were
Mozart's G minor, Beethoven's "Eroica," and Schu-
bert's Ninth.

Four years later the Thomas Orchestra was disbanded, for reasons stated elsewhere, but the next
year came the national testimonial, and a widespread
popular demand that the concert tours should be
revived.   For the testimonial tour Mr. Thomas organized an orchestra in which were some of the members
of the old organization, but the "Thomas Orchestra," as it had been known so many years, had
closed its labors.   Two years later, the Chicago
Orchestral Association was incorporated, the incorporators being N. K. Fairbank, E. B. McCagg, A. C.
Bartlett, C. D. Hamill, and C. N. Fay, who constituted the first board of trustees.   It is no injustice

to any of the incorporators to give Mr. Fay the credit of being the originator of the Association. He gave generously of his time and labor and money to it, secured the original subscriptions, and was largely instrumental in maintaining it until it was able to stand on its own feet. Contracts were made with Mr. Thomas to serve as director for three years, beginning July 1, 1891, with Mr. Milward Adams to serve as manager for the same time, and the Auditorium was secured for the concerts. Fifty-one gentlemen assured the finances. These fifty-one original sponsors of the Chicago Orchestra were: Marshall Field, C. N. Fay, E. B. McCagg, N. K. Fairbank, H. H. Porter, A. A. Sprague, T. B. Blackstone, Walter C. Larned, George A. Armour, O. S. A. Sprague, R. T. Crane, John M. Clark, Thomas Murdock, Edson Keith, Franklin MacVeagh, John R. Walsh, O. W. Potter, Henry Field (estate), Charles Counselman, C. L. Hutchinson, N. B. Ream, T. W. Harvey, C. W. Fullerton, Henry W. Bishop, Dr. Ralph N. Isham, Eugene S. Pike, C. R. Cummings, George M. Pullman, P. D. Armour, Victor F. Lawson, A. C. Bartlett, S. A. Kent, Henry W. King, L. J. Gage, Norman Williams, Albert Keep, Martin A. Ryerson, H. W. Higinbotham, Cyrus H. McCormick, E. W. Blatchford, Byron L. Smith, Carl Wolfsohn, J. McGregor Adams, Allison V. Armour, J. J. Glessner, S. E. Barrett, J. M. Loomis, W. G. Hibbard, L. Z. Leiter, Charles H Wacker, and O. W. Meysenburg.

The story of the Chicago Orchestra, of its struggles and vicissitudes, of the patience and courage of

its leader, of the noble generosity of the little band
of guarantors,— for the original number was largely
reduced after the three years' contract expired,— of
the arrival at the parting of the ways, and of the unprecedented popular tribute of Chicago to the orchestra bearing its name, and of its attachment to its
leader, is familiar to every one.   Mr. Thomas lived
long enough to dedicate the permanent home which
Chicago had given to its orchestra, and passed away,
knowing that his life-work had not been in vain, and
that the purposes which had been nearest his heart
for fifty years were at last realized.

## XI

### DISAPPOINTMENTS

THERE were three great disappointments in Mr.
Thomas's life growing out of his connection with
the Cincinnati College of Music, the American Opera
Company, and the World's Columbian Exposition
Bureau of Music.   These disappointments were all
the more bitter because in each case he had planned
musical schemes upon the broadest foundations, and
for the highest and noblest purposes, and in each
case he hoped for results which should not only
justify the time and labor and money expended, but
should be far reaching in their influence.   In other
words, he looked forward to a college which should
be not merely a conservatory, but a university of
higher musical learning; to an opera organization of
a national and purely American character, which, in

time, should give a great and much-needed impetus to musical composition, as well as performance, in this country; and to such an exposition at the famous White City of musical progress, that its evolution should be marked, and its promise made clear to every one. All three projects failed, but not because of his fault. His plans were too great for one man to carry out unaided.

It would be a thankless task to stir up the old embers of strife — all the more thankless now that Mr. Thomas is not here to make answer. In each case, when he saw that persistence in his plans must involve a long and bitter contest, and that these plans were either misunderstood or antagonized, he resigned, and bore his disappointment with philosophical composure. He cherished no resentments, but turned to the great purpose of his life with fresh courage and renewed activity. I have had letters from him during these three periods, but only in one of them does he refer to his troubles, and in that he merely says: "I cannot tell you what pain these attacks have given me. My age and my record should have protected me from them. But let it pass. Art is long." So, as the Master said, "let it pass." It will not revive strife nor pain any one now, however, to define his relations to the three schemes mentioned, all of which were nobly conceived, and to show what he intended, though his plans failed.

Mr. Thomas, in his autobiography, refers to the unpleasantness of his connection with the Cincinnati College of Music in a general way. It was the only unpleasantness he ever had there.   He went to that city as a young man.   He conducted every one of its biennial festivals from 1873 to 1904, the last one with a series of programmes so colossal, so grandly conceived, so perfectly put together, so admirably executed, as to excite the wonder and attract the admiration of the whole musical world.   If he had left no other great achievement behind him, the programme book of the sixteenth Cincinnati festival would have been a sufficient memorial of his greatness.   What the Festival Association thinks of him, how it cherishes his memory as musician and friend, how proudly it recalls his triumphs, how faithfully it promises to follow in the course he laid out for it, is stated in its beautiful and dignified memorial contained in the appendix of this volume.   There were no disappointments in his connection with the Musical Association; with the College, unfortunately, it was different.

The College was incorporated under the laws of Ohio in the summer of 1878, its directors being R. R. Springer, John Shillito, George Ward Nichols, Jacob Burnet, Jr., and Peter R. Neff.   Mr. Nichols was made president.   On August 16 of that year the following letter was addressed to Mr. Thomas by many leading citizens of Cincinnati, inviting him to take the position of musical director:

CINCINNATI, August 16, 1878.
MR. THEODORE THOMAS, NEW YORK:

DEAR SIR: — The undersigned, citizens of Cincinnati, on the part of the College of Music of Cincinnati, cordially invite you at the earliest opportunity to make your residence in this city, and accept the musical directorship of the college. It is proposed to establish an institution for musical education upon the scale of the most important of those of a similar character in Europe; to employ the highest class of professors; to organize a full orchestra, with a school for orchestra and chorus, and to give concerts.

This city has superior advantages for the success of this project. We have the new Music Hall, where the College will be held, and the great organ, which offers decided attraction. Our community is cultivated in music; living is cheap and comfortable here.

In this invitation we recognize your especial fitness for a trust so important, and believe if you accept that you will be taking another step forward in the noble work of musical education to which your life has been so successfully devoted.

| | |
|---|---|
| R. R. Springer, | Peter Rudolph Neff, |
| Joseph Longworth, | Joseph Kinsey, |
| John Shillito, | A. Howard Hinkle, |
| George K. Shoenberger, | Lawrence Maxwell, |
| Robert Mitchell, | Gordon Shillito, Jr., |
| David Sinton, | Jacob Burnet, Jr., |
| W. H. Andrews, | Julius Dexter, |
| Rufus King, | Robert F. Leaman, |
| William Resor, Jr., | M. E. Ingalls, |
| C. H. Gould, | Charles Short, |
| T. B. Resor, | Geo. Ward Nichols. |

Mr. Thomas promptly accepted the invitation, and signed a contract for five years, because he believed that the College would be just such an instituton as he had long desired for the cultivation and diffusion of knowledge of the higher music. He organized it upon the basis of a great musical university. In addition to the tuition in all the common branches of music, he organized an orchestra of large proportions, a quartette for chamber music, a chorus for oratorio work, and provided for regular recitals upon the great new organ. The College was soon humming like a hive, and there were no drones in it. In the first season (November 7, 1878, to May 29, 1879), there were twelve orchestral concerts with programmes of the highest order, and eminent soloists, twelve chamber concerts in which Mr. Thomas took part, with Jacobsohn, violin, Baetens, viola, and Hartdegen, violoncello, besides choral, closing examination, and miscellaneous concerts, and organ recitals by Mr. George E. Whiting, three or four times a week. During the second season there were eight orchestral and six chamber concerts, organ recitals twice a week, and miscellaneous concerts.

A letter to "Dwight's Journal of Music," January 25, 1879, says:

"The influence exerted by Theodore Thomas in his new field of labor cannot be overrated. A faculty has been formed of local teachers, and in addition Jacobsohn, Baetens, and Hartdegen, with Theodore Thomas, make a strong quartette. Mr. Whiting has been engaged as organist, Signor and Mme. La Villa as vocal instructors, and Perring as teacher of oratorio. It is also a success from a business point of view. Its most potent influence is exerted through the orchestral, chamber, and organ concerts, and the College choir. Every member of the latter is rigidly examined, and discipline is strict. In the orchestral concerts Beethoven's Second, Haydn's Ninth, Schumann's Fourth, and Brahms's C minor symphonies have been performed; in the chamber concerts, quartets by Beethoven, Mozart, Haydn, Schubert, and Schumann, and a quintet by Brahms; and at the organ recitals the best works of Bach, Mendelssohn, Hesse, Thiele, Fink, Lemmens, Best, and Smart."

A second letter to the same paper, written February 8, 1879, says:

"In the instrumental and vocal departments, the system in vogue in European conservatories is adhered to, except that more attention is paid to the individual. The chorus classes are instructed in musical notation, sight singing, etc. Theory is thoroughly taught, and the attendance in classes is controlled by carefully kept registers. For the orchestral concerts, Mr. Thomas took the standing orchestra, which had been directed by Michael Brand, and supplemented it, and made Jacobsohn concertmeister."

In February, 1879, Mr. Thomas, owing to his manifold and engrossing duties, gave up his place in the string quartette to Eich, a resident violinist. In March of that year the College choir was studying Handel's "Hercules," Schubert's E flat Mass, Verdi's "Manzoni Requiem," Beethoven's "Ruins of Athens," and other important works. Mr. Whiting, the organist, had added to his department instruction in church music. Apparently all through 1879 everything was prosperous, but early in 1880 sinister rumors were afloat, and there was talk of disagreement between Mr. Thomas and the Board of Directors. The correspondence "connected with the withdrawal of Mr. Theodore Thomas from the College of Music of Cincinnati" explains the disagreement. In February, 1882, Mr. Thomas submitted certain recommendations to the Board of Directors. The report they made upon them was not satisfactory to him, and on the 27th of that month he wrote to the Chairman of the Board as follows:

CINCINNATI, *February* 27, 1880.

MR. A. T. GOSHORN, CHAIRMAN:

DEAR SIR:— I am in receipt of your communication of the 25th, inclosing the report of your committee for my examination, and requesting me to make such further suggestions as I wish, concerning said report, before its return by your Committee to the Board.

There are some minor matters of detail, concerning the curriculum and prospectus, which will require further consideration. But there are two matters of fundamental importance, as to one of which my former suggestion is disregarded, and as to the other of which the report is ambiguous.

In the first place, I am clear that the school year cannot be divided into more than two terms. According to regulation No. 2 of your report, the Musical Director is to be charged with, and held responsible for, the musical conduct of the College. I am willing to assume this responsibility, but I must insist upon being intrusted with the *exclusive* direction of the school in all its departments, reserving, of course, to the Board of Directors all questions involving the expenditure of money. In other words, I insist upon occupying that relation to the school which is ordinarily involved in the office of President of a College, and I expect the Board of Directors and its officers to sustain the relation ordinarily sustained by the Trustees of a College.

Under these conditions, with a curriculum established and discipline maintained, I have confidence in the prospect of building up a great musical College. Under any other conditions, I consider further effort in that behalf futile, and I therefore desire to know at the earliest convenient day whether my suggestions are acceptable. If they are, I think it important that the changes which they involve in the office of the College should be made at once.  I shall be glad to receive an answer, by, say, next Tuesday.                    Yours truly,

THEODORE THOMAS.

Mr. Goshorn replied to this letter, asking Mr. Thomas to explain more definitely his understanding of the relations of the President of a College to the Board of Trustees.  In his reply Mr. Thomas explained at length, and as his letter contains the reasons for his subsequent resignation, I append the most important portion of it.  Mr. Thomas says:

"With the experience which you say you have had in such matters, I must assume that you are familiar with the usual character of the office of President of a College, and I beg to assure you that your apprehensions of an erroneous understanding on my part are groundless.  I understand, as you do, that the President of a College is an executive officer who is appointed by the Board of Trustees, and administers the affairs of the College under authority derived from them, and conformably, of course, to any rules and regulations adopted by them.

"But the Trustees of a College never come in contact with the students or take any personal part in the administration of the internal affairs and government of the College.  All that is confided to the President and Faculty, and that is what I desire to have done in our College.  I must have exclusive direction of the school in all its departments.  Everybody connected with the school must be under my control, and receive his instructions from me, and be accountable to me alone.  I in turn would expect to be accountable for my administration to the Board of Directors.  I would not expect to submit my judgment to theirs in musical matters, and in everything concerning which I would be obliged to consult them, I would rely upon mutually sympathetic coöperation.  I believe that I could easily administer the affairs of the office of the College with the assistance of a Secretary. An additional Clerk or Treasurer might be necessary for a few days at the opening of each term.

"In view of your allusion to my contract, I beg to say that rumors, which have not escaped my ears, to the effect that I am desirous of being relieved from it, are entirely false. I assure you that it is my earnest desire to adhere to my contract, and go on with the College, in whose success, under proper organization, I lack no confidence.

"But you must appreciate that my professional reputation is at stake, and that I cannot, in justice to myself, consent to continue longer responsible for a school whose direction is not confided in me; and that therefore I am entitled to know, without delay, whether that will be done. I simply insist upon being in fact what I am now only in name, viz., Director of the College. That office I am entitled to under my contract, and I decline longer to act as Assistant or Associate Director."

Several more letters passed between Mr. Thomas and various members of the Board, but at last he wrote March 4, 1880, the following letter of resignation:

CINCINNATI, March 4, 1880.

THE BOARD OF THE DIRECTORS OF THE COLLEGE OF MUSIC
    OF CINCINNATI:

GENTLEMEN:— I am in receipt of the letter of your committee dated 2d instant. I regard it as a misrepresentation of my position and an evasion of the real issue. That position and issue you certainly cannot misunderstand in view of the communications, written and verbal, which I have had with your committee and the President of your Board. I, therefore, deem further negotiations useless, and respectfully request that you relieve me from my duties October 1, or as soon thereafter as will enable you to secure a successor. Yours truly,

THEODORE THOMAS.

The directors accepted the resignation, but not the date named by Mr. Thomas, and after consultation with them his official relations with the College terminated April 8, 1880, and, with one exception, they parted good friends.   He had differed from them in his views as to the scope of a Director.   To carry out the purpose he had in mind, he needed more personal authority than the trustees were willing to concede to him.   But even had they conceded all he asked, it is doubtful whether Cincinnati was ready for such a great university as he had planned, which, if he could have carried out those plans, would have been one of the greatest seats of musical learning in the world. Nor was there the student material for such an institution.   Simply, the time was not ripe for such a great project, and from that point of view the contest was immaterial, and left no rancor behind it, disappointing as the result was to him.   He had greater and in many respects more important work to do, not alone for Cincinnati but for the whole West, and work for which no other city in the West but Cincinnati could give him the opportunity of doing.   Nobly and most generously she stood by him and maintained those great festivals which have made her name famous, and shed added lustre upon his renown.

Mr. Thomas's experience with the American Opera Company was a bitter one, not alone because of the disappointment entailed by its failure but also because of the exasperating litigation and petty persecution to which he was subjected for some time after the collapse by those who thoughtlessly assumed that he was financially responsible. Mr. Thomas's only financial connection with the enterprise was a salaried one, and he sacrificed several months' salary in order that the orchestra should receive its pay. The American Opera Company, though a distinct institution from the School of Opera, which was incorporated as the National Conservatory of Music, was conducted under the same patronage and in sympathy with its practical workings. The prospectus shows that the American Opera Company, Limited, was incorporated in 1878, for the purpose of permanently supporting "opera sung by Americans." Its capital was $250,000. Its officers were: President, Andrew Carnegie; Vice-Presidents, Mrs. August Belmont, Mrs. William T. Blodgett, and Mrs. Levi P. Morton; Secretary and Treasurer, Mrs. Jeannette M. Thurber; Musical Director, Theodore Thomas. It was not a local but a national enterprise. The leading artists came from twenty different cities, and the chorus, originally selected from six hundred and thirty applicants, represented twenty-three different States of the Union. The distinct features of the Company were enumerated in the prospectus as follows:

"FIRST. Grand opera sung in our own language by the most competent artists;
SECOND. The musical guidance of Theodore Thomas;
THIRD. The unrivalled Thomas Orchestra;
FOURTH. The largest regularly trained chorus ever

employed in grand opera in America, and composed entirely
of young and fresh voices;

FIFTH.   The largest ballet corps ever presented in grand
opera in America, and as far as possible American in its composition;

SIXTH.   Four thousand new and correct costumes for
which no expense has been spared in fabric or manufacture;

SEVENTH.   The armor, properties, and paraphernalia, the
handiwork of artisans employed solely for this department,
and made from models designed by the best authorities;

EIGHTH.   The scenery, designed by the Associated Artists
of New York, and painted by the most eminent scenic artists
in America.

In a word, the object of the American Opera Company is
to present ensemble opera, giving no single feature undue
prominence to the injury of others, and distinctly discouraging
the pernicious star system, long since discountenanced in con-
tinental Europe."

The purpose of the American Opera Company
was most commendable.   It was one which had been
contemplated by other eminent musicians, among
them Anton Seidl.   At this writing it is again on trial
by Mr. Savage, and its latest manifestation is the
ambitious attempt to produce "Parsifal" in English.
While opera in English is still an experiment, yet it
has been the dream of many conductors.   Mr.
Thomas entered upon the work with enthusiasm.
He had an ensemble the like of which had never been
seen in opera in this country before — an orchestra
splendidly trained, a most capable chorus of young,
fresh voices, artists who, if not great, were yet efficient, the largest and best-trained ballet ever seen
on the American stage, and scenery, costumes, and

properties in lavish profusion, and at the head of all this was the most accomplished conductor in the country. Surely he had reason to begin his work enthusiastically, and good grounds for hope that it would be supported by the American people and prove a success. And yet, before two years had elapsed, he wrote upon the back of the programme of his last performance, "the most dreadful experience I have ever had!"

The principal singers engaged for the first season, which began in New York January 4, 1886, and closed at Albany June 27 of the same year, were as follows:

*Sopranos* — Pauline L'Allemand, Helene Hastreiter, Charlotte Walker, Annis Montague, Kate Bensberg, May Fielding, Christine Dossert, Minnie Dilthey, and Emma Juch.

*Mezzos and Contraltos* — Mathilde Phillipps, Mathilde Muellenbach, Sara Barton, Helen Dudley Campbell, and Jessie Bartlett Davis.

*Tenors* — Charles Turner, William H. Fessenden, Whitney Mockridge, Albert Paulet, George Appleby, and William Candidus.

*Barytones* — Alonzo E. Stoddard, William H. Lee, George Fox, Homer A. Moore, Eugene E. Oudin, and William Ludwig.

*Bassos* — William H. Hamilton, John Howson, Edward J. O'Mahony, and Myron W. Whitney.

The repertory for that season included Goetz's "Taming of the Shrew" (given for the first time in this country, New York, January 4, 1886), performed five times; Gluck's "Orpheus," thirty times; Wagner's "Lohengrin," fifteen times; Mozart's "Magic Flute," five times; Nicolai's "Merry Wives of

Windsor," fourteen times; Delibes's "Lakmé," twenty-five times; Wagner's "Flying Dutchman," eighteen times; Massé's "The Marriage of Jeannette," and Delibes's spectacular ballet, "Sylvia," given together, fourteen times — in all, one hundred and twenty-six performances.

The principal artists engaged for the second season, which began at Philadelphia, November 15, 1886, and ended in collapse in Toronto, June 18, 1887, were as follows:

*Sopranos* — Mme. Fursch-Madi, Emma Juch, Pauline L'Allemand, and Bertha Pierson.

*Mezzos and Contraltos* — Cornelia Van Zanten, Mathilde Phillipps, and Jessie Bartlett Davis.

*Tenors* — Charles Bassett, Henry Bates, Charles Wood, William Candidus, and C. W. Lenmane.

*Barytones* — William Ludwig, Alonzo E. Stoddard, and John E. Brand.

*Bassos* — Myron W. Whitney, D. M. Babcock, and William H. Hamilton.

The repertory for the second season[1] included "Faust," "Orpheus," "Lakmé," "Lohengrin," "Flying Dutchman," "Aïda," "Galatée," "Bal Costumé"

[1] I am unable to assign the number of representations of each opera, as in the first season, because the last two or three months' programmes are missing from the Thomas collection. In common with sundry other property of the American Opera Company, a trunk containing them was either carried off by the manager to keep it out of the sheriff's hands, or the sheriff levied upon it and carried it off for the benefit of creditors who were growing uneasy. Little incidents of the kind were so common in the Spring of 1887 that the librarian of the orchestra, who was responsible for programmes, is uncertain as to the fate of these missing ones.

music of Rubinstein for ballet, "Marriage of Jeannette," "Sylvia," "Huguenots," "Merry Wives of Windsor," "Martha," the ballet "Coppelia," and Rubinstein's "Nero," the latter given for the first time in this country at the Metropolitan Opera House, New York, March 14, 1887. To this performance, which was given upon a most brilliant scale, the composer was invited. His reply to the invitation was as follows:

St. Petersburg, February 4.

Dear Sir:—I was extremely happy to hear from your letter that you intend to perform my "Nero" this season in the American Opera. All I wish for my work is that the American public should be as kind to it as it always was to my piano playing.

It pains me very much indeed not to be able to cross the ocean and be present on this occasion in New York, but the names of Mr. Hock, *régisseur*, and Mr. Theodore Thomas, conductor, insure the perfection of the performance and quiet me entirely as for the artistic wants.

I shall be all the time in a feverish impatience to hear about it, and hope you will let me know instantly of the result of the performance for *fas* and *nefas*.

I humbly pray Mr. Hock and Mr. Thomas that the *coupures* they surely intend to undertake in the work (and some are indispensable, as the work is long and fatiguing) should not become amputations. Believe me, dear sir,

Yours very sincerely,

Ant. Rubinstein.

During the second season, notwithstanding Mr. Thomas's herculean efforts to make American opera successful, and notwithstanding the brilliant manner in which every opera was staged, troubles arose and

rapidly increased.  The management was speedily
in arrears to every one, from stage hands to soloists,
but Mr. Thomas, who was unswervingly loyal to his
orchestra musicians, succeeded in keeping them paid,
though, as I have said, he sacrificed his own salary
for months to accomplish it.  Strikes among the
stage hands, the chorus, and the ballet followed in
quick succession.  How to provide for transportation was a difficult problem.  Sheriffs had to be
dodged.  Hotel and lodging-house keepers had to be
satisfied.  Constables with writs had to be evaded.
The original backers of the enterprise had long ago
backed the other way, all save one, who was so financially involved that she was unable, or at least unwilling, to get out without saving something from the
impending wreck.

Mr. Thomas held on to his unsalaried position,
and worked faithfully to save the organization, but at
last, when the affairs of the American Opera Company, Limited, were in a condition for which there is
no other name but anarchy, he left it at Buffalo, June
15, 1887.  The poor old organization, which had
just vitality enough left to get to Toronto, gave one
last convulsive, expiring performance, and then col-
lapsed and went to pieces, fortunately for the name
of the thing, in a foreign land.   Even then, some un-
wise persons sought to galvanize it into life again —
but it was dead beyond all hope of resurrection,
leaving behind it a long array of bills, levies, lawsuits, and sheriffs' sales.

On the ninth of July, 1887, nearly a month after

he had resigned his position, Mr. Thomas wrote a letter to the management of the company, in which he said: "We have had in ourselves all the elements for good work and prosperity if only the first and vital condition of success in any undertaking had been observed by the directory and managers of the National Opera Company, namely, prompt payment of all employes. The National Opera Company owes me between five and six months' salary, and I have put the matter into the hands of my lawyer. The directors have had ample time to make arrangements to meet their indebtedness to the members of the company."

For the first time Mr. Thomas speaks of "my lawyer." He had to employ a lawyer, who vainly tried to collect his back salary, but was more successful in warding off the many suits brought against him by creditors who supposed that he was responsible for the debts of the company. On the thirtieth of July of that year, Mrs. Thurber filed a bill in the Court of Chancery at Trenton, N. J., to have the company declared insolvent and a receiver appointed. August 27, the ill-fated American Opera Company disappeared from the musical world. Its assets were sold under foreclosure of mortgage made by Mrs. Thurber to Mr. Frank R. Lawrence. The total original value of all these assets was $150,000. They were sold for $26,101.

The failure of this scheme, so nobly conceived and with such a legitimate and praiseworthy object in view, was a source of keen disappointment to Mr.

THEODORE THOMAS IN 1888

THEODORE THOMAS IN 1898

Thomas, the more so because it happened from no fault of his, and because he had to suffer for the faults of others.   He gave the American people an operatic ensemble such as they had never seen before and an orchestral accompaniment such as they had never heard before.   It was an experience he did not like to talk about.   Once, in our consultations, I said to him: "Mr. Thomas, to what shall I attribute the American Opera Company disaster?"   He replied: "To inexperienced and misdirected enthusiasm in business management, and to misapplication of money.   It is not necessary to say more than that."

Mr. Thomas's experience with expositions was unfortunate.   He records in his Autobiography that his musical scheme for the Centennial Exposition at Philadelphia in 1876 was "a dismal failure."   Seventeen years later he undertook the duties of Musical Director at the Columbian Exposition in Chicago, but adverse circumstances forced him to resign his position before the great work he had planned was accomplished.   When, in 1904, he was consulted by the Commissioners of the Louisiana Purchase Exposition at St. Louis, he advised them to give plenty of military band music out-of-doors, as people did not go to expositions to be educated but to be amused. The commissioners wisely followed his advice. Some went to hear the great organ in the Festival Hall, but the thousands were entertained at the plaza bandstands and in the Tyrolean Hall, where the orchestra served as an accompaniment for private and public banqueting, certainly not as an educational institution.

Every one who has the interests of music at heart, and who recognizes the far-reaching importance of the scheme which Mr. Thomas sought to carry out at the Columbian Exposition, must regret its unfortunate outcome. He gave a great deal of time and labor, after his appointment as Musical Director, to the preparation of a complete exhibit of musical art. In this exhibit he proposed to show all that had been done in music, excepting opera, from an early period in its development to the present. Two large music halls were built on the Exposition grounds, one for symphony and chamber concerts, the other for festivals and daily free popular concerts. An orchestra of one hundred and forty players was engaged, and all the elements of a great musical exposition, such as had never been attempted elsewhere in Europe or America, were provided.

With a liberal equipment of material, and with encouraging prospects before him, Mr. Thomas organized his bureau, and June 30 issued the following outline of the scope which music would have at the Exposition:

"Recognizing the responsibility of his position, the musical director groups all intended illustrations around two central ideas:

"1. To make a complete showing to the world of musical progress in this country in all grades and departments, from the lowest to the highest.

"2. To bring before the people of the United States a full illustration of music in its highest forms, as exemplified by the most enlightened nations of the world.

"In order to carry out this conception of the unexampled opportunity now presented, three coöperative conditions are indispensable:

"1. The hearty support of American musicians, amateurs and societies, for participation on great festival occasions of popular music, and for the interpretation of the most advanced compositions, American and foreign.

"2. The presence at the Exposition of many of the representative musicians of the world, each to conduct performances of his own principal compositions and those of his countrymen, all upon a scale of the utmost completeness.

"3. A provision on the part of the Exposition authorities of the means necessary for carrying out these plans, in the erection of the halls indispensable for successful performances, and in the engagement of solo artists, orchestras, and bands."

The general classification of concerts during the six months, May to October, was announced by the Bureau as follows:

1. Popular orchestral concerts.
2. Symphony concerts.
3. Festivals, with chorus, orchestra, and eminent soloists.
4. Concerts by famous visiting orchestras, bands, and choral societies from other cities.
5. Concerts by famous European or American artists and composers, exhibiting their own works.
6. Open-air band concerts.
7. Chamber concerts.
8. Amateur concerts.

To what extent this scheme was carried out the programmes of Volume II. of the present work will show.

The inaugural ceremonies took place October 21, in the stately Manufacturers' and Liberal Arts Building. The dedication music, which was performed under Mr. Thomas's direction, included "Columbus March and Hymn," written for the occasion by Prof. John K. Paine; dedicatory ode, music by G. W. Chadwick; Mendelssohn's cantata, "To the Sons of Art," accompanying the award of medals to the master artists of the Exposition: Haydn's chorus, "The Heavens are telling"; Handel's "Hallelujah" chorus; the "Star Spangled Banner" and "Hail Columbia," with full chorus and orchestral accompaniment; and Beethoven's chorus, "In Praise of God." The musical forces for the occasion were composed of the following musicians of Chicago: Apollo Club and auxiliary, 700; the World's Fair Children's Chorus, 1,500; surpliced choirs, 500; members of quartette choirs, 200; German societies, 800; Scandinavian societies, 200; Welsh societies, 200; orchestra and bandsmen, 300, besides 100 drummers for a few phrases in the Chadwick music, and six additional harps.

As a further evidence of the comprehensiveness of Mr. Thomas's scheme, an exhibition, of which Mrs. Thomas was the executive, was planned which was designed to show the musical standard of the American people in their homes and private life — the standard of the audience in contradistinction to that of the stage. To illustrate this idea, Mrs. Thomas organized a convention of the amateur musical clubs of all parts of the country, the sessions of which extended through four days in May. Its object is defined in the following paragraph, quoted from her address at the opening meeting:

"The Bureau of Music believes that these meetings of women's amateur musical clubs from widely separated parts of America will be productive of important results by showing the world the character and quality of the educational work being accomplished by women in this direction; by stimulating the formation of similar clubs in places where they do not yet exist, and by the interchange of ideas which will take place amongst clubs whose homes, objects, and methods of work are so widely diverse."

This convention was successfully carried out. Many clubs accepted the invitation, and each was assigned forty minutes in which its president read a short paper before the Convention, sketching its organization and work, followed by a programme rendered by its delegates, illustrating its standard of musical performance. The eight sessions of the Convention were of great interest, and those who attended them all were astonished to find that the musical standard of the clubs farthest removed from the great centres, such as those of Tacoma and Los Angeles, in the far West, or Portland, Maine, in the far East, were as high as those of New York or Chicago, and their performances equally good.

Several years later, a number of musical women, most of whom had been delegates to this convention, and desired to perpetuate the good work inaugurated there, organized the ''National Federation of Women's Musical Clubs,'' under the presidency of Mrs.

Edwin F. Uhl, of Grand Rapids, Michigan, which now numbers many thousands of members in all parts of America; and thus one of the objects of the Convention has been realized. Mrs. Thomas was not connected actively with this work, which was carried out chiefly by Mrs. Uhl, and Mrs. Sutro of New York, but in recognition of her services at the Columbian Exposition Convention, of which it was the offspring, she was elected its Honorary President.

Such were the general outlines of this great World's Fair music scheme, nobly and artistically conceived and successfully carried out from May until August. It is unnecessary to explain the reasons for the discontinuance of the scheme. Adverse influences gradually undermined and destroyed the Bureau of Music after three months of concerts which those who heard will never forget, and on August 4 Mr. Thomas resigned his position and sent the following manly communication to the Chairman of the Music Committee:

CHICAGO, August 4, 1893.

JAMES W. ELLSWORTH, ESQ.,
    CHAIRMAN COMMITTEE ON MUSIC.

DEAR SIR: — The discouraging business situation, which must of necessity react upon the finances of the Fair, and which makes a reduction of expenses of vital importance to its interests, prompts me to make the following suggestions, by which the expenses of the Bureau may be lessened. The original plans of the Bureau, as you know, were made with the design of giving, for the first time in the history of the world, a perfect and complete exhibition of the musical art in all its branches. Arrangements were made for regular orchestral and band concerts; for performances of both American and European master-works of the present day, under the direction of their composers; for concerts by distinguished European and American organizations; for chamber concerts and artists' recitals; for women's concerts, etc., besides a general review of the orchestral literature of all kinds and countries, in symphony and popular concerts throughout the season.

The reduction of expenses at the Fair has obliged the Bureau to cancel all engagements made with foreign and American artists and musical organizations, and to abandon all future festival performances, thus leaving very little of the original scheme except the bands and the great Exposition orchestra, with which are given every day popular and symphony concerts. My suggestion is, therefore, since so large a portion of the musical scheme has been cut away, that for the remainder of the Fair music shall not figure as an art at all, but be treated merely on the basis of an amusement. More of this sort of music is undoubtedly needed at the Fair, and the cheapest way to get it is to divide our two fine bands into four small ones, for open-air concerts, and our Exposition orchestra into two small orchestras, which can play such light selections as will please the shifting crowds in the buildings and amuse them.

If this plan is followed, there will be no further need of the services of the musical director, and in order that your committee may be perfectly free to act in accordance with the foregoing suggestions, and reduce the expenses of the musical department to their lowest terms, I herewith respectfully tender my resignation as musical director of the World's Columbian Exposition.

Should, however, any plans suggest themselves to you, in furthering which I can be of assistance, I will gladly give you my services without payment.

Very respectfully,<br>THEODORE THOMAS,<br>Musical Director.

Mr. Thomas's resignation was accepted, the orchestra was disbanded, and he went to his country home for much-needed rest until the regular winter season of symphony concerts with the Chicago Orchestra opened.

It will never cease to be a matter of regret to those interested in the progress of music that this great scheme could not have been carried out as Mr. Thomas planned it. It would have marked an epoch in the musical history of the world. How resolutely he upheld his standards of performance, and what persistent stress he laid upon the elevation of music, is shown in this extract from one of his many bureau instructions:

"The musical director holds that while coöperation is asked of all grades of attainment, every musical illustration there produced must be justifiable upon artistic principles; that is to say, it must be what it honestly purports to be. The ounce or the pound of progress will be regarded as art, and every step, from the lowest to the highest, will be acceptable provided it faces in the right direction, thus fulfilling its true use and popular ministry."

Through his entire career, whether in a garden concert, a symphony concert, a festival, or a World's Exposition, he never lost sight of the importance of elevating the standard of music and educating the popular taste. That was his ambitious determination when, in 1855, a young man of twenty, he set the standard, and though it cost him well-nigh half a century of labor, and he had to face disappointments and overcome obstacles that would have daunted almost any other musician, he lived to see his work accomplished, and knew it would endure. He "hitched his wagon to a star"—and it remained there.

## XII

### THE MUSICIAN

THEODORE THOMAS began his musical career as a violinist, and during the years of his boyhood and youth not only supported himself but helped support the family by playing anywhere and everywhere that he could find the opportunity. He has said himself that he has no remembrance of a time when he was not playing. The earliest recorded appearance on his programmes as a violinist is in 1852, he being at that time in his seventeenth year, but he had played in concerts before that, and was even then so well known that his services were in frequent demand in theatre and opera orchestras, as well as in concert-rooms. He had played before he was out of his teens in the accompaniments of nearly all the great singers of his time, some of them the greatest singers of all times. His ability was so reliable, his musical endowment so unmistakable, and his qualities of leadership so convincing, that he was soon promoted from the ranks to the position of concert-meister, or "leader," as it was called at that time. More than once, in the absence of the conductor, he had to take his place, and at such times never failed to give signs of those extraordinary abilities which

were destined to be manifested in after years, when
the bow was finally exchanged for the baton.
Doubtless had he continued playing the violin he
would have become a famous virtuoso, but "Frau
Musica" had other work and other triumphs for
her favorite. His musical knowledge, his accurate musicianship, his perfect ear, and his ability
in producing absolute purity of tone, as well as his
great love for tone-color, fitted him to become a great
violinist; but back of all these qualities and dominating them was the noble ambition to make people acquainted with the higher music, as well as that
perfect mastery of self and sure knowledge of his
own power which impelled him to become the leader
of men, the interpreter of the great composers, a
player upon the orchestral choirs rather than a player
upon a single instrument. He had all the ability
and all the knowledge to make himself one of the
best of violinists, but his temperament urged him to
become not a player but a leader of players — not an
Ysaye or Wilhelmj, but the master of the Ysayes and
Wilhelmjs.

I never heard Mr. Thomas play in his days of
mastery. There are few living who have. I have
been with him on social occasions, and at suppers
with his orchestra, when, upon urgent request of
friends, or to entertain his own players,— for he was
always in the best of humor on these informal
occasions,— he would take the violin and gratify
them, but of course these were not examples of his
real skill, when fingers had grown stiff from want

of practice for years, and arms had been used so long for time-beating. But even on such occasions there were evidences of his old-time skill and purity of tone. It is upon the old accounts, therefore, that we must rely to ascertain his position as a violinist. He was first violin in the famous Mason-Thomas Quintette for many years, and two members of that quintette, Bergner, the 'cellist, and Mason, the pianist, are still living. Bergner enthusiastically said upon one occasion, "One of the best violinists in the world was spoiled to make the best conductor in the world." In his "Memories of a Musical Life," William Mason more critically says:

"Thomas's fame as a conductor has entirely overshadowed his earlier reputation as a violinist. He had a large tone, the tone of a player of the highest rank. He lacked the perfect finish of a great violinist, but he played in a large, quiet, and reposeful manner. This seemed to pass from his violin playing into his conducting, in which there is the same sense of largeness and dignity, coupled, however, with the artistic finish which he lacked as violinist."

Some contemporary notices of his playing may help the reader to form an idea of his ability and style as a violinist. Of his playing in the Beethoven Quartet in F, op. 59, at one of the Chamber Concerts in 1855, "The New York Times" says:

"Mr. Thomas is a young and praiseworthy artist who reads with great accuracy, but who is not quite so steady in the upper part of the instrument as a sensitive ear requires. There was nothing, however, to call for condemnation, and very little even of false intonation to mar the effect of a great and thoroughly appreciable work."

"The Musical Review and Gazette," in a notice of a sacred concert given April 14, 1856, at the City Assembly Rooms, in which Carl Bergmann was conductor and Mr. Thomas "leader," says:

"Mendelssohn's interesting concerto for the violin was played by the talented leader, Mr. Thomas, in a superb manner, much better than we ever heard it before in this country. The only objection we would make is to the somewhat thin tone of the player, but this, we presume, was more the fault of the instrument than of the performer." [1]

At the closing concert of the Mason-Thomas season, in 1856, Mr. Thomas played the Bach "Chaconne." The correspondent of "Dwight's Journal of Music" says:

"Decidedly the most wonderful performance of the concert was Mr. Thomas's playing of the celebrated Chaconne by Bach. This young artist (and very young he is, although the stamp of genius matures his almost boyish face) bids fair to rise high in the musical world. . . Young Thomas played the whole unfalteringly, without notes, and consequently with all the more freedom and abandon. His mechanism, too, gives proof of untiring industry in practice, but more than all, his evident enjoyment of what he was playing, and his thorough entering into the spirit of the music, showed the true artist in him. His choice of pieces also betokens real art love and reverence. He never plays any but good music. Such men are or ought to be the missionaries of art in this country." [2]

[1] Upon the programme of this concert in the Thomas collection is a notation in which Mr. Thomas complains of the inferiority of his instrument.—EDR.

[2] Dwight's correspondent prophesied better than he knew.—EDR.

Referring to a Mason and Thomas matinee at the Spengler Institute, April 19, 1858, "The New York Tribune" says:

"Mr. Theodore Thomas, a young and rising artist, whose modesty is only equal to his merit — indeed, he is hardly conscious of his own powers — and who is well known as a devoted and enthusiastic laborer in the higher walks of art, played a solo upon the violin, by Bach, admirably, and received an encore. The chief points in Mr. Thomas's style are a pure, full, rich tone, and unexceptionable bowing; he is also an irreproachable timeist and has great powers of execution."

Mr. Thomas appeared at a concert in Philadelphia, June 10, 1858, with Carl Formes, the basso, and Musard. "The Evening Journal" of that city says:

"Mr. Theodore Thomas created a very pleasant impression at this concert by his correct and spirited conductorship. Mr. Thomas is a young man of large and brilliant promise. He is wedded to his art, and devotes himself to it with assiduity and enthusiasm. As a violinist he is already eminent. Thus much in all sincerity for the young and modest leader, whose name does not appear on the bills in letters a foot high."

Mr. Thomas was in Chicago in 1859, and played at a concert March 28, in which Carl Formes, Satter, the pianist, and Mlle. Poinsot, vocalist, also appeared. "The Illinois Staats Zeitung" says:

"Theodore Thomas, a worthy associate of these artists, develops an extraordinary volume of tone, and also displays extraordinary skill in bowing. Mr. Thomas's art shows that he has devoted himself to the study and understanding of musical theory with unwearied industry. During the last two years he has become America's most accomplished violinist. His beautiful staccato and admirable performance of the Kreutzer Sonata are worthy of the highest praise."

November 24, 1860, Mr. Thomas played in one of the famous Wolfsohn [1] Chamber Concerts in Philadelphia, of which the correspondent of "Dwight's Journal of Music " says:

"Mr. Thomas came next, playing Schubert's 'Tarentelle' with a vigor and execution unsurpassed. As a leader we had heard him before in the opera orchestra, and had remarked his perfect coolness and self-possession when the conductor was most nervous and perplexed, and by his bowing they were several times prevented from coming to a dead halt. With his solo every one was delighted, and for an encore he played a beautiful reverie by Vieuxtemps."

March 2, 1861, he again played in the Wolfsohn concerts, and the Philadelphia correspondent of the "Deutsche Musikzeitung" says:

"Mr. Theodore Thomas was in his best form, and the public, whose favorite he has become, lavished upon him the heartiest applause and frequent recalls. The Berlioz 'Reverie' which he played is as restless as a butterfly, and abounds in rich tone-color, as well as in difficulties which, however, were not difficulties for him."

At the first concert of the twenty-third season (1862) of the New York Philharmonic Society, Mr.

[1] Mr. Carl Wolfsohn is a resident of Chicago and is still teaching. Chicago owes much to him for his important musical service. He was one of the first to guarantee the Chicago Orchestra concerts, and has ever been a stanch friend of Mr. Thomas, in whose earlier concerts he often played and with whom he gave very successful chamber concerts in Philadelphia in the early days.

Music Hall, World's Fair, Chicago, 1893

FESTIVAL HALL, WORLD'S FAIR, CHICAGO, 1893

Thomas played the Mendelssohn Concerto, op. 64. "The New York Times" says:

"The second solo was performed by Mr. Theodore Thomas, a worthy and prominent member of the Society who, we are glad to find, is at length acknowledged to be able to play the fiddle. Mr. Thomas produced a firm tone and stops absolutely in time, and plays without any affectation of sentiment. He was completely successful."

A correspondent of "Dwight's Journal of Music" writing January 6, 1868, of his playing at one of the Mason-Thomas Chamber Concerts, says:

"Mr. Thomas played superbly. We have gradually become so accustomed to that gentle preëminence in anything which he undertakes that we sometimes overlook the fact that he is one of our first violinists. His performance did not compare unfavorably with that of Joachim in this same sonata (Beethoven's op. 47, for violin and piano). He deserves the greatest credit for acquitting himself so well, because just in the middle of the first movement one of his violin strings snapped, and a delay of some minutes was thereby occasioned. Mr. Thomas's ease and insouciance of manner were enviable."

The most important pieces in Mr. Thomas's violin repertoire which I have been able to find in his programmes are:—Lipinski's "Concerto Militaire"; Ernst's "Élégie" and "Otello" theme and variations; Tartini's "Trille du Diable"; Mozart's Symphony Concertante, for violin and viola; Berlioz's "Romance" and "Reverie"; Raff's Sonata, op. 73; Vieuxtemps's "Reverie," "Fantaisie Caprice," and Concerto in E major; Schubert's "Tarentelle" and "Rondo Brillante," op. 70; Mendelssohn's Concerto, op. 64; Bach's "Chaconne" and Double Concerto;

Beethoven's F major Romanza, Kreutzer Sonata, and Concerto in D; Schumann's "Fantaisie," op. 131; and several of the first-violin parts in chamber music of Haydn, Mozart, Beethoven, and Brahms.

The citations I have made from contemporary sources of information may serve to answer the question frequently asked during the latter part of his life—how did Mr. Thomas play? Before leaving this period of his career, the following letter, which he wrote about two years ago to a prominent music house in Chicago, with regard to the well-known Hawley collection of violins, will be of interest, particularly for its information concerning violin bows and the Cremona instruments.

CHICAGO, October 19, 1903.

GENTLEMEN:—The well-known collection of violins, formerly owned by Mr. Hawley, of Hartford, and which you have purchased with the intention of placing them on the market, I have known of from boyhood. I am glad that they will now fulfil their mission, and pass into the hands of artists and art-loving amateurs, instead of being silent, locked up in the cases of a collector. The undertaking can hardly be called a speculation, as there are risks in such a venture which make it difficult to manage successfully. But if it does pay, you should be welcome to the profits of the transaction, for the public is the gainer thereby.

It is safe to say that without the Cremona instruments of the seventeenth century the world would not have had the master-works, quartets, and symphonies of Haydn and Mozart. It was, in particular, Stradivari who created a tone which appealed to musicians, and François Tourte, born 1747, died 1835, who invented a bow which made the modern orchestra—with all its shading and nuances—and a Beethoven, possible.

Without these instruments and the Tourte bow, invented over a century later, the music of to-day would have been developed on altogether different lines. One cannot help thinking of a quotation from Pascal, that if Cleopatra's nose had been shorter, the world's history would have been different.

The best Cremona violin is as much an art work as a great statue, and an expert will derive as much pleasure from contemplating its form as from a fine piece of sculpture. The tone of these instruments in master hands has never been equalled, and as an interpretative vehicle of great compositions they are a necessity. It is also well to bear in mind that they are becoming daily rarer. Many have been ruined by ignorance and Europeans are not willing to part with these art treasures any more than with their national paintings and sculptures.

Of the thousands of men and women studying music, but very few show any sign of having a soul. Even the first step toward artistic expression, light and shade, and beauty in tone-color, is only achieved by a small percentage, and consequently they make no impression. I am convinced that the prime reason for this defect amongst violinists was the lack of a good instrument in early life, which might have awakened a sense of tone-quality, instead of noise. The production of a full, soft, warm tone cannot be taught. We can only cultivate and develop the sense for tone-color. Johann Joachim Quantz, a musical authority — born 1697, died 1773 — and teacher of Frederick the Great, says, "Auffassung ist die Kunst mit der Seele zu spielen." [1]

In placing such fine instruments within the reach of American musicians, your undertaking should meet the appreciation and encouragement which it deserves.

Yours truly,

THEODORE THOMAS.

In the early days of his career, Mr. Thomas had a strong ambition to be a composer, but after he

[1] Freely translated, "Conception is the art of playing the soul of music."—EDR.

knew his own powers better and came to understand the needs of the time, he felt convinced that he could do better work for his country as an executant than as a creator.  He did not feel that his creative ability was of the highest order, and so he deliberately made his choice, though he wrote several pieces for "occasions."  As an arranger of piano and other solo instrument compositions for full, or string orchestra, however, and an adapter of the old music for the modern orchestra, his work was of the highest importance, because of his absolute knowledge of orchestral resources and his musical scholarship and interpretative ability.  He seemed to read the very soul of the composer in a score, and to have an intuitive sense of what the composer would have freely expressed had he not been hampered by the comparative lack of instrumental resources in his time.  In this respect he followed in the steps of Mendelssohn, Robert Franz, Esser, and others.  A publication of the works which he has thus adapted for orchestra, as well as of his markings and revisions to supply omissions or fill out mere suggestions in the works of the old masters, would be extremely valuable for conductors and musicians generally.

Among Bach's works, he adapted the cantata, "Ein feste Burg," for performance at the fourth Cincinnati Festival, in May, 1880.  In this cantata he substituted modern instruments for the obsolete ones which Bach used, such as the viola d'amore, viola da gamba, oboe d'amore, oboe da cassia, etc., filled in harmonies, transposed where it was necessary for a modern instrument, divided the instruments variously, and augmented where strength was effective — and all this without violating the traditions, or introducing any foreign matter or new motives, or in any way destroying the balance between chorus and orchestra. Such work is scholarly, but like much scholarly work, it passes unnoticed. He has also adapted three of Bach's violin sonatas — the andante and allegro of No. 2, which is set for the full violin section of the orchestra, with the correction of some errors; the No. 3, E major, for violin and cembalo (piano), in which the accompaniment has been filled out in the genuine Bach spirit; and the No. 5, in F minor, in which Mr. Thomas has assigned the solo-violin part to the violins and violas and the pianoforte part to the wood winds and basses. Besides these sonatas, Mr. Thomas, using the copy belonging to the Leipsic Bach Gesellschaft, restored the Suite No. 2, in B minor, to its original form by correcting phrasing and expunging the numerous errors which had crept into the score from time to time, and adapted it to the needs of the modern large orchestra without sacrificing any of the Bach spirit. He was always a great student of Bach. In his earlier years his aim was to adapt Bach to the modern orchestra, but during the last few years of his life he returned to the old forms by adapting the modern orchestra to Bach, and by making a most careful study and reproduction of the classic ornaments. This was evidenced in his arrangement of the Passion Music, and especially in

the great D minor Mass, in which he restored the
balance of the Bach orchestra and its quality of tone.
The composition of his orchestra for the production
of this mass in the Cincinnati Festivals was as follows: Four first flutes; four second flutes; two oboes
d'amore; six first oboes; six second oboes; two third
oboes; two D clarinets and four A clarinets, to take
the place of the old high trumpets in the original
score; eight bassoons; two horns; six cornets; four
tympani, and the usual string section.  His markings
and additions to the score are extremely interesting,
and, although numerous, he has not once violated the
Bach spirit.  On the other hand, he produced this
mass as nearly as possible as Bach produced it.  It
was his purpose, and had he lived longer he would
have carried it out, to give Bach's music with a Bach
orchestra, Mozart's with a Mozart orchestra, and the
same with that of Beethoven, Wagner, Strauss, and
other composers.

One of the most popular adaptations made by
Mr. Thomas is that of the andante and variations
from Beethoven's "Kreutzer Sonata," with which he
was particularly familiar, not only from frequent
performances of the violin part himself, but from
having conducted it on so many occasions when
played by prominent artists — most prominent of all,
Rubinstein and Wieniawski.  In this arrangement,
the theme is stated by the English horn, first violas,
and 'cellos, and the variations are assigned to a
variety of instruments, the trumpets, bells, and
violins pizzicato taking the theme in the first variation.

The analyst of the Chicago Orchestra programmes, Mr. Hubbard William Harris, said of this adaptation when it was first performed: "Throughout the entire movement, the modifications and enlargements of the original score necessary for the present style of performance are handled with fine musicianly skill, and with an accuracy of judgment which is acquired only through long experience with the manifold complexities of the modern orchestra" — a statement which is characteristic of all Mr. Thomas's adaptations.   The arrangement was made in one of his summer vacations at his much-loved "Felsengarten," in New Hampshire, and is dedicated to his friend, Mrs. J. J. Glessner.   The title-page bears the inscription, "Beethoven's Theme and Variations from the 'Kreutzer Sonata,' adapted for Grand Orchestra, and dedicated to the Mistress of the 'Rocks,' by Theodore Thomas, July, 1900," and the last page, the annotation, "Fine, July 11, 1900, Felsengarten."

Mr. Thomas's felicity in adaptation is also shown by his arrangements of the Chopin Polonaise in A flat, and the "Marche Funèbre" by the same composer.   When Rubinstein was in this country he besought him to orchestrate the Polonaise, but he could not then find the time.   Subsequently, at Mrs. Thomas's request, the work was done at Felsengarten, and is dedicated to her.   The "Marche Funèbre" arrangement, with which every one is familiar, is dedicated to Mrs. E. D. Gillespie, his friend and an enthusiastic promoter of music and the arts, who died in Philadelphia a few years ago. Mr. H. M. Finck, the accomplished critic of "The New York Evening Post," said of this adaptation, when the Chicago Orchestra played it in New York:

"The funeral march, wonderful and pathetic as it is on the piano, nevertheless seems to call for the sombre colors and the overwhelming power of the orchestra to give full vent to its bitter grief. In those thrilling fortissimos which follow the slow dull thuds of the march movement, and which Mr. Thomas has assigned to the brass choir, there is a world of heartrending agony that would convulse even those to whom music is usually an unknown language. For the funeral of a great man of genius, the grandest piece in existence is the Chopin Funeral March as orchestrated by Theodore Thomas." [1]

Among lighter works, Mr. Thomas adapted Schubert's three marches, op. 40 — No. 1 for full modern orchestra, No. 2 for a reduced orchestra, strings the most prominent, and No. 3, same arrangement as No. 1, but without drums; also a concert ending for the overture to Mozart's "Don Giovanni"; Schumann's "Träumerei"; Schubert's "Serenade," "Erl König," "Am Meer," "Der Doppelgänger"; Wagner's "Träume," and several settings of scenes as well as of single numbers from his operas, among them a beautiful arrangement of "Siegmund's Love Song," and other songs and piano compositions.

Mr. Thomas was not a creator in the sense that

[1] Mr. Thomas once said in conversation with a friend: "The Chopin Funeral March is growing hackneyed. The 'Eroica' march is for 'a great man.' The Siegfried march is for a demigod. What shall we plain people have for our dirge? Let it be the Beethoven A flat Sonata March." His adaptation of the last named is extremely impressive.

the great composers are, but he was the interpreter of the messages of the composers, with the ability to transmit them to the world, to make those understand who might misunderstand, to make those listen who are indifferent, to rouse thousands of people from their prejudices or their lethargy, and make them acquainted with the great thoughts of great souls, and to read what is to them a sealed book, so that they shall not only understand but come to love it.  In this sense he was the re-creator.

It was as the conductor, however, as the interpreter of the composer's message to the people, that Theodore Thomas greatly excelled and nobly crowned his mission, though in the supreme moment of his career the cypress was interwoven with the laurel. Few have come to that position more richly endowed. Practically he was a self-educated musician, as he was a self-made man.  From the first he was master of himself, and there is no higher quality of leadership than this.  In the concert orchestra he was the dominant player.  In the theatre orchestra he was the self-possessed one when others were nervous. When he took his place in that famous Mason-Bergmann organization, he dominated it at once. He dictated its programmes, inspired the performance, and his four associates, though older musicians, never disputed his supremacy.  He was born to command.  He had great power over men, and that extraordinary gift of making men obey, and at the same time holding their respect and admiration. Add to this his skilled musicianship, his knowledge of the resources of an orchestra, his wonderful musical perception, which enabled him to interpret so accurately, and his rare gift of absolute pitch, it is not remarkable that at the first opportunity he dropped the bow for the baton, and never relinquished it, never faltered in his great task, never missed a concert or a rehearsal, until death summoned him. He had taken the baton in hand forty-three years before for a lofty purpose, namely, to give the people the best music, played in the best manner, to make them acquainted with it, to make them interested in it, to make them like it, and finally, to make them impatient of the trivial and unworthy. He never wavered in the belief that he could do this, and the end crowned his work.

Mr. Thomas also brought to his work as conductor great strength and simplicity of character, a nature not given to the emotional or sentimental, but rather intellectual, forceful, and temperate. He had strong passions, well under control. Under great provocation, his wrath would fairly blaze, especially if he were provoked by an act of cruelty or injustice; but he was usually philosophical and patient. Finally, he had the same faith in the people that he had in himself. He was sure that he was right, and he was sure that the people would see he was right. It might take ten, twenty, fifty years, but he knew that in the end truth would prevail. I met him once at the time of the great railroad strike, in Chicago. It was during the summer night concerts, and that evening I went to the Exposition Building much earlier than

THE CHICAGO ORCHESTRA IN ORCHESTRA HALL, CHICAGO

(PHOTOGRAPH TAKEN AFTER MR. THOMAS'S DEATH)

Chicago, Ill.
April 13th /92.

My dear Mr. Upton,

At last I can make
the time to write a few lines to
you, acknowledging your letters and
also thanking you for the enclosed
newspaper clip. I do not care to
dwell long on the subject, but I
will say that I have neither sympathy
nor patience with those so called
musicians, whose education begins
with and ends with Wagner.

FACSIMILE OF A LETTER

It is also a great drawback in this Country that the "musical public" is either too busy or too Phlegmatic to treat Music as an Art, but look upon it only as an amusement and a passtime. Conditions change, but progress is slow.

Very sincerely Yours

Theodore Thomas.

WRITTEN BY MR. THOMAS IN 1892

FACSIMILE OF MR. THOMAS'S PENCIL ORIGINAL OF PROGRAMME
DEDICATING ORCHESTRA HALL, DEC. 14, 1904.

usual.   One end of the huge structure was occupied by troops.   At the concert end a solitary person was sitting at one of the tables with his head bowed upon his hands.   As I came nearer, in the dim light, I saw it was Mr. Thomas.   He looked up, and beckoned to me.   I sat down by him.   He said: "I guess I am a little blue to-night.   I have been thinking, as I sat here, that I have been swinging the baton now for fifteen years, and I do not see that the people are any farther ahead than when I began, and, as far as my pocket is concerned, I am not as well off.   But," and he brought that powerful fist of his down on the table, "I am going to keep on, if it takes another fifteen years."   That was the kind of man needed for the kind of work before him — pioneer work in a most unpromising soil, sowing seed apparently among the stones, hard work, discouraging labor, but making the way easier for all who follow him.   In any estimate of the work he did, this should not be lost sight of. He had no precedents, no traditions, no experiences of others to aid him in his great task.   He was doing the kind of work for music in this country that the first settler does who ploughs his furrows in the primeval wilderness.   It is not difficult now for others to follow in the way he opened.

It is probable that to most people Mr. Thomas appeared impassive and unemotional in the concert-room.   They could not see his face, and perhaps they did not observe the significance of his quiet and graceful motions.   They had not seen him in rehearsals, where the real work was done — and well done, or he would not have allowed it to be done in public. Some persons, observing the quietness of his beating, his easy pose, and the absence of physical gesticulations or frantic demonstrations, have fancied perhaps, that the orchestra could have played just as well without him. The secret of his ease and quietness, however, was that the players had learned their lessons before they came to school, and that with such players as constitute the Chicago Orchestra, drilled and trained in his methods, as well as being competent musicians, it is not essential that there should be any extraordinary demonstrations with the baton, jack-in-the-box jumpings, or sensational motions of the head, arms, and feet. These sometimes indicate that the conductor is posing for effect, or that he is not confident of his players' ability — perhaps not of his own. An "impression" of his conducting, which appeared in "The Outlook" for February, 1905, illustrates this point. The writer says:

"In his conduct of an orchestra in the concert-room Mr. Thomas had always seemed to me impassive and imperturbable. The perfection of his orchestra's work I recognized; but he seemed to be not only without passion, but without feeling. . . . I had, therefore, entertained a notion, the truth of which, however, I always suspected, that the excellence of the interpretation and the rendition was in the orchestra rather than in the leader. Mr. Thomas seemed to me simply a kind of human metronome, beating time. I learned the contrary on one occasion, when I was permitted to witness one of his private rehearsals. At a certain point in the symphony, which the orchestra was playing in perfect time and in perfect tune, but with a certain mechanical effect of crescendo and diminuendo, which, however, I had not noticed, he suddenly rapped on the music-stand before him.   The orchestra stopped; with hand and foot acting together, he imitated the movement of an organ-grinder; then, with only a word to indicate the bar at which the orchestra was to take up the music, he struck the music-rack before him again for attention, then, with the movement of his baton, gave the orchestra the signal, and they repeated the passage the execution of which by dumb signal he had criticized.   The orchestra repeated the passage with the spirit and fire, before lacking, infused into it.   It was a trifling incident, but a significant one."

Mr. Thomas was the least demonstrative of all the great leaders of his day, but he was the most graceful, dignified, and easy of them.   He knew his players intimately, their physical and moral defects. If their defects were incurable, he soon found it out, and supplied their places.   He never tolerated scandals of any kind in the orchestra.   With moral defects he had little patience, and once displayed in hours of duty there never was opportunity for a second display, no matter how excellent the player might be.   They, in turn, knew all his ways almost intuitively.   He really had no code of signals, for there was no need of it.   His right hand was the indicating member, his left hand the persuasive one — and how gracefully and eloquently persuasive it was, whether in the Fifth Symphony of Beethoven or the "Village Swallows" waltz of Strauss!   Some of his players have told me that they could feel his beat, so completely was he in touch with them, and so intimate the sympathy between them.   It was a kind of magnetic leadership.   The impression which he made

upon others, others sometimes made upon him.    In
an interview he once said:

"Before the first note is played, there is a something in
the air that whispers what sort of a concert we are going to have.
Sometimes I breathe it in, and know that the night is going to
be a triumph, and that every man waiting to respond to the
baton is determined to find the true meaning in every note he
plays.   Then again there are times when the music, though
technically correct, is mechanical, the audience restless and un-
sympathetic — an indefinite, intangible something hovering over
everybody that says as plainly as if it had a human voice, 'You
cannot win hearts to-night, Theodore Thomas.   Nature is out
of sorts.' "

Sidney Lanier, the poet, also musician, has put on
record one of the best descriptions ever written of
Theodore Thomas's leading.   He says:

"To see Thomas lead is music itself.   His baton is alive,
full of grace, of symmetry; he maketh no gestures, he readeth
his score almost without looking at it, he seeth everybody,
heareth everything, warneth every man, encourageth every instrument, quietly, firmly, marvellously.   Not the slightest shade
of nonsense, not the faintest spark of affectation, not the
minutest grain of effect is in him.   He taketh the orchestra in
his hand as if it were a pen, and writeth with it."

It has been said that he was a martinet in his discipline, and kept his players at such a distance that
they stood in fear of him, and felt that they were mere
machines.   It is true that he was autocratic so far as
music was concerned.   His word was law, and he
would brook no opposition.   If any player discovered that he knew more than the conductor, and did
not keep that knowledge a secret, known to himself

only, he speedily found that a player with such vast knowledge was not needed, even though he might be the concertmeister, as once or twice happened. When some one was commiserating him upon the loss of his first violin, he coolly replied: "I never lose any one." He was intolerant of any trifling, or boy's play, among his men at rehearsals. He disapproved of the eccentricities of dress and manner affected by some musicians. He was sometimes merciless in his musical demands, but he never asked his men to do anything he was not ready to do himself. His rebukes were always brief, but pointed. Once in a rehearsal of a Mozart symphony, the attack was not prompt enough to suit him. "Some people," he said, "are born behind time and never catch up with themselves." At one rehearsal the playing did not suit him. It was careless and mechanical. Suddenly he raised his hand — he rarely rapped upon his desk as a signal either to begin or stop — and the music ceased. With a significant look over the ranks he said: "Young men, I am sixty-eight years old, and am still advancing. There are some of you who will lose your places right away if you continue standing still." It is needless to say that progress was made. Upon another occasion Beethoven's Ninth Symphony was in rehearsal, and he had set his heart upon an excellent performance of it. Some extra players had been engaged who manifested inexcusable carelessness in not coming in promptly on the beat. He remonstrated with them several times, and, finally, losing his patience, threw off his coat and announced that he would "thrash" the next man who came in out of time. The certainty that he would do so had its effect, and from that time the precision of the outsiders was admirable.

He was also rigid in his ideas of musical decorum so far as audiences were concerned. He has explained, in his introduction to the second volume of this work, why he disapproved of encores. He began opposing them at his very first concert, and in all the years which followed, he never yielded where an encore would injure the effect of his admirably constructed programmes. Many have been the contests he has waged with audiences upon this point. It is a proof of the high esteem in which he was held that they always submitted good-naturedly. Late coming was another of his aversions. He laid down the law to fashionable patrons, and to those "born late," in his Central Park Garden programmes forty years ago. At the first Cincinnati Festival, in 1873, he said to the committee on the opening day: "When I commence the 'Te Deum,' you will close the doors and admit no one until the first part is finished." The committee remonstrated some, as they were afraid of its effect upon the public. Mr. Thomas replied firmly: "It must be done. When you play Offenbach or Yankee Doodle, you can keep your doors open. When I play Handel's 'Te Deum,' they must be shut. Those who appreciate music will be here on time. It makes little difference to those who come late how much they lose." He was rigid, also, in the enforcement of rules for rehearsals. In his long service as

conductor he not only never was absent but he never
was tardy at a rehearsal.  Promptly on the minute
he was in his place, and he demanded of his players
that they should be equally prompt.  No outsider
was allowed in his rehearsals.  He once explained to
me the reasons for this rule.  Often he had to
rehearse by sections, sometimes by small groups, and
occasionally he had to call a single player to account.
Such a player, he said, would not mind going over a
passage again and again before the orchestra, but it
would not be just to him to make him do it before
outsiders.

Never was leader more strict, but never was
leader more just and kind.  The men knew that he
had their interests at heart, that he was thoroughly
loyal to them, that he would sacrifice himself for
them, as he did more than once, and that in moments
of success he always unselfishly sunk himself out of
sight and awarded them the praise.  When off duty
and enjoying himself with his players at their informal functions, he was a boy with them, and led
their mirth as enthusiastically as he led their music.
Even in rehearsals, when all was going well, he
kept his players in the best of humor with his hearty
jokes or quiet sarcasms, but when things were not
going well, Jove frowned.  But the strongest reason
why his men not only respected, but had a feeling of
affection for him, was because they never questioned
his superior attainments, and appreciated the kind,
humane, loving nature behind his austere seeming.

The following incident shows the extraordinary

quickness with which his players responded to him.
In a festival given in a southern city a choral number
with instrumental prelude was on the programme.
The chorus came in four bars ahead of time, causing
a frightful discord; but in an instant singers and
orchestra were moving smoothly along as if nothing
had happened.   After the performance the manager
inquired of Mr. Thomas how it was done.   "Oh,"
was the reply, "I just jumped the orchestra ahead
four bars."

He also had a quick ear for false notes, and never
failed to locate the offender, even when the full orchestra was in action.   Once in rehearsing the "Good
Friday Spell," from "Parsifal," he suddenly dropped
his hands, and the music stopped.   Glancing at a
player in the front row he simply said to him, in his
peculiarly high pitched tone of voice, "Well?"   The
offender well knew what he meant.   "It was only  a
wrong note, sir," he replied, "that was all."   "Oh!
Only a wrong note!   That was *all*, was it?"   with
a world of sarcastic meaning in his voice.

In July, 1904, he went to Milwaukee from his
summer home in New Hampshire to conduct the
festival of the North Western Sängerbund.   He had
considerable trouble with some of the local players,
who had been hired to reinforce his own orchestra,
and who were bent upon earning their salaries as
lightly as possible.   While rehearsing, he noticed one
of these shirks drawing his bow in a peculiar way.
He listened, but could hear no tone from him.  Stop-
ping the orchestra, he called  him to the front rank,

where he had to play.  The orchestra had hardly begun, before it was stopped again, and Mr. Thomas wrathfully addressed the man: "First, you don't play at all.  Then, when you do play, you play all wrong." He did not put in an appearance again.

His recognition of any new peculiarity in the player, or any change, however slight, in an instrument, was most extraordinary.  Unger, one of his 'cellists, had had his instrument repaired, without Mr. Thomas's knowledge, and the repairer had changed the position of the sound-post.  After the rehearsal of the first number, he turned to him and said: "Is that a new instrument you have there, Mr. Unger ?"  In his autobiography he has himself related an incident, which occurred in the New York Festival of 1882, illustrating his quickness of sight as well as of hearing.  His gift of absolute pitch was infallible.  While he was walking with a friend one day in the street a whistle sounded.  The friend asked him if he could give the tone.  "Oh, yes; the tone is C sharp; the overtone is F sharp, or, rather, G flat."

In a letter, written by him December 1, 1889, Mr. Thomas, referring to the first New York Philharmonic concert of that season, tells some of his tribulations.  He writes:

"I had a curious rehearsal this morning, and I had to do a good deal of fighting.  I could not get the men to play as I wanted, and finally I slammed the score on the floor and took up another number with the same difficulties; but at last, by talk and insistence, and making stands play alone, I began to

get the effects I wanted, and behold, it went to the ears and
hearts of the men, and then, of course, it was easy.  They were
more delighted than I was when they heard the result and
understood what I wanted; but that is a terrible fight—over a
hundred men of ability trying for something, and one man
beating the stand, shouting at the top of his voice, scolding,
entreating, etc., and finally taking out his watch to show them
all that it has taken an hour.  The trouble is, they can play
elsewhere as they please, and when they come to me after a
short interval it always takes half of the first rehearsal time before they again realize the proportions and proper conditions.
Well, I feel better for the fight, and it is also a satisfaction to
have the whole profession stand and own it up."

William Mason is right when he says, in his
"Memories of a Musical Life," that Mr. Thomas's
"talent for programme making, by putting pieces in
the right order and sequence, thus avoiding incongruities, was unsurpassed."  He showed this ability at the
outset of his career, when he was making programmes
for the Mason-Bergmann concerts in his twentieth
year—programmes of a kind that led Bergmann to
say, "You have lifted the veil from our eyes."  In
one of his earliest symphony concerts in Boston
(1866), they played the following perfectly constructed programme: Overture to "Manfred," Schumann; concerto for two pianos, Mozart; introduction
to "Tristan and Isolde," Wagner; and Fifth Symphony, Beethoven.  After the concert "The Boston
Orpheus" said:

"And now let me say one word in regard to the taste with
which Mr. Thomas had made the programme, even if I run
the risk of being denounced as partial and in favor of that
gentleman's ruling the instrumental music in New York.  The

programme is short. It comprises music from a period of more than two hundred years. The classical and romantic schools are well and equally balanced. There is a unity of character in the whole programme — a character of loftiness and nobility, and properly the programme ends with the jubilant and soaring flight of the soul in the finale of the Fifth Symphony. It is my opinion that it is just as difficult to make a good programme as it is to conduct well. In this art Mr. Thomas has not been outdone by any one in this country."

This is high and merited praise for this one programme, but it is equally due to thousands more in his half-century of programme making. Instances of his consummate skill are thickly strewn through the programme groups in the second volume of this work. Though the old music constituted the principal part of their framework, and Beethoven and Wagner were his "pillars," yet he was always on the alert for new music. Some pieces he read through and never tried. He had his orchestra play through others for a surer test, and many of these pieces were carefully consigned to Mr. McNicol, his librarian, with the remark, "More stuff for the closet, Mac." And yet, of late years, he rarely made a programme which did not contain new music. I asked him once why he played so much of it. He replied: "People cannot read the new music, but they should keep abreast of it, and the only way to know it is to hear it. It does not follow that I approve or indorse it because I play it. It is due to the public to hear it once. This has been a lifelong idea with me."

In this connection attention may be called to the chronological list of works which Mr. Thomas produced for the first time in this country, and which will be found near the end of the second volume. Since that compilation was made, I have received from Mr. Bernhard Ziehn, the well-known musical theorist and scholar, a list made two years ago showing the dates at which Mr. Thomas produced noted compositions, and the time at which they were first heard in European cities, which are usually supposed to be progressive. The list is as follows:

Franck, "Les Éolides" . . Chicago, 1895; Vienna, 1903
Strauss, R., "Eulenspiegel" . Chicago, 1895; Vienna, 1903
Bruckner, Symphony No. 7   Chicago, 1893; Dortmund, 1903
Charpentier, "Impressions d'Italie" . Chicago, 1893;
    Frankfurt a'M., Sondershausen, 1903.
Liszt, "Mephisto Waltz" . . Chicago, 1893; Hanover, 1903
Tschaikowsky, "Francesca da Rimini" . Chicago, 1896;
    Vienna, 1903.
Franck, "Le Chasseur Maudit" Chicago, 1898; Hanover, 1903
Glazounow, "Le Printemps" Chicago, 1898; Munich, 1903
D'Indy, "Istar" . Chicago, 1898; Sondershausen, 1903
Dukas, "L'Apprenti Sorcier" . Chicago, 1900; Dresden-
    Munich, 1903.
Franck, Symphony, D minor . Chicago, 1900; Frank-
    furt a'M., 1903.
Bruckner, Symphony No. 3 . Chicago, 1901; Dessau-
    Leipsic, 1903.
Fibich, "Evening" . . . Chicago, 1901; Vienna, 1903
Schillings, "Prologue to King Œdipus" . Chicago, 1901;
    Stuttgart, 1903.
Weingartner, Symphony No. 2 . Chicago, 1901; Berlin, 1903
Humperdinck, "Dornröschen". Chicago, 1902; Berlin, 1903
Hausegger, "Barbarossa" . Chicago, 1902; Bremen, 1903
Sibelius, "Christian II." . . Chicago, 1902; Munich, 1903

Mr. Ziehn also says:

"Furthermore, for some years the Chicago Orchestra, under the direction of Theodore Thomas, has been the only orchestra in this, as well as foreign countries, which executes the ornaments of classic compositions correctly as explained by Quantz, Leopold Mozart, C. Ph. Em. Bach, and others, and before that time there was none since the classic era. These two out of a great many items of importance are sufficient to answer the question, 'Shall this orchestra go?'" [1]

In describing his system of programme making, Mr. Thomas speaks of Beethoven and Wagner as the two "pillars" of his programmes in earlier years. In later years, they were not so necessary. His programmes, so to speak, could stand alone, so great had been the progress of popular taste and appreciation. He could introduce more new matter and freely acquaint his hearers with what was going on in the musical world without any danger of their "running after false gods." He knew that they would accept his standards of taste. So of late years he gave much attention to the works of American composers, drew liberally from the Russian, Bohemian, and Scandinavian schools, and prominently brought out the music of the advanced style, represented by Richard Strauss and others, as well as the much disputed works of Bruckner and his disciples. What French art also owes to him is shown by a letter of condolence to his widow from the celebrated composer Vincent d'Indy, in which

[1] This was written at a time when the existence of the orchestra was at stake.—EDR.

he says, "Accept, Mme. Thomas, this expression
of profound sympathy for the cruel loss which
musical art has sustained by the death of the illustrious master to whom French composers and
M. d'Indy in particular, are solely indebted for
their recognition in America."

Nothing that was new and worth hearing escaped
his vigilant eye. His programmes, especially since
the organization of the Chicago Orchestra, are a
record of musical accomplishment during fourteen
years in every field of music. Thus his audiences
have been kept abreast of musical thought and creation. It is doubtful indeed whether any other audiences in the world have been as well "posted" in
contemporary musical literature. And yet he never
neglected the old for the sake of the new. To the
end Beethoven remained the foundation of his programmes and Wagner was their strong dramatic
support, but at the same time what other conductor
has done a greater and more enduring work for
Mozart, Haydn, Schumann, Schubert, and Brahms,
as well as Liszt, Berlioz, Tschaikowsky, and Rubinstein? What other conductor has done the musical world more important service in making it acquainted with Bach through the medium of scholarly adaptations and arrangements, to which I have
made reference elsewhere in this volume? He had
that broad catholicity of taste which recognized the
value of the best modern works as well as of the
accepted classics.

While studying his immense half-century col-

lection of programmes I was continually impressed
with his preference for Beethoven, not alone for his
symphonies but for his overtures and incidental
music, his readings of which came at last to be
authoritative.   Who ever studied him more closely,
more intelligently?   It was a labor of love, almost
a labor of life with him.   He had conducted the
Fifth Symphony hundreds of times, and yet every
time that he took it up the performance showed
the influence of fresh care in phrasing or tone-quality,
to make it more effective, and more elasticity in
conducting.   He has been criticized by the conservative for his tempos, but the fact remains that
he had no equal as a conductor of the Beethoven
symphonies, especially of his favorite three, the
"Eroica," the Fifth, and the Ninth, and no equal
as a conductor of the "Fidelio" overtures, the
"Coriolanus" overture, the "Egmont" music, the
"Prometheus" ballet, or, among the choral works,
the Mass in D.   In his hours of leisure during the
last few years he prepared analyses of the first five
symphonies and had intended to prepare the other
four in a similar manner, but death prevented the
fulfilment of his purpose.   The five which he has
finished, however, are masterpieces of musical study
and skill, and it is to be hoped that some day they
may be given to the musical world.

In this connection, the following extract from a
letter written to me by Dr. Julius Fuchs, the musical
scholar and writer, who was a friend of Mr. Thomas
many years, is of special interest:

"It should be a duty to keep his library intact.[1] The works, of course, may be replaced for money, but what has been written down by this giant with his meritorious and technical additions to the classics, can never be rebought. These so exact works — exact in the smallest details of art, should be kept intact and unchanged as models. All the live experiences of Liszt, Bülow, Klindworth, Riemann, etc., are accessible to the public in the editions of the classics for piano music of Robert Franz for vocal music.

"Thomas was, as you know best yourself, a man of practical deed. He mastered work which would have taxed the powers of many. Hence the singleness of his work, the singleness of his unexcelled orchestra. The means and ways for this model singleness are not published. As yet, we have no 'Edition Thomas' of the orchestra work of the classics. Now, what can be done so that this life-work shall not be lost to art, as was, for instance, the work of the old Müller String Quartette in Germany? Every great leader has to offer the classic works together with his own individuality in order to influence the public. To this end, however, the technical means of execution will always change, as we may observe in the various conceptions and the technical material of the classics of piano music, from Liszt to the present time.

"Now, in case the contents of the Thomas library should be made use of for public performances, permission should be granted only with the special proviso that absolutely no changes should be made in any direction so that the additions made by Thomas may remain as an inheritance of his conceptions until a 'Thomas Edition' is published. I mean that only the works contained in a 'Thomas Edition,' or such as are already supplied by the composers themselves with all technical material, as, for instance, the Russian compositions of the present

[1] Steps have already been taken in this direction, and all musicians will be glad to know that his scores will soon be collected and classified by expert hands so that they will be available for reference.—Edr.

time, should be open for public performances or technical changes. It may not be possible to keep together the entire library and to supplement it in such a way that all the prominent works of the present time will be contained in it, but as it stands it is unique and can be made the nucleus of a library to which students will come from far and near as they do to the library of the Vatican — there for the old, to America for the new.

"When the 'Amen' of the 'Hallelujah' for Thomas has died away on the heights, there will probably be no end to questions. Beethoven will say, 'How have you conquered this violin passage, even if transposed to C minor?'

"And Thomas will answer: 'How could you write so impractically?'

"Beethoven will say then: 'Had I known that you were to have such an orchestra, I should have written still more difficult music. In my time there was no Chicago, no Thomas.'"

Mr. Thomas gave frequent expression to his admiration for Beethoven. It was his belief that "the man who does not understand Beethoven, or has not been under his spell, has not half lived his life." In an interview he once said:

"Take Beethoven's music, it is something more than mere pleasure; it is education, thought, emotion, love, and hope. I do not doubt that when my orchestra plays one of his symphonies, every soul in the audience is stirred in a different way and by a different suggestion. I care not from what station in life come the thousands who sit back of me. Beethoven will touch each according to his needs, and the very same cadence that may waft the thoughts of one to drowsy delight or oblivion may stir the heart of another to higher aspirations — may give another hope in his despair, may bring to yet another a message of love."

At one of the rehearsals for the Cincinnati May Festival of 1904, the Bach B minor mass and the Beethoven Mass in D were taken up. Just before beginning, Mr. Thomas, turning to the chorus, said:

"Ladies and gentlemen, we have a difficult programme to perform, but with due attention from your side to the conductor, I think this Festival will be memorable in history. By due attention I mean you must not take your eye from the conductor, that you may be in sympathy with him. With Beethoven, music becomes a language, which is the most emotional, and never sentimental. There is none of that so-called 'rubato' desirable in his style, but the constant light-and-shade expression marks are needed to give life to every phrase, which you cannot do without the aid of a conductor. As I have remarked to you before, you must often allow time for expression marks, but immediately take up the tempo again. For the music of the eighteenth and nineteenth centuries you must allow time for ornamentation; since Beethoven, for expression."

While the music of Bach, Mozart, and Beethoven held the highest place in Mr. Thomas's esteem he did a great work for Wagner, and for what in Wagner's day was called "the music of the future." The credit for giving the first performance of a Wagner composition (the overture to "Tannhäuser") in this country belongs to Carl Bergmann, but Mr. Thomas was the first to make the country well acquainted with that composer's music. With the persistence always characteristic of him, he played it over and over, season after season and as rapidly as he could procure the manuscripts. When they were accepted only under protest and he was told

that people did not like them, he coolly replied:
"Then they must hear them till they do." He
did not have to force them upon his audiences,
however, after the New York Festival of 1882,
when he gave selections from some of the Wagner
works with Frau Materna for his soloist, and the
Wagner festival tour of 1884, in which he had the
assistance of Winkelmann, Scaria, and others, and
performed selections from all the music-dramas,
including "Parsifal." In his concerts, also, he
greatly advanced the Wagner cult by his fine settings
and arrangements for the concert stage and at last
made his music so popular that the "Wagner nights"
were excelled in point of attendance only by the
"Beethoven nights." He was for a long time
accused of being "a Wagnerite," when that word
conveyed something like a reproach, but he was in
no sense a Wagnerite. He exploited Wagner's music
because it was a new revelation in the musical world
and some hailed it as the dawning of a new light
which was to eclipse all others. This he never
believed. He knew that Bach and Beethoven and
Mozart had laid the foundations of music and that
they never would be disturbed. But he thought
it due to the people that they should be well informed
and keep pace with what was going on, and so he did
for Wagner what he later did for Richard Strauss,
and in both cases did it more promptly and more
thoroughly than any other. In a letter to me,
reproduced elsewhere[1] in facsimile, he says: "I do

[1] Page 230, Vol. I.

not care to dwell long on the subject but I will say that I have neither sympathy nor patience with those so-called 'musicians' whose education begins and ends with Wagner." In another letter, written in 1877, when he was busiest with Wagner's music, he writes: "I am a Wagnerite, but not in the modern and New York sense. Your New York Wagnerite tramples under foot everything that is not Wagnerian. I do not think I can be accused of showing a lack of appreciation for Wagner's works but I still think there is something else besides Wagnerian music; so, in that sense, I am possibly not a Wagnerite."

Before closing this appreciation of Mr. Thomas, the musician, I should like to quote another impression from "The Outlook," because it makes an interesting comparison between his interpretation and that of Mr. Gericke, a conductor for whom he had high respect. The writer says:

"Sometime in the eighties I happened to notice in a New York paper the advertisements of the Thomas Orchestra and the Boston Symphony Orchestra, which were to play on the same day. Mr. Gericke was to give his concert in the afternoon at old Steinway Hall, and Mr. Thomas, his concert in the evening at the Metropolitan Opera House. As I looked over the programme announced in the paper I saw that each programme had on its list of compositions to be given, Goldmark's 'Sakuntala' overture. Such an opportunity to hear two of the great orchestras of the world play the same composition on the same day was not to be missed, and so, although I had to consider the expenditure both of time and money in my concert going, I got tickets for both performances. It was well worth making the effort to hear this splendid overture performed by two great conductors. I purposely say performed by two great conductors, because the concerts were convincing illustrations of the fact that a conductor of skill and genius plays upon his band of men as an organist plays upon his organ.  Both orchestras were composed of musicians of the first rank, and of expert, technical skill;  both scores were exactly the same;  the same instruments were used, and in the same number and with the same volume of tone.  But there was quite as much difference, both sensuously and intellectually, between the two renderings as there would be between a reading of Hamlet's Soliloquy by Sir Henry Irving and by Edwin Booth.  Mr. Gericke's interpretation as I recollect it, was the more definite and elegant;  Mr. Thomas's the more temperamental and impressionistic.  Both were beautiful and satisfactory in their respective ways.  I learned, I think, one lesson from this experience — that music is a plastic art and that it is folly to lay down rigid lines with which any given composition shall be performed and insist that all conductors shall follow those lines.  It is perfectly logical and reasonable for an auditor to say that he prefers Irving's Shylock to Edwin Booth's, but it is unreasonable for him to assert that preference as a proof that his friend who may prefer Edwin Booth's interpretation is ignorant or stupid.  Interpretative art has a very wide range.  If this were not so, the best way to hear a Beethoven Symphony would be when it was performed upon an orchestrion instead of by an orchestra.  Theodore Thomas's genius was not that of a mere disciplinarian of a band, although some critics have laid emphasis upon his skill as a disciplinary officer; it lay in the power of his imagination to penetrate a composition and discover its hidden and poetic meaning and then to inspire his men with an understanding and appreciation of that meaning."

Mr. Thomas's most active, personal work for music was measured by the span of fifty years. Forty-two of these years he conducted an orchestra, in addition to performing many other duties

connected with the progress of music in this country.
He reached the highest standard of success ever
attained by a musician in America, and left an
impression upon his art which can never entirely
disappear. To him and to his two orchestras—the
Thomas Orchestra in the East and the Chicago
Orchestra in the West,—this country owes its education and its progress in instrumental music and
to a large extent in vocal music also. He accomplished this great work because he believed in himself and in it. Upon the very threshold of his career
he announced his high purpose and no obstacles
were too great, no disappointments too bitter, no
antagonism too severe to cause him to swerve from
it. Often despondent, sometimes almost despairing,
he struggled on year after year. He reached the
goal when the years had come which have "no
pleasure in them" and the physical powers were
waning, but his eyes did not close in final slumber
until they had seen the triumph of that cause to
which he devoted himself in the strength of his young
manhood, and he had heard the approving "well
done, good and faithful servant." He has told us
himself how he accomplished it — "by perseverance,
hard work, and stern discipline." He has told us
what was his greatest pleasure — "to render perfect
music perfectly." He has told us, though not with
that intention, of what must have been his great
consolation in his dark hours — "the power of good
music! Who among us can tell or measure it?
Who shall say how many hearts it has soothed,

how many tired brains it has rested, how many sorrows it has taken away? It is like the power of conscience — mighty, immeasurable."

In closing this sketch of Theodore Thomas, the Musician, let some of his great contemporaries, whose words are authoritative, declare the full value, the real meaning, and the actual accomplishment of the two orchestras he founded:

"I have found in America something that I least expected to find. . . I had no idea that such a new country had an orchestra like Theodore Thomas's. Never in my life, although I have given concerts in St. Petersburg, Vienna, Berlin, Paris, London, and other great centres, have I found an orchestra that was as perfect as the organization Theodore Thomas has created and built up. When he accompanies me with his orchestra, it is as though he could divine my thoughts and then as though his orchestra could divine his. It is as perfect as the work of some gifted pianist accompanying a singer with whom he has often rehearsed. I know of but one orchestra that can compare with that of Theodore Thomas, and that is the orchestra of the Imperial Academy of Paris, which was established by the first Napoleon in the year 1808, into which only artists, when young, are admitted; and they may have any number of rehearsals until they arrive at absolute perfection. It is that orchestra alone which is as perfect as Theodore Thomas's — but, alas, they have no Theodore Thomas to conduct them."— *Anton Rubinstein.*

"I can give you no better idea of my opinion of the Orchestra than by saying that when I was listening to it I said to myself, 'I wish Wagner himself were here to hear his music so perfectly rendered.' It was magnificent, grand, nothing could have been finer. When I sang in Berlin and Vienna, Wagner rehearsed with the orchestra most carefully until it was near perfection. But that Theodore Thomas should, here in America, and without having heard Wagner, so faithfully reproduce the very effects which I heard Wagner teach his musicians, amazes me. It was simply perfect."— *Frau Friedrich-Materna.*

"I have always supposed the Vienna Orchestra to be the best in the world, but it cannot be compared with the Chicago Orchestra. Thomas plays upon his orchestra as other artists play upon a solo instrument."— *César Thomson.*

"I have never in my life been so wonderfully accompanied as by Theodore Thomas and the Chicago Orchestra."— *Eugene Ysaye.*

"It is a duty as well as a pleasure to compliment this Orchestra, which for sight-reading, promptness of attack, broadness and steadiness of tone, firmness and delicacy of touch, has no superior in the world; and I consider it an honor to have conducted it."— *Hans Von Bülow.*

"*Gentlemen:*—I came here in the pleasant expectation of finding a superior orchestra, but you have far surpassed my expectations, and I can say to you that I am delighted to know you as an orchestra of artists in which beauty of tone, technical perfection, and discipline are found in the highest degree. I know that this is due to your, by me, most highly revered meister, Theodore Thomas, whom I have known for twenty years, and whom it gives me inexpressible pleasure to meet again in his own workroom. Gentlemen, such a rehearsal as that which we have held this morning is no labor, but a great pleasure, and I thank you all for the hearty goodwill you have shown toward me."—*Richard Strauss's address to the Chicago Orchestra.*

"Theodore Thomas, under whose leadership I first appeared [season 1898-99] a full-blooded musician of the Hans Richter type, should serve as a model for our modern timebeaters. His style of leading is a convincing proof that shades of expression and tonal effects may be produced without hysterics, contortions, and such foolery. He has his excellent band under wonderful control and produces the most impressive effects without apparent effort. This gifted man, whose services for the musical life of America cannot be overstated, is as unostentatious and sensible in everyday life as he is at the desk."—*Emil Sauer.*

"The greatest conductor in the world is Theodore Thomas." —*Ignace Jan Paderewski.*

"Thomas's Orchestra is in truth what Americans love to call it with national pride 'the unrivalled orchestra of the world.' Not only the works of the great masters are played with spirit and inspiration, but even the waltzes of Strauss are given with a piquancy unequalled anywhere. This, the writer says, in view of the fact that he has himself been a member of Strauss's own Vienna Orchestra and other great European Orchestras."— *Berlin "Allgemeine Muzikzeitung."*

Bernhard Ziehn, resident in Chicago, and well known in Europe as in this country as a profound musical theorist, scientist and scholar, is an expert in all matters pertaining to the higher music. Very intimate musical, as well as personal, relations existed between him and Mr. Thomas, for the latter had great respect for his opinions and judgment and when in doubt was accustomed to consult with his friend, though it must not be assumed that they did not have some pretty strong contests together. I recently asked Mr. Ziehn to put in a few words his estimate of Mr. Thomas as a conductor. He did so and I give his statement in his own words. The characterization could hardly be more accurate or comprehensive. Mr. Ziehn says:

"Theodore Thomas treats the compositions, whether classic or modern, with the same conscientiousness, earnestness, and accuracy. There is no sentimentality, no affectation, no mere calculation, no animosity, but veracity and true cognizance. Under his baton the works were safe. He never undertook alterations of any kind, arbitrary omissions or additions, to show 'a genial conception.' Still his genius was continually at work to put life in the dead scores, and one receives the impression — this interpretation is the proper one. I know of only one man, who can be compared with Thomas as conductor — it is d'Albert as pianist."

Upon another occasion, Mr. Ziehn said:

"A score could not be in safer hands than those of Mr. Thomas. Such violence as has been committed recently by famous conductors of Germany and Austria upon the scores of Beethoven and Bruckner could not have been committed here."

# XIII

## THE MAN

FEW pictures of Mr. Thomas are satisfactory to those who were well acquainted with him. His earlier portraits bear little resemblance to the later, and the later sometimes differ widely from one another. His moods were many, and his expression depended largely upon the interest of the occasion. It is quite certain that the photographic process had little interest for him when he was the victim of it. If the camera could have caught him at one of those Olympian feasts when he was thoroughly enjoying the *Gemüthlichkeit* of the occasion, or in the height of a discussion, or when the triumphant measures of the finale of Beethoven's Fifth Symphony were surging upwards to suit him, then we might have had a picture of the real Theodore Thomas.  It is still more difficult to draw a pen picture of him.  Though he seemed tall upon the concert-stage he was only of medium height, but he carried himself like one born to command.  He stepped to the conductor's desk as of right, his bow was courtly, his presence always dignified, his gestures always graceful, and the lines of his figure in leading, statuesque.  It all spoke of authority, self-mastery, the gift of leadership, the certainty of accomplishment, the freedom of the "art to conceal art" — in other words, the respose of art, which is the consummation of the highest endeavor.  Nothing could be less ostentatious than his manner in the concert-room.  He walked in an easy but dignified way to the desk, turned and made a graceful bow to his audience, then turned to his players who were always in readiness, simply lifted his arms, gave the signal and the work began.  There was no fuss, no disorder, no desk rappings, no instructions to his concertmeister, no waiting for this man or that man to get his instrument ready, no nervousness, no hesitation. You could settle down to your seat with the absolute conviction that everything was right and everything was going right.  Everything he did was sure, strong, sane, healthy.  It was never necessary for his hearers to feel anxious about results.

He was a man of sturdy physique, as he was a

man of sturdy character, with strong shoulders, a well-set head, powerful arms, full chest, resolute mouth and chin, strongly marked face, earnest in repose, intense in listening, radiant when in good humor, and eyes of shifting hue that had ways at times of flashing, again of darkening, and sometimes of looking through you. His strength was extraordinary. It was probably due in the beginning to his perfect health, for his last sickness was in reality his first one, and was still further developed by his long years of violin playing and his still longer years of conducting. While I was walking with him one day in Chicago, four hoodlums approached us abreast and taking up the whole width of the sidewalk. To get by them it was apparently necessary to go out into the muddy street, but Mr. Thomas was not in the habit of making such concessions. Squaring his elbows in front of him he collided with the unsavory quartette directly in the centre. Two of them were flung against the building on their right and the other two went sprawling into the gutter. They were too much dazed by the suddenness of the onset to assail him and meanwhile he went on as unconcerned as if he had only brushed four straws out of his path. At the conclusion of the second Cincinnati festival some of his friends gave him a supper ''over the Rhine'' at which many musicians were present. It was the famous "tenth symphony night," so called because it followed Beethoven's Ninth Symphony, which had been excellently given earlier in the evening. At one time the talk turned upon strength of wrists and fingers. Andres, the pianist, placed his hand flat down upon the table and raising his third finger, brought it down like the hammer of a piano, producing an extraordinary degree of sound. Others tried the same thing but none equalled Andres, until Mr. Thomas brought his finger down with such force that he not only excelled the sound Andres had produced but made the glasses on the table fairly dance. It was this tremendous physical power that enabled Mr. Thomas to bear a burden of labor for fifty years that would have soon broken down any ordinary person.

Mr. Thomas was simple and unpretentious in his dress and never indulged in any of those eccentricities of garments or physique or personal habits which so many professional musicians affect to produce sensation. When he first went to "Felsengarten," his New Hampshire home, a neighboring farmer who had been very anxious to see him told a gentleman, who had a summer home near by, that he didn't believe Mr. Thomas was a musician for he didn't look like one, showing that among people in general the eccentric type has come to be regarded as the normal type of the professional. There was nothing in his make-up to indicate that he was a musician, but there was something in his appearance, that indefinable distinguishing mark of greatness, which impressed even the most casual passerby.

In the tide of being that sweeps through the street he would instantly have been singled out by a stranger as one in authority, and who had achieved greatness in his calling. Upon one occasion, while he was travelling to his summer home, the regular conductor asking for his ticket addressed him as "judge"; not long after, the sleeping-car conductor called him "professor"; a gentleman near by soon hailed him as "general"; and the porter was profuse in his appellation of "boss." Foreign artists who played under his direction always addressed him as "meister" or "maestro." The simplicity which marked his own dress and manner he also sought to cultivate among his players. He strongly disapproved of any affectations or eccentricities among them, and his rebukes were so prompt and sometimes so sharp that no orchestra ever exhibited a saner or more normal body of players than the Chicago.

He was one of the most modest and unpretentious of men. He was elected an honorary member of the Italian Society of Artists at Milan, which was under royal patronage. He was also elected a member of the "Verein Beethoven Haus" in Bonn, the object of this union being the preservation of Beethoven's birthplace, the collection of all his works, pictures, busts, and literature concerning him, and the erection of a memorial to him. Other European cities and societies had honored him. In this country he received the degree of Doctor of Music from Yale College in 1880, and from Hamilton College in 1881, as the following letters attest:

YALE COLLEGE.

New Haven, Conn., Sept. 27, 1880.

THEODORE THOMAS, ESQ.,

Dear Sir: It is my duty to inform you officially of the action of the President and Fellows of Yale College at the recent commencement, the conferring upon you the honorary degree of Doctor of Music, by way of recognition of the substantial service which you have rendered to musical culture in the United States. The diploma certifying to this degree is sent by mail herewith; and I must apologize for the long delay in forwarding it, owing to my ignorance of the fact that you had returned from Europe.

I have the honor to be, very respectfully, your most obedient servant,

FRANKLIN B. DEXTER,
*Secretary.*


HAMILTON COLLEGE.

Clinton, Oneida Co., N. Y., June 30, 1881.

THEODORE THOMAS, ESQ.,

Dear Sir: I have the honor to announce that the Board of Trustees of Hamilton College have this day conferred upon you the honorary degree of Doctor of Music. May I express the hope that this recognition of eminent services in the cause of music may be agreeable to yourself and your friends? If it should tend, even in the remotest degree, to bring that noble art into closer connection with the college, and into still higher esteem, it would bring to us also another degree of satisfaction.

I have the honor to remain, very respectfully, your obedient servant,

S. G. BROWN,
*Pres't of Hamilton College.*

While Mr. Thomas was greatly pleased, especially with the American honors, because they signified appreciation of the work he had done for music in his own country, he never used the degrees in any way. It would have been an exhibition of personal vanity of which he was utterly incapable. He preferred to be plain Theodore Thomas, and as such he remained to the end of his life.

He was not a demonstrative man and his brusqueness and impatience of manner sometimes repelled people; but once a friend, he was always a friend. There was one associate, William Mason, the pianist, whom he always called "William" whenever he spoke of him to me. I never knew another similarly favored. After more than thirty years of friendship with me he one day suggested that it was unnecessary to use the prefix "Mr." in addressing each other. "We know each other well enough to drop these stupid formalities," said he with a smile. Probably, as Mr. Mason once said of him, it was not that he meant to be short with people but he simply felt that he did not have time to be anything else. The consciousness of his work was always with him. Naturally, like many forceful men, he had a violent temper, but he kept it well under control. He would exhibit it only under great provocation as when he was misrepresented, or his orders were disobeyed, or outsiders interfered with his business, or singers and players aired their ignorance or displayed their vanity before him. He never recognized or permitted a man to speak to him who deliberately misrepresented him.

Two little incidents illustrate his impulsiveness. In a rehearsal at one of the Cincinnati festivals a tenor, who was not a professional, but an amateur who had an exaggerated opinion of the character of his singing and of his musical knowledge, and was by no means backward in airing it, offended Mr. Thomas several times not alone by his airs but also by his gross mistakes.  When the rehearsal was finished he accosted the singer: "Are you a professional singer?" "No, sir." "What do you for a living?" "I am a mechanic." "Well, you had better go home to your trade.  What are you doing here?  The shoemaker should stick to his last."

Upon another occasion a prominent soprano was rehearsing with him for an important concert. She sang her aria through and Mr. Thomas did not interrupt her, but at the close he asked, "Is that the way you have always sung this aria?"

"Oh, yes," she somewhat loftily replied, "it is the way we artists always sing it."

Mr. Thomas asked her to repeat the aria and she did so, singing it exactly as before.  "Do you think you sang the aria right?" he asked.

"Oh, yes, I know I have, I always have sung it that way."

"Then you had better take your music home and study it.  Come again to-morrow morning and we will try it again."

The lady returned the next morning in a less confident state of mind and asked Mr. Thomas if he would not show her how the aria should be sung. "Certainly," said he.  Patiently he explained to her just how she should sing it, both for phrasing and for expression, and when at last she sang it properly he cordially shook her hand. She told me some years afterwards that she never had a better friend than Theodore Thomas and that she owed her concert success to him. There are other singers who have had similar experiences.

Mr. Thomas was not a fluent conversationalist except when he was interested in the subject discussed, and then his crisp, epigrammatic, emphatic manner was delightful, for it was always accompanied, especially upon purely social or convivial occasions, by his strong sense of humor and his pleasure in the good stories of others. He was not at home in public speaking. Once in Cincinnati, at a banquet given to him he was called upon to reply to a toast to his health. It is said that he arose, tried to speak, murmured a few words and sat down, like Thackeray at the Boston banquet, whereupon Michael Brandt, the 'cellist, rose and said that Mr. Thomas ought not to be expected to make a speech,—"He is a 'Lieder ohne Worte.'" But his pithy epigrammatic style of talking and writing, and his ability to express his meaning precisely and say much in the fewest possible words, are shown in such examples as these:

"How great a gift God gave to the world when music was breathed into creation!"

"Music has the strongest influence of any art if properly controlled, because of its powerful appeal to the emotions. It can also do great harm where there is no character."

"Music, in its psychologic aspects, is little understood as yet, but we are gaining in our knowledge. Some feel only the emotional influence, others realize that a powerful character-building force has by its uplifting influences put them on a higher plane."

"I have always worked hard and always work ahead, and know little about the past."

"To play correctly, that is something. But to find the soul in music and play it — that is everything."

"In art the first rule is system and form."

"In art you cannot count your time."

"We don't work for the penny."

"The world is moving in music; we must keep pace with the change."

"By permanent work alone can we accomplish our purpose."

"For artistic work the surroundings must be artistic."

"I agree with the present time and prefer truth to European (culture) hypocrisy; but I also admire to some extent good manners, and confess that I am in my inner self enough a German that it makes me feel better if I can treat some one or some thing with respect."

"Everything revenges itself on this earth. Wagner fights just as much to-day as when alive — perhaps when he wants peace; and Berlioz, with whom we have thought we were through, had his centennial fall at a time to force the world to make up for lost time at the other end."

"I shall soon be ready to spend most of my time in Chicago. It is the old story — what New York offers, I refuse; what I demand, she refuses."

"I have suffered much these weeks playing before the iron curtain[1] and placed as we are, besides being sick with a cold. I began to think that there was a vacancy in the angel choir, and that I was preparing to fill it. Well, I hope I shall be able to help the new scheme along until it is safely launched. That will be enough."[2]

He was very fond of social gatherings in his home and of little dinners, with a few chosen friends, and at such times he was always "the bright, particular star." Like Dickens he was continually discovering a place where the chop was done to a turn, and like Thackeray he could take you to the restaurant where the wine was something rare, and bouillabaisse was excellent. How well I remember one invitation, "Come and have a good time and drink to the gods as the Greeks did, who loved only the good and the true," and his radiant humor and genial comradeship that night. And all save one who were at the board — "all, all are gone, the old familiar faces!" This side of his nature was for his friends, as well as a certain healthy German poetic sentiment which rounded out his character so finely.

While music was the work of his life, and he

---

[1] This was written shortly after the Iroquois Theatre fire in Chicago, when the fire ordinances were rigidly enforced.

[2] Referring to the permanent orchestra and the new Orchestra Hall in Chicago.

devoted himself to it almost continuously for half a century, yet he found time for general culture. In literature, as in music, only the highest appealed to him. This is all the more peculiar because he had no literary traditions or inheritance. His studies were in history and philosophy, and Shakespeare, Goethe, and Schiller were his literary favorites. At one time, when everything looked darkest and he saw no way of escape from financial ruin, he took down his Shakespeare and read far into the night. The next morning he awoke with renewed hope and devoted himself to his work with fresh courage. His sense of humor was also a saving grace to him. A dinner was once given him in Toledo at which a gentleman persisted in introducing his son, an infant phenomenon, who could play two cornets at once. After the youth had performed his feat, Mr. Thomas was asked by the proud parent what he thought of it. "Better learn to play on one before he takes two," was all he replied. In making out his list of players for the permanent Chicago Orchestra the ranks were filled with the exception of one 'cello player. In order that the vacancy should not appear on a programme list, he inserted the name "Fr. Stelle." For a long time his players wondered who "Franz" or "Friedrich" Stelle might be, and why he did not appear, and what kind of a player he would be when he did appear. At last the secret leaked out,—"Fr. Stelle" was simply "Freie Stelle"—or "open place."

German born, associated with German musicians

all through his life, meeting them daily, and living as it were in a German atmosphere, yet he was the strongest of Americans in sentiment, disposition, feeling, and patriotism. Many a time have I heard him resent foreign slurs upon American institutions and defend the national government's policy against its critics. His love for the United States, where he had lived from boyhood, and his respect and admiration for the broad-minded views of its people as well as their public spirit, was deep, sincere, and hearty.

Notwithstanding his sternness of demeanor, he was in reality the kindest hearted of men. He had great sympathy with suffering humanity and animals. In her pleasant little book, "Our Mountain Garden," Mrs. Thomas tells of his love for animals. After much labor he had made a pond near the house, which he jocularly used to call his "ocean." A friend, visiting him, suggested that he might stock it with trout and thus supply his table. His reply was, "What! First feed a creature and then eat it? I do not like that idea. I wish we could get on without this everlasting killing and eating of meat, but, since that is not practicable, let us at least not devour our friends." Let me tell another incident in Mrs. Thomas's own words:

"My private opinion is that it would take a champion squirrel to handle any of the Felsengarten birds, for they are past masters of the noble art of self-defence, and keep their claws and beaks in good practice by fighting each other all day long. One day the Meister looked out of the window and beheld two of them lying prone upon the grass, clutching each other so fiercely by the throat that they paid no heed to his pounding on the window, nor yet when he went out and shouted to them from the piazza; and it was not until he had descended to the ground, and almost reached them, as they lay struggling in the grass, that the combatants finally let go their savage clinch and flew off. This exhibition of ferocity on the part of creatures he had hitherto supposed to be the gentlest and most delicate examples of animated nature, was, I regret to say, such a shock to all his preconceived ideas, that it seriously cooled his ardor towards our birds and caused him to regard them as ruffians and swash-bucklers.''

A few weeks before he died he entertained two other gentlemen and myself at lunch. The immediate object was to settle some business matters. These were quickly finished, and then a social afternoon was spent. During the pleasant talk—and he never was a more gracious host than on that occasion, for he was feeling very happy because he was so soon to go into the new Orchestra Hall—the conversation turned upon Port Arthur and General Stoessel, who was upon the eve of surrendering the fortress to the Japanese. One of the gentlemen spoke of Stoessel as a hero, because he had held out so long and made such a stout defence. Clenching his fist, a habit he always had when he wished to emphasize his remarks, Mr. Thomas replied: ''Hero! not at all a hero. He is a brute. A general who knows that his case is hopeless, that there is no possible relief, and that he must surrender, and yet continues to sacrifice thousands of men, nine-tenths of whom do not know what it is they are fighting for, to

starvavation, to sickness, and to death from shot and
shell, is to me a brute. When Stoessel surrenders
he will march out of Port Arthur with all the honors
of war and will be lionized as a hero. But what of
the dead and wounded, the lifelong cripples and
invalids, so uselessly made victims of his so-called
bravery?" He was evidently not an enthusiastic
lover of the military, for on that same afternoon,
he took a cutting from the morning paper out of his
pocket and read that the civil courts in Germany
had justified an officer who had killed a private
soldier for some petty reason. "More brutes," said
he; "it almost makes me sorry that I am a German."

Like his favorite composer, Beethoven, Mr.
Thomas was ardently fond of nature, and he looked
forward to his long summer vacations at "Felsengarten" with all the eagerness of a child. As the
time drew near for the annual journey he could
hardly wait for the conclusion of the final concert.
In an interview he once said:

"How do I get my inspiration? Why, up in the White
Mountains of New Hampshire I have a cottage hidden away
from the world. A cunning little bypath runs through the
woods, and without a guide you cannot find your way in.
And when you are in, you do not want to find your way out.
I go in the morning and at night and talk to my trees, and my
mountains that I love. And I catch a little bit—just a little
bit—of what they answer me.

"What is it they say? Ah, that is it. It is nothing, and
yet everything. Nature is all music, and whatever she whispers to us is the heart of melody and the soul of rhythm. Some
of us are lucky enough to catch a few of her disjointed words,

"FELSENGARTEN," MR. THOMAS'S SUMMER HOME IN NEW HAMPSHIRE

ORCHESTRA HALL, CHICAGO

and are allowed to tell them to our brothers.   That is called inspiration."

Mrs. Thomas, in the work already mentioned, gives us an entertaining picture of his indefatigable industry in redeeming the wild tract of rocky land and making it a pleasant summer retreat.   She herself took charge of the building of the cottage and the making of the garden, while he devoted himself to the grounds, laying out avenues and making wood paths, turning a marsh into a pond, cutting away unsightly growths, felling useless trees, cutting, pruning, and digging like a common laborer.

"Before leaving Felsengarten in the fall," says Mrs. Thomas, "he would select the locality he meant to improve the following summer, and wander over every inch of it until he was familiar with all its features; and its trees and boulders, humps and hollows, and general topography were 'photographically lined on the tablet of his mind.'   During the winter he would plan his improvements, and the following spring he was ready to put them into execution.   First he would clear the section of rubbish, ragged growths, inferior trees, dead branches, and other unsightly objects.   Then he would stake out the path or avenue to be constructed, and, beginning at one end, he and his young assistant would work at it quietly, day by day, and as the work progressed the embellishment of the adjacent land naturally suggested itself."

He spoke of this "recreation" once in a quietly humorous way.   It was evidently before he had become well acquainted with the possibilities of stones "in the old Granite State."   "I don't seem to make any impression upon the stones of New Hampshire.   For years I have spent my summer

days with a pick in one hand and a crowbar in the
other. I have been attempting to clear a small
place of all the stones and have found it impossible.
Somehow, when I go there at the beginning of the
summer, it always seems to me that there are more
stones upon that patch of ground than when I
left."

Those were happy days in Felsengarten "under
his own vine and fig-tree"—days of quiet enjoyment
of nature, of healthy outdoor work which was a
grateful remedy for overstrained nerves, and a rest
after the hard round of a season's rehearsals and
concerts. At Felsengarten also he met his children,
who, having homes of their own, were separated from
him at other seasons of the year, and with his boys
he was like an elder brother. It was his delight
after the day's work to sit upon his piazza and watch
the mountain horizon line in the afterglow of sunset, so strangely contrasting with the darkness
settling down on the slopes below. In his last
moments he saw this picture again and said to his
companion who had labored with him and helped
to transform those waste lands into a mountain
garden, "I have seen a beautiful vision." And
then he smiled and his voice was hushed forever-
more. And soon the sun set and "all the land was
dark." He had passed to the heights where great
souls rest. "Ueber allen Gipfeln ist Ruh."

Thus passed from our midst the great musician
who had wrought so long, so devotedly, so courageously for the things that make for the refinement of

life and for the ennobling of the spirit, never once
degrading the great gift which had been given him,
never yielding to a sordid consideration, nor com-
promising his art with commercialism.  His life is
an example for American youth of a great purpose
nobly striven for, nobly won, of work for civic and
individual righteousness, of patience in well-doing,
of honors modestly received, of success richly earned.
He has affected the lives of thousands of men and
women for good, by diverting their tastes from the
trivial and meretricious to nobler and purer things,
for great music is a moral influence whose extent
can hardly be measured.  Life and music may be
more intimately related than we know.  Music helps
to keep body and soul in health, and no man's education can be called complete without it.  As Wilhelm
Hoffman says in "Serapionsbrüder": "No art, I
believe, offers so much evidence of the spiritual
in man as music, and there is no art that requires
so exclusively means that are purely intellectual and
ethereal."  Measured by every standard, viewed
from every standpoint, tested by every canon of
music and of morals, Theodore Thomas's career
tended to the elevation of popular taste and the uplifting of the national life.  His work was a public bene-
faction.  His life is a noble example.  His memory
will be cherished by his contemporaries, and history
will record his name as that of the pioneer of the
higher music in America.

# CHRONOLOGY

## THEODORE THOMAS'S LIFE WORK

1835    Born at Esens.

1843    Began playing the violin.

1845    Family came to America.

1845–47 Played in concerts.

1847–52 Played in theatres and at opera, and travelled in the South.

1852    Soloist at a Dodworth Band concert.

1854    Elected a member of the New York Philharmonic Society.

1855    Mason-Thomas chamber concerts began.

1856    Leader of concert orchestra in sacred concerts.

1857–58 Travelled with Thalberg, Formes, and other artists.

1858    Conductor of Ullmann opera season.

1860    Concerts with Carl Wolfsohn in Philadelphia.

1861    Operatic conductor in New York.

1862    Classical soirees in Orange, N. J. First concert with his own orchestra at Irving Hall, New York.

1862    Alternate conductor with Th. Eisfeld, of the Brooklyn Philharmonic Society.

1863    Matinee concerts at Irving Hall.

1864    Begins symphony soirees.

1865    Musical director of the New York Institute for the Blind.

1866    Elected conductor of Brooklyn Philharmonic Society. Garden concerts at Terrace Garden.

1867     European visit. Founded the Thomas Orchestra.

1868     Elected conductor Mendelssohn Union. Began Central Park Garden concerts.

1869     Symphony concerts closed. First concert tour.

1870     First Wagner concert.

1872–78 Symphony concerts resumed in Steinway Hall.

1872     Musical festival in New York.

1873     Cincinnati festival inaugurated.

1876     Philadelphia Centennial concerts.

1877     Conductor of the New York Philharmonic Society.

1878     Director of Cincinnati College of Music.

1879     Returned to New York. Conductor of the Philharmonic Society.

1880     Organized New York chorus.

1882     Festivals in New York and Chicago.

1883     Tour to Pacific coast.

1884     Wagner festival concerts.

1885     Director of American Opera Company.

1891     Removed to Chicago and founded Chicago Orchestra.

1893     Director of the World's Fair Music Bureau.

1904     Dedicated Orchestra Hall, Chicago.

1905     Died January 4.

# APPENDIX

# APPENDIX

## MUSICAL POSSIBILITIES IN AMERICA

[A paper written by Theodore Thomas for "Scribner's Magazine," March, 1881, at the special request of its editor.]

THE Americans are certainly a music-loving people. They are peculiarly susceptible to the sensuous charm of tone, they are enthusiastic and learn easily, and with the growth in general culture of recent years, there has sprung up a desire for something serious in its purpose in music, as in the other arts. The voices of the women although inclined to be sharp and nasal in speaking, are good in singing. Their small volume reveals the lack of proper training, but they are good in quality, extended in compass, and brilliant in color. The larger number are sopranos, but there are many altos, and there would be more and they would be better were it not for ruinous attempts to make sopranos of them. The men's voices do not compare favorably with those of the women. They lack strength and character, and a well-balanced chorus is hardly possible as yet without a mixture of English or German voices to give body to the tone. Of late years, probably because of the growing attention to physical training, there has been a marked improvement, and many good and beautiful voices have been developed, chiefly barytones or high basses. The incessant pressure of work which every American feels, prevents the men from paying much attention to music, but as the country advances in age and begins to acquire some of the repose which age brings, there will come possibilities of development which cannot now be estimated.

In considering, therefore, the present condition of musical development in this country, I am led naturally to speak first of vocal music. Although the contrary has been asserted, I think it is in the vocal direction, and not in the instrumental, that the present development of the art tends. We have no public instrumental performers of American birth who can rank with our singers in public estimation, nor is there at present more than a very limited demand for instrumentalists. New York is the only city in the country in which an orchestral player can make a living, and even here he must give lessons or play at balls and parties, thereby losing or injuring the finer qualities of an orchestral player. Boston, in spite of many efforts, cannot support a large, well-balanced orchestra. Philadelphia has no standing orchestra, and in Cincinnati and Chicago the orchestral musician must eke out a living by playing in beer-gardens and saloons. The only demand for piano players, except of the highest order, is as teachers, and of those we have many and good ones, who do what may be called missionary work. Singing, on the other hand, appeals to almost every one, and there is a certain demand, even if limited, for singers in the churches.

When we consider that music is taught in the public schools throughout the country, we might expect some evidence or result of this teaching among the people. Much money is spent in our schools for instruction in this branch, and what does it amount to? Many of the children learn like parrots, and soon forget the little which they have learned. Those who retain this knowledge find it a drawback when wishing to go on in the study of music. The fault is not in them, but in the system taught.

So faulty is that system that it would be better to abolish singing entirely from the schools than to retain it under the present method. It does more harm than good. I consider the system at present followed in this elementary instruction, called the "movable *do* system," fundamentally wrong, and experience has confirmed me in this opinion. It is a make-shift, invented by amateurs. Pupils should learn something about absolute pitch of tones, instead of merely their relative pitch. The "movable *do* system" shuts the door against this knowledge. The first tone of the scale in every key is *do*, and that term *do* never suggests to one who has thus studied music any fixed, absolute conception of pitch; for example, *do* is sometimes C and sometimes D, while to the musician C and D are as distinct sounds as the vowels a and e. The system will enable a pupil to sing a simple hymn tune which has no accidental sharps or flats, but it is wrong thus to limit pupils to so restricted a capacity. In my experience, those who have learned to read music according to this method never free themselves altogether from it. It should be considered as necessary to be thorough in the study of music as in that of mathematics. I do not say that it should be carried to the same extent, but that, so far as it is carried, it should be taught understandingly and well — taught so as to pave the way for future study, when desirable, and not so as to block it up. I attach a great deal of importance to this matter of correct musical instruction. If we start right in the schools, the public taste will soon advance to a higher standard. It is from the young that the church choirs and singing societies must be recruited, and if a correct foundation is laid when the rudiments are learned, the progress to a more advanced position is natural and easy.

While singing under proper direction is a healthy exercise, great injury can be done to the throat and vocal organs by allowing the children to sing, or rather scream, at the top of their voices. Most of the school singing which I have heard in this country is screaming, not singing, while in England and Germany I heard nothing of the kind. On the principle that no person can teach another what he cannot do himself (a principle which I believe in to a great extent), I hold to the opinion that the teachers of singing should themselves be singers, with a good method. Singing ought also to be taught without the aid of an instrument, unless it be occasionally to support the pitch.

At present, the musical standard of the American public, taken as a whole, must be pronounced a low one. If we should judge of what has been done in music by the programmes of concerts given in the larger cities, we might rightly claim for this country a high rank in cultivation. Those concerts, however, appeal not to the general public, but to one class only, and that a limited one, as any one who observes the audiences can easily see. This class is growing in numbers as well as in cultivation, but it is still far too small to support more than a limited number of concerts, as at present those of the New York and Brooklyn Philharmonic societies. The general public does not advance in music, partly from want of opportunity, partly from the habits of the people. The average American is so entirely absorbed in his work that when he goes out in the evening he looks for relaxation in some kind of amusement which makes little or no demand upon his intellect, and he has no difficulty in finding it.

As regards general musical culture, the public may be divided into two classes — those who go to the theatres, and those for whom the church is the social centre. In both church and theatre, the standard of music is a low one. In the church, where first of all sincerity should prevail, and where nothing but healthy food should be given, the music is looked upon as an attraction and given as an amusement. It is largely operatic, it appeals to the senses only, and is too often of the sickly sentimental order. In those churches only which have congregational singing is the sense of what is suitable and decorous not offended. In this criticism I do not include some of the Roman Catholic churches. The priest estimates at its full value the power of music over the masses, and coöperates with the organist to produce a good musical service. Why cannot this be done in the Protestant churches? Pleasing music need not be trifling or sentimental; there are many beautiful works, not suited for the concert-room, which are intended for devotional use. But the greater part of the church music is a sort of patchwork — a little piece from this composer and another piece from that, put together by an amateur. A higher aim ought to be set, if not in the first place because of the art itself (though why this is not a praiseworthy purpose I do not see), at least for the sake of truth and propriety. The most exalted and artistic church service is the most proper one. The music that will inspire those feelings which ought to fill the soul of every worshipper is noble, good music — not sentimental, not secular, but lofty and devotional. That this low standard of church music exists is not owing to the want of competent organists, for we have many of ability, but rather to the fact that they are hampered in their attempts to introduce better music by the solo singers, as well as by the want of interest on the part of the minister, and, in many cases, by the desire of the business committee to "draw" and please the congregation. Recent years have also given us composers of undoubted merit.

It can hardly be expected that the managers of our theatres will carry on their business solely on art principles, nor can they afford to make the theatre an educational institution; but they ought to try to have the music in keeping with the general character of their houses, and, as far as possible, appropriate to the plays given. A small but well-proportioned band of twenty pieces, for which the leader can adapt and arrange music,— such as opera selections, overtures, dances, with solos for different instruments,— is competent to furnish music which will give pleasure to the educated ear, and be at the same time an educator of the popular taste. If an orchestra of twenty is too expensive, it would be better to reduce the number to a half-dozen players, and have, in addition to a piano and a cabinet organ, a fair violinist, a violoncellist, or some other solist. Instead of that, we have now a blatant cornet or trombone, drums, bells, wood and straw instruments, every one making the greatest possible noise, headed by an important conductor, with a baton in his hand instead of a violin bow. We had better music in the theatres twenty years ago than we have at present. Why appeal in music to a lower class, or allow in the orchestra a lower standard than is in keeping with what is presented on the stage?

I have mentioned thus hastily some of the defects of our methods of musical instruction, and pointed out some of the obstacles to our advancement to a higher musical standard. What are the remedies? I was once asked by a gentleman what he ought to do to make his children musical. He perhaps expected me to advise him to send the girls to Italy to study vocalization, and to set the boys to practising the violin so many hours a day and studying harmony. I told him to form for them a singing class under the care of a good teacher, that they might learn to use their vocal organs, to form a good tone, and to read music; after they became old enough, to let them join a choral society, where, for two hours once a week, they could assist in singing good music; and, above all, to afford them every opportunity of hearing good music of every kind. This gentleman knew nothing of music, but thought the advice "sounded like common sense."

If we have arrived at that point where it is considered necessary to give music a place in the common-school education, it is time that something like organized work should be done for the general cultivation of taste. The formation of singing societies would reach the people, and the knowledge which the children are supposed to gain in the schools would be sufficient for participation in such societies. So far as the singers themselves are concerned, everybody who has ever sung in a chorus knows that nothing so awakens an interest in music as helping to make it. The sympathies of hundreds are enlisted through their personal relations with the singers, and gradually a correct taste is formed and developed. If the proper means be put in use, and those who are willing to do something for music will organize for work with a purpose in it, such is the power of music that the growth will be steady until the general state is one of worth and dignity. In European countries, while the highest mark attained by the advanced class is no higher than here, the love for and understanding of music is more widely diffused. The Philharmonic concerts do not appeal to the general public; they are for this advanced class, and are well supported. But this class does not grow in numbers as rapidly as it ought.  The steps by which the people can be led up to the plane of these concerts are lacking.  They were once partly supplied by the Central Park garden concerts, which were managed in a way that gave no offence to the social ideas of the people, and hence had their support.  It is of great importance at present to give the people the right kind of food.  Their taste has been awakened and they are willing to be led.  The way in which music is often taught is an insult to any person of common intellect. The intelligence is not appealed to, but the pupil is treated like a child, and often remains, musically speaking, a child his life long.

The value of a visit to Europe, at the proper time, is of course great for those studying music; but pupils should not be sent there for technical instruction, but for the knowledge of other schools and methods — in short, for the experience.  A great many singers are sent to Italy; and what results have we?  If they devote themselves to vocalization and really learn to vocalize — and many do not — they come back without a repertory of practical value.  They display their acquirements in some show pieces of operatic airs to which they have given all their attention, and for which there is no demand.  Many singers are excluded from opportunities of appearing in good concerts, because they have no pieces in keeping with the character of the programmes.  Why send them so far to acquire that which is of no use to them?  What a waste of money and, more serious still, what a dreadful ruin of moral character often results!  No teacher in a foreign country can rightly understand how to prepare pupils for practical work here.  Though the taste for singing was awakened by Italian opera, and though the Italian method of using the voice commends itself to us, the educated

American is not satisfied with the Italian repertory, and soon outgrows it. I am satisfied that we shall never have a standard opera, that will take hold of the people, until we educate our own singers for the stage, and choose our repertory from the best Italian, French, and German works.

We want home education and thorough home education of a kind suited to the needs and demands of our people, and calculated to promote the new life which we hope is opening before us. We want an end of amateurism in teachers and other professionals. Those who present themselves to guide the people must have thoroughly studied music, not dabbled in it. We need some provision for the talent which is developing every day — we need institution, well endowed, which will not be obliged to adopt a mere commercial standard for want of the means of support. We need the influences coming naturally from such institutions. We need them, not only to give instruction to pupils, but to keep up a high standard of excellence. We need them for our numerous earnest teachers to come to from time to time, to rub off the rust of teaching, and refresh themselves by contact with those who live in a musical atmosphere. The greatest enemy to fight is mediocrity, and an institution of standing is the only sure defence against it. Such an institution would afford an opportunity for public or semi-public performances, by which ability would be tested and experience gained. It would also give us — what we have not now — a suitable place for the performance of the works of young composers. A concert of a society like the Philharmonic is not the proper place for experimental music.

There are many ways in which such an institution would be of national advantage. It would not only develop our native talent and give us a true standard of excellence, but it would also give fresh impetus to the mechanical branch of the art, wherein this country already occupies an enviable position. It is generally acknowledged that we make the best pianos. Our organs are good, and our brass and reed instruments are of a superior quality. But the most noteworthy fact of all is that we are making the best violins. Some of the first living violinists claim that the violins made by George Gemünder are worthy to rank with those of the famous Italian makers, needing only age to prove their great excellence. Mr. Gemünder, who has shown himself a master in this most difficult art, says that we have an extraordinary variety of woods suitable for instrument-making, and that his experience, which he has dearly bought by indefatigable labor since 1847, shows our woods to be in no way inferior to the best used by the old Italian makers. We have, furthermore, an abundant supply, whereas in Europe there is a great scarcity. The rough tone of the violins of German manufacture is due largely to the inferior quality of the wood. A striking tribute to the superiority of Mr. Gemünder's work is furnished by the following authentic anecdote: At the Vienna Exhibition there was a collection of the best specimens of violin-making. It included not only the famous instruments of the Italian makers, but those of modern workmanship. Mr. Gemünder sent a remarkable violin, made by him after the pattern of Joseph Guarnerius. The judges, who had been selected from all parts of Europe to pronounce upon the merits of the various instruments, refused to admit this particular one to competition, declaring that the competitor was trying to deceive them with a genuine old instrument in an unusually good state of preservation.

It will be seen, therefore, that we have in this country the possibilities of a great musical future. We have the natural taste of the people for music, their strong desire to have only the best, and their readiness to recognize what is the best when it is presented to them. We have exceptional natural resources for the making of musical instruments. Nature has done her part of the work generously; it remains for us to do ours.

## MUSIC IN CHICAGO

[Written by Mr. Thomas for "The Chicago Tribune," January 23, 1894.]

I have always regarded Chicago as a music-loving city, and although when we first began to come here, many years ago, comparatively few persons knew much about music, we found here a widespread love for it, which very soon developed into an appreciation of and desire for music of the best kind.

During the old summer night concerts of former years, I noticed each season a marked advance in musical taste, as expressed in the "requests" sent in for our weekly "request programmes." Indeed so high a class of music was asked for in the last few seasons of these concerts, that I could have made up a regular symphony programme of the most classic order, every week, without departing in the least from numbers actually requested, had it seemed wise to do so. As an instance of this I might mention one of the most largely attended and warmly applauded "request programmes" we ever gave, the first part of which contained six successive numbers by Bach, and the Dvorak Symphonic Variations; the second part, compositions by Beethoven, Brahms, and

Wagner; while the third and lightest part asked for
nothing more popular than Liszt's "Twelfth Rhapsody"
and a portion of Moszkowski's Suite, op. 39.  I remember
that this programme called forth some comment from
some of the Eastern papers, whose editors refused to
believe that its numbers were really requested by the
audience of a summer night concert.

The interest thus early manifested in music has steadily
advanced, as the public have had the opportunity to hear
it more frequently.  No surer proof of this is needed
than the recent successful effort to establish a great permanent orchestral organization on lines of the very highest
art.  I have been very much encouraged by the attitude
which the Chicago people have taken in regard to this
work.  Only those who are directly interested in the
management of such an organization have any idea of the
many difficulties which have to be surmounted in order
to make its maintenance possible.  In Chicago these
difficulties are increased a hundredfold, because the city
is situated so far from all other large cities that the great
expense of transporting the orchestra makes it impossible
to take engagements for single concerts in them, and so we
cannot look for any assistance from outside sources, but
our city has to bear the whole burden alone.

Under these circumstances, and when it is also taken
into consideration that the orchestra has been maintained
as an art institution, and not, as an amusement bureau, it
naturally follows that the expense has been a large one to
those generous and cultivated citizens who have supported it.  But I have not yet heard one murmur of dis-
content on this head from any one who has given liberally in
either money or time toward the support of this institution.

But one spirit seems to pervade the minds of those

who are working together in this noble cause — it is the best Chicago spirit which has made realities of such vast undertakings as the Art Institute, the Chicago University, the World's Fair, and the Field Columbian Museum, and which thinks only of establishing something ennobling and refining in our great Western metropolis, to temper the influences of the daily struggle of life and to lighten its sordid cares. Such a spirit does not seek to cramp its artistic standards within the limits of the means provided, but rather to enlarge the means to meet the requirements of the standards.

When Chicago men start a good work, and are convinced that it is good, they do not pull it down because it is more costly than they supposed it would be. On the contrary, they merely make a stronger and more determined effort to maintain and develop it to its highest perfection. The architecture of the World's Fair was the most extraordinary instance of this peculiar characteristic. Rather than lower its artistic standard a jot, they threw millions into the work without a thought of ever getting back a dollar. How wise this policy was the sequel proved, for in the financial stringency of last fall only a meagre crowd would have come to the Fair without the glories of the Court of Honor and the enchantment of its fairy palaces.

It is this scorn of mediocrity and this indomitable determination to have the *best*, and maintain only the highest standard in all its enterprises, which makes the greatness of this city. I believe, therefore, that having once had the best in music, Chicago will not go backward in this art any more than in any other, but will find the means of continuing the good work so auspiciously begun, and of constantly enlarging its field of usefulness.

That the musical taste and culture of the people here will advance from year to year as the art grows more familiar to them naturally must follow. Already I have observed a very marked change in the conduct of our audiences, showing a far better understanding of the work than was apparent three years ago. At that time our audiences regarded the Orchestral Association concerts in the same light as they had formerly regarded the summer night concerts, and acted accordingly. They came late, or went early, constantly moved about, talked, and in general kept up a little restless disturbance throughout the entire programme which seriously marred the performance. Also, they were all the time clamoring for the old summer night programmes, and complaining because they had to pay more than the old scale of summer night prices. It was some time before they could understand that a great symphony orchestra of ninety men could not be supported through the whole winter for the same price paid to the little orchestra of less than sixty for a month at midsummer. Nor could they at first appreciate the vast artistic difference between the standards of the two organizations, or comprehend that a standard of programme which might even be high in a garden concert would be as wholly unsuited to our winter concerts as a chromo hung among the Dutch masterpieces at the Art Institute.

But already this has changed. Our audience has learned that the master works of the great composers contain more good for brain and soul than the prettiest waltzes that ever were penned; it has discovered that there is a deeper joy and a nobler spirituality to be gained from familiarity with the higher art forms than it ever dreamed of seeking in the lower. It has discovered that while Strauss or Bizet will charm the ear, Beethoven and Wagner will warm and thrill the whole nature. Hence we find that our popular programmes do not now draw as large an audience as our symphony programmes; the largest audiences in the three years having been those of last winter, when Beethoven's Ninth Symphony was performed — with the exception of those at which Paderewski played.

And having learned to value and appreciate the music, our audience now wishes to hear it all. The late comers are much fewer, and are content to wait for a pause in the music before disturbing others by taking their seats. Talking has almost wholly ceased, and only those leave early who are obliged to take suburban trains. When the orchestra gives an especially fine rendering of any number, we generally find now that the audience takes notice of it, and very few people have any idea how intelligent and discriminating listeners react upon the performers. A stupid audience kills the orchestra dead in five minutes, as water kills fire, whereas an intelligent and responsive audience will stimulate the musicians at once to their best efforts.

In conclusion, I need hardly say that the musical future of Chicago looks to me full of the brightest promise. That this promise may find ample realization is my earnest hope.

## FAREWELL BANQUET IN NEW YORK

[As a testimonial of respect and admiration many leading citizens and musicians of New York tendered a farewell banquet to Mr. Thomas at Delmonico's, on the evening of April 22, 1891, Hon. George William Curtis occupying the chair. Among the guests were many of the most distinguished citizens of New York. Mr. Curtis made the following speech in proposing the health of "a public benefactor." The other speakers were Mr. Parke Godwin, Mr. William Steinway, Rev. Arthur Brooks, and William Mason.—EDR.]

"I rise to propose the health of a public benefactor — an artist whose devotion to a beautiful, refining, and ennobling art has greatly distinguished his name and given great distinction to the city in which he lives — the health of the central figure of the musical life of New York for a generation, and your hearts go before my tongue in saluting Theodore Thomas. He has made the conductor's baton an imperial sceptre, with which he rules, not only an orchestra but an ever widening realm of musical taste and cultivation. In his hand it has become an enchanter's wand which has transformed our musical ignorance and crudity into ample knowledge and generous appreciation. While it has introduced us to the learned and acknowledged masters of the past, it has summoned and revealed the still shadowy figures of the future. Musical artists have come and gone. Virtuosos of every kind have appeared, have charmed us and have vanished. Our private accomplishment has advanced from the "Battle of Prague" and the variations of Henri Herz to the symphonies of Schumann, the songs of Rubinstein, the Schubert transcriptions of Liszt, and is still pushing on and on like Columbus, sailing beyond the horizon into unknown seas. But the one figure which has remained, the laureate of the past and the herald of the future, is Theodore Thomas.

"I suppose there are very few guests at these tables of memories so daring as mine, which recalls the coming of Jenny Lind to this country. I remember her always with a certain selfish pleasure, because I heard her, I believe, every evening that she sang in this city, and when on the last evening she sang her farewell to America at Castle Garden, she held in her hand a bouquet that I had sent her, and which still perfumes my recollection of that

incomparable singer. A few years before, when Fanny
Ellsler was here, bewitching the heels rather than the
heads or hearts of the golden youth of that time they un-
harnessed the horses from her carriage and drew her across
the street to her hotel, merely substituting, as an elderly
cynic of the time remarked, jackasses for horses. We
did not draw Jenny Lind in her carriage, but the youth of
her day — of whom my friend Parke Godwin was one, who
paid her tribute in the charming tale of "Vala"— have
borne her in their hearts across a generation, and their
hearts still rise at the mention of her name as the Garde
du Roi sprang cheering to their feet when the Queen
appeared.

"There is one story of Jenny Lind which I always recall
with entire confidence in its truth, because it ought to be
true. After her return from her American triumph she
was in Italy, and went one day from Florence to the con-
vent at Vallombrosa, to which the young Milton went when
on his travels. When she came to the chapel the monks
with courteous and deprecating regret told her that no
woman could enter. She smiled as she said: 'Perhaps
if you knew who I am you would let me in.' 'And who
might the gracious lady be?' returned the monks. But
when she said, 'I am Jenny Lind,' every head was bowed
and the doors were flung wide open. Then when she
seated herself at the organ and sang where Milton had
sat and played, I can imagine the heavenly visions that
floated before the minds of the monks and that they
crossed themselves reverently as they listened and believed
that St. Cecilia had descended.

"That is what I have always thought of her visit to
America. St. Cecilia descended upon these shores, coming to give the right impulse to our musical development.

But St. Cecilia would have descended in vain if there had been no continuing personal force in the country of her own spirit in art, of a kindred enthusiasm and lofty purpose. Happily in the orchestra at her concerts there was a youth who played the first violin, and who has continued to play it ever since, everybody else playing second fiddle, and to the genius, the untiring devotion, the intelligence, the energy, the masterly skill of that youth, more than to any other single force, we owe the remarkable musical interest and cultivation and the musical preëminence of New York to-day.

"I do not mean, of course, that there have not been other admirable artists and effective influences coöperating to this noble result. Certainly I do not forget Bergmann and Damrosch. I do not forget those upon whom my eyes fall at this moment. But during all this time the constant dominating personality has been that of Theodore Thomas. It was Thomas with Bergner, Mosenthal, Matzka, and Mason in the old Dodworth salon. It was Thomas in the Central Park Garden; Thomas in the Philharmonic Society; Thomas in the great festival of 1882. It was always Thomas and his orchestra, and always Thomas and his baton, like the valiant Henry of Navarre and his white plume waving in the van of victory.

"The great works of the great composers, the mighty music of the masters who have given to their art an equal renown with the kindred arts of literature and painting and sculpture; the music of Bach and Handel, of Mozart and Haydn and Beethoven—names that in their kind shine in equal lustre with those of Raphael and Angelo and Shakespeare — has been played continuously from year to year under Thomas's direction in a manner not often surpassed at the Conservatoire or the Gewandhaus; while the music of a later day and of another charm has been so interpreted by him that after the great Wagner afternoon at the Festival Mme. Materna said to me that Wagner had never heard that work of his own so magnificently rendered. Thomas's whole career has been a campaign of education. If he has revealed to us more fully Beethoven, whom we knew, it is he, also, who first showed us that there was a Wagner who might be worth knowing. He has given to New York a musical distinction without which no great city is a metropolis; and Chicago has shown the true metropolitan instinct in securing his musical leadership. It is because of the dignity of his career, its absolute fidelity to a high ideal, its total freedom from charlatanry of every kind that his service to this city has been so signal a public benefit and that his departure is a public misfortune.

"But a great interpreter of music — and such is a great conductor — wherever he goes carries his own welcome with him. It is not as a stranger that he goes to Chicago; it is because he is not a stranger, because Chicago knows him well, that she asks him to come. And he does not go alone. He takes with him our gratitude, our admiration, and our affection. He goes wreathed and garlanded with our cheers and hopes and our perfect confidence in his return. For New York only lends Theodore Thomas to Chicago. With metropolitan magnanimity she decorates with one of her own precious jewels her younger and successful competitor for the prize of the great Fair. But presently she will reclaim it and restore it to her crown with a fresher lustre gained from her sister's coronet. Therefore on your behalf, on behalf of the great multitude of New Yorkers who follow him with a pang of farewell, but with a hearty godspeed, I say to him in a language familiar

to him before he knew that in which I am speaking:
'Wir sagen nicht, Lebewohl; wir sagen nur, Gott be-
fohlen, bis auf Wiedersehen!'"

## THE NEW YORK FESTIVAL OF 1882

[George William Curtis, in the "Editor's Easy Chair,"
"Harper's Magazine," July, 1882.]

From the Philharmonic concerts of the last generation
in the old Apollo Rooms upon Broadway below Canal
Street, and from the Italian opera, and opera singers, of
which Mr. Richard Grant White, the master critic of that
day, is giving us charming reminiscences, to the Music
Festival of 1882 in the Seventh Regiment Armory, is a
step of progress which is amazing and incredible. The
Philharmonic audience was a pleasant little assembly,
which listened doubtfully to the music of Beethoven
pleasantly played by a moderate orchestra. The Festival
audience was a vast multitude bursting into a tumult of
delight over the music of Beethoven, Mozart, Schubert,
and Wagner, played incomparably by a vast orchestra of
three hundred exquisitely trained musicians, and the
mighty Handelian choruses rolled sublimely forth from
a host of three thousand voices.

It was not the first music festival in the country.
There had been festivals in Cincinnati and Chicago, and
a monster performance in Boston, and the admirable
Damrosch Festival in New York. But the legitimate
grandeur of the Festival of this year, the symmetrical
precision and perfection of the orchestra, over whose wonderful richness of effect the spirits of the great masters
might well have hovered, satisfied and approving; the
vast chorus gathered from different cities, which, suddenly

brought together, blended under the magic baton of the
conductor in a majestic and inspiring volume of sound;
and the solo singers, greatest of the world in their various
kinds, from the grand dignity of Materna to the exquisite
delicacy and grace of vocalization of Gerster, and from
the broad, manly, fresh vigor of Candidus to the sweet and
fervid charm of Campanini — all these combined to make
the first week of May memorable, and to indicate the high-
water mark in the musical annals of the country.

We have mentioned the various musical elements of
this great success, but we have not mentioned the supreme
organizing and directing force. Many things were important to the result, but one thing was indispensable.
That was the conductor. It was a misfortune that Miss
Cary was unwell, and could not appear until the last day.
It would have been a serious blow had Madame Materna
been prevented by any reason from appearing, or had she
failed to justify the high anticipation that awaited her
coming. But it would have been fatal had any mishap
befallen Theodore Thomas. In the sense that Napoleon
was Austerlitz, Thomas was the Festival. Without Napoleon there had been no Austerlitz; without Thomas,
no Festival. For him, indeed, it was a peculiar triumph.
To those who have known his long, unwearied, most
efficient, and most unselfish devotion to the development
and education of the best musical taste in this country, it
was a profound satisfaction to feel the immense musical
success of this Festival. The long selection of music to
be performed was of sustained excellence. There was no
attempt to catch a cheap applause, or to tickle the ears of
a multitude. The purpose was not superficial entertainment, but the enjoyment that comes from the highest art.

As those who were directly interested in the preparations saw the leader massing his vocal and instrumental lines to scale the rugged and perpendicular heights of the most inaccessible Beethoven and Handelian chorals, or to thread the weird and bewildering labyrinths of the Wagnerian orchestration, they could not but feel that at least the director was no doubting Thomas, and his courageous confidence inspired the enterprise. Indeed, that is the secret of Mr. Thomas's success. He believes in his cause, and therefore he conquers. He believes that the public will accept and enjoy the best music, and he makes them enjoy it. When it was asked of a certain concert whether it was not beyond the public taste, the answer was, "This is the only way to lift the public taste." Like the old warrior who hurled his javelin far into the ranks of the enemy, and fought his way forward to recover it, Thomas flings his baton higher and higher toward the pure and awful peaks, and we all gladly press after, up, up, into a more inspiring air and a broader and grander horizon.

As the week's performances ended toward Saturday midnight amid a tumult of delight from the thousands that crowded the vast hall, and after five minutes of a continuous roar of demand from the audience that would not depart until he appeared, Mr. Thomas came forward to receive such a greeting as we have never seen surpassed upon any occasion. Amid the tornado of excited applause, the retiring auditor of a philosophic and contemplative turn undoubtedly asked himself what was the real permanent result of so great a musical triumph. The result, however, was evident. It is shown that a festival need not be merely a series of "big," or "monster," or "mammoth" concerts, but that larger numbers both of instruments and singers may greatly increase the true effect of the music.

Indeed, the grandest choral effects require vast space and a mighty volume of sound, which are possible only under the conditions of a festival, and most of the finest contemporary instrumental music contemplates an immense orchestra. Nor is an adequate voice and a noble manner lost in a festival, however large the space.

## ORCHESTRA HALL DEDICATION

[Address of Hon. George E. Adams upon the occasion of the dedication of Orchestra Hall, Chicago, December 14, 1904.]

"The president and trustees have asked me, as a former president of the Association, to bid you welcome to the dedication of the permanent home of the Chicago orchestra.

"It is an event to which we have looked forward with hope, hope sometimes discouraged but never entirely cast down, for the last fourteen years.

"Fourteen years ago the Orchestral Association was formed. It was founded on an agreement between Theodore Thomas and five gentlemen of Chicago, the charter members of the Association. They were N. K. Fairbank, E. B. McCagg, A. C. Bartlett, Charles D. Hamill, and C. Norman Fay. Between Mr. Thomas and these gentlemen there was the mutual pledge that in the concerts of the orchestra the highest standard of art should be maintained whatever the effect on the box office receipts might be. I need not say that that pledge has been kept.

"It involved a serious pecuniary loss to Mr. Thomas, and it was known beforehand that it would involve a serious pecuniary loss to the Association. Annual deficits were expected, and they came. They were made up willingly. They were paid willingly in the hope that if the orchestra could be supported from year to year, sooner or later a movement would be started to establish it in a permanent home. Such a movement was started two years ago, and the result is the beautiful hall where we are gathered to-night.

"The erection of this home of music is notable in more ways than one. That in this eager, driving, industrial city nearly three-quarters of a million dollars could be raised by voluntary contributions, not for profitable enterprise, but to aid the highest manifestation of the most spiritual of all the arts is in itself significant. But the true significance of the fact lies in the source from which the money comes. It is not the easy gift of millionaires. There are more than eight thousand contributors. They represent the rich, the well-to-do, and the poor. And the poorest contributor of the smallest sum has the same right as any other to look on this beautiful building with pride and a sense of personal ownership.

"Much of this money has come directly from individuals, but it is significant of one of the social forces of our time and country that a considerable sum comes from associations of individuals. It comes from musical societies and from social and literary clubs; from all trades and professions, from railroads, from the public schools, from janitors, and scrub-women. It comes from Chicago and its suburbs; from Evanston and Aurora and other towns of Illinois; from Iowa and from other States, and part of it comes from Europe.

"But why, it may be asked, is it necessary to ask or to receive these contributions from those who perhaps can never expect to listen to music in this hall? There are those who have said that an orchestral association, like a vaudeville company, ought to be supported by its box

office receipts, and that if it cannot be so supported it has
no right to exist at all. Those who think so forget that
orchestral music is a means of education as well as a
means of amusement, and that its influence for good, like
the influence of a great university, is indirect as well as
direct, and spreads far beyond the circle of its immediate
hearers.

"I have read somewhere that more than half of the
wealth of Oxford University comes from the gifts of
charitable women, gifts to the cause of higher education,
the direct benefits of which these women could not expect
to share. But for such gifts neither Oxford nor Cambridge would have existed — no, nor Yale, nor Harvard,
nor any other great institution of learning.

"As it has been with the higher forms of learning, so
it has been with the higher forms of art. Painting,
sculpture, architecture, and music were for centuries upheld by the mighty hands of the church — and when the
influence of the church declined, and the Renaissance
followed the age of faith, it was the splendid personal
generosity of popes and Italian princes that gave
Michael Angelo and Raphael for an eternal possession.

"Disinterested patrons of art there must be whenever
and wherever art is to find its highest expression. The
difference between former times and now is that then the
patron of art was a pope or a prince, while now and in
this country the most effective patron of art is an association like this, in which rich and poor, learned and un-
learned men and women, merchants and bankers, professional men and workingmen, join hands to serve the
higher life of the community in which they live.

"Nor need we suppose that a contributor, large or
small, to this orchestral fund, is moved solely by love of

music. He may be moved partly or altogether by civic pride. When the merchant princes of the house of Medici adorned Florence with paintings and statues and beautiful buildings may we not believe that they were moved not only by the love of art, but also by pride in their beloved city?

"So it may be with us. Whatever Chicago may be hereafter, up to this time she has been the most public-spirited city in the world. We are proud of our rapid growth in wealth and population, but we are not satisfied with the merely industrial achievements of our city — we demand something more and something better.

"We look through the dust and smoke of Chicago as she is, to see the fair and noble form of our city as she will be, a centre of influence, intellectual and artistic as well as industrial, a school of the nation, as Pericles declared that Athens was the school of Greece.

"One thing more. We have built here a noble hall of music. It is a merely material structure of brick and stone and steel. We have not and we cannot put into this building its living soul. That is a task for other hands than ours.

"How can I fitly express the sense of our obligation to the members of the orchestra and their great leader for what they have done for this community and the greater community that lives around it?

"Mr. Thomas and Gentlemen of the Orchestra, we hope and believe that this building will outlive every one of you and every one of us. We hope and believe that it will stand for generations to come. But if it stands for centuries, it will not outlast the beneficent influence which you have bestowed upon the higher life of the American people."

## THE CHICAGO ORCHESTRA'S TESTIMONIAL

[In November, 1904, the members of the Chicago Orchestra decided to give their leader a banquet in the latter part of January, 1905, and passed a series of resolutions, which were beautifully engrossed by the artist Rascovitch. These were to have been presented to him on that occasion as a testimonial of esteem and loyalty, but he did not live to receive them. After his death they were presented to Mrs. Thomas.—EDR.]

RESOLVED, That we place on record the gratitude we owe to you as our respected and revered leader in our own campaign of education, for your patience, so untiringly displayed, for your help so freely given, for the vigilant watchfulness with which you have always guarded our interests.

RESOLVED, That we place upon record our admiration of the high musical standard you have maintained and of your straightforward, unswerving course, and of our love for the man who has never "trifled with his gifts" and who has never sacrificed the honor of his art to gratify personal ambition or further personal ends.

RESOLVED, Now that your reward has come and leader and players are in their own home, given to them by lovers of music, that we extend to you our heartiest congratulations. Fifty years of honest work have not been wasted. You have come to your own, nobly striven for, nobly won. You are recognized and will be remembered for your self-sacrificing, courageous devotion to the highest in our noble art. None recognized it sooner, none will remember it longer than those who have worked with you.

RESOLVED, That as a token of our admiration for you as a musician, of our loyalty to you as our leader, and our affection for you as a man, we ask you to accept this tribute with the wish that we may have many happy and useful years together in the new home, which stands as a testimonial of the popular love and respect for an honored leader under whose baton we have served so long and pleasantly.

## MEMORIAL OF THE CINCINNATI MUSICAL FESTIVAL ASSOCIATION

"Theodore Thomas died at his residence in Chicago on Wednesday, January 4, 1905, after a short illness. His funeral was held at St. James Church in that city on Friday, January 6, and was attended by President Hinkle, Directors Rawson and Wiborg, former President Hobart, and Mr. Glover, representing this Association. The Directors have met to-day for the purpose of recording on the minutes of the Association their acknowledgment of the services of the great leader to the cause of music in Cincinnati, and of expressing their sense of personal bereavement at his death.

"Mr. Thomas has been musical director of the festivals from the beginning. He conducted the first concert of the first festival, on Tuesday evening, May 6, 1873, and every concert of every festival thereafter until he laid down his baton after the memorable performance of Beethoven's Missa Solennis and Ninth Symphony, with which he brought the sixteenth festival to a glorious close on Saturday night, May 14, 1904. What he accomplished for the education of the public and for the cause of music in this city during those years of service is not recorded in any written annals, and cannot be; it is part of the history of Cincinnati, and of the lives of her citizens, which he enriched and made purer and better and happier by inspiring them with an appreciation of the highest and best forms of music, and by revealing to them the ineffable beauties of the art to which he devoted his life with noble and unselfish purpose. His upright character, his high ideals, his sound judgment, matured by years of study and labor, his indefatigable energy, his courage and patience in time of trial, his catholic spirit, his faith in the people, and his confidence in the ultimate triumph of his appeals to their intelligence, and of his efforts to raise the standard of art in their midst, are the qualities of heart and mind which have endeared him to his associates, and have laid the foundation of his enduring fame as a benefactor of mankind.

"He came to us when he was a young man; he gave to us a large part of his life; he has gone, full of years and honor. He fought a good fight and kept the faith. We deplore the loss of our leader and mourn the death of our friend. In the shadow of his death we pledge ourselves to continue the work which he began, and to maintain the Cincinnati Festivals on the plane of excellence where he placed them, and in the spirit of conscientious endeavor and high artistic purpose with which he endowed them."

### TRIBUTES TO THEODORE THOMAS

[The following are selected from the many tributes paid to the memory of Theodore Thomas on account of their close insight into the character and results of his work.—EDR.]

#### FROM "THE NEW YORK TIMES"

"It is hard to estimate the debt that this country owes to Theodore Thomas. It is the debt of a pupil to a teacher; or it is the debt of a people led out of a wilderness to the prophet who has shown them a sight of the promised land. To Mr. Thomas more than to any other single force is due the present state of musical culture in this country. To an amazing persistency in the face of repeated discouragement and piled-up difficulties he joined the fine and catholic taste, and most of all, the willingness to make his propaganda gradually, that were precisely the qualities necessary for his success. He knew that there were many kinds of good music; and that the love and appreciation of the greatest kinds were best attained by a gradual uplift through the lesser. . .

"The older generation of music-lovers learned to know their classics through Mr. Thomas's temperament and methods. To them he was the ideal conductor; and his breadth, repose, and clarity of view gave to his conducting artistic qualities that could never be invalidated. Other ideals have arisen in later years. Some accused him because he did not remould his artistic nature nearer to their hearts' desire; because he was not, and in the nature of things, could not be the 'modern' conductor that has been evolved from Wagner's influence, and the movement set going by his famous essay. But in grasp of all that pertains to the direction of an orchestra, in authority over men, in knowledge of his own mind and purposes and the way to get them realized, and most, perhaps, of all, in full possession of that subtle art that is called programme-making, there were few who were the superiors of the great artist who is dead. The immediate loss is Chicago's; but the whole country, and New York in particular, will not let the Western city mourn alone."

"The most remarkable characteristics of Mr. Thomas as a musician were his catholicity of taste and consequent versatility. No one ever interpreted the oldest masters —Bach, Handel, Gluck, Haydn, Mozart—more impressively than he, or with a keener insight into the antique spirit of music. Beethoven and Schubert he worshipped, and he made propaganda for them every week of his life. At the same time he was an enthusiastic champion of modern music. He did missionary work for Wagner, Liszt, and Berlioz, at a time when it meant money out of his pocket and the incurring of critical censure. And he kept his interest in new music to the last moment, his latest *protégés* having been Elgar and Strauss. In this catholicity of taste and ability to interpret the old and the new equally well, Theodore Thomas resembled Franz Liszt. He had chosen for his Philharmonic programme in this city, in March, Beethoven's 'Eroica' symphony, and Richard Strauss's 'Death and Glorification,' thus exemplifying his liberal-mindedness. Had there been room he might well have added some work like Professor Paine's 'Island Fantasy,' by way of calling attention to the fact that he did more for American composers than any other conductor has done.

"Theodore Thomas was a born commander. As a general he would have held Port Arthur as long as Stoessel held it. His stubborn determination to carry out his plans and wishes frequently got him into trouble, and he made many enemies; but they were for the most part enemies to be proud of. He was not without jealousy, and when Anton Seidl came to America he looked on him, unfortunately, as a rival rather than as a helper.

But when he became more familiar with Seidl's admirable work (with the Thomas orchestra) at some of Mr. Grau's operatic performances in Chicago, he cordially offered his colleague his friendship and praise. Dr. William Mason, speaking of the early days when he and the future conductor played chamber music together, says that Mr. Thomas 'rapidly developed a talent for making programmes by putting pieces into the right order of sequence, thus avoiding incongruities. He brought this art to perfection in the arrangement of his symphony concert programmes.' Here, indeed, lies one of his chief distinctions."

### FROM "THE OUTLOOK," NEW YORK

" . . . More than any other man Theodore Thomas educated the public of New York to an appreciation and love of the best music. He made no concessions to popular taste; but he was so thoroughly the master of the art of conducting, so profoundly imbued with the musical spirit, so firm in his faith in the power of the highest music to appeal to and satisfy even those who were musically uneducated, that he built up rapidly a devoted constituency, and accustomed them to the best interpretation of the best music.

"It is to Theodore Thomas, more than to any other man, that the intelligent appreciation and understanding of music which characterize New York are due. His taste was wonderfully catholic. He held to the old with tenacity, but he welcomed the new with hospitality. No man loved Beethoven more, no man interpreted Bach with the orchestra with greater sympathy; but, on the other hand, no man so persistently, and finally so victoriously, interpreted and popularized the music of

Wagner. The large number of men and women in New York who went to school to Mr. Thomas and gained their insight into music from his baton have not forgotten the quiet, persistent enthusiasm with which in those days he made Wagner's music familiar in New York City.

"This catholicity Mr. Thomas retained to the last day of his life, together with unworn enthusiasm and freshness of feeling; his latest programmes included the oldest and the newest music. What he did in New York in the earlier part of his career he repeated in Chicago in the later years; and to him more than to any other single man, as a result of his earlier work in Cincinnati, and his latest work in Chicago, is due the widespread and growing enthusiasm for music in the Central West."

### FROM "THE BROOKLYN EAGLE"

"The hands are folded at whose beck great music once filled our halls. Theodore Thomas is dead. America owes more to this man for its musical taste and knowledge than it can ever owe to another, and the glory and the pathos of his death is that he passed in the hour of his best success.

"Brooklyn came to know him well, for he conducted our Philharmonic concerts for years, and he had the personal friendship of scores of our citizens. His concerts at the Academy, always decorated for the occasion with flowers, palms, and sometimes with fountains, were events, for there was no better music in the world than we heard then. His programmes were models, his mastery of the orchestra was complete. In private life Theodore Thomas was modest, conscientious, quiet in manner, obstinate in what he deemed to be right; in short, a good citizen, a fond husband and father, a man of clear name, and of the best ideals. Had it been possible to pay the debt we owe to him he would have died rich; but he died better, in the knowledge that he had enriched the world. The placing of a laurel on his bier is but a form, yet as a tribute to his art he would have prized it. Earthly music is still for us, but for what he did to make the inheritance sublime, 'he sings to-day the Trisagion in heaven.'"

FROM "THE BOSTON TRANSCRIPT"

"In these days of endowed symphony orchestras in some of the wealthier cities of the country, it is difficult for younger generations to understand the honor in which the name of Theodore Thomas has been held by his contemporaries. Nowadays it is merely a matter of setting aside a million or so and issuing the fiat, and an orchestra exists. In Thomas's day, the taste and desire for good music had to be built up in the first place. In New York there was, to be sure, the old Philharmonic, and in Boston there was the old Harvard Musical Association, giving symphonies and other classical music to subscribers. It was Theodore Thomas's destined life work to create the broader popular base for musical culture, on which alone it can have any vital relation to or influence on the national character and refinement. . . .

"Many were the devices he had to resort to to obtain support by the public, for our 'benevolent feudalism' had not risen as yet in the seventies. His strategetics included luring the public to one of those popular resorts called 'gardens,' introduced in New York and the West from Germany. He also sought maintenance for his permanent organization in tours, and many were the leanly recompensed or downright disastrous visits of the Thomas Orchestra to Boston — then, to him, it is sad to recall, 'the enemy's country.' Good Mr. John S. Dwight, as the champion of the then decadent Harvard musical symphonies, and as the leading musical critic of his day, used to insist that 'a certain rugged naturalness' in the interpretation of symphonies was, after all, superior in appeal to a really refined appreciation to the mechanical perfections of the Thomas men!

"Thus all of Thomas's efforts to make a financial surety of fine music in America were, one after another, year by year, doomed to disappointment. It is this pathetic and heroic struggle, during all of which it never occurred to him to give it up, that accounts for his being held by those who witnessed it all, one of our American heroes, a man to be ever remembered and looked up to as a public character and benefactor. Of course, there were with him the usual 'defects of his qualities.' A born leader fit for such a struggle must be made of the sternest stuff, and Theodore Thomas, though personally modest to shyness, was a dictator in matters of music, and a hard master with his players. Nor did he ever lower his crest after those great musical foundations of Cincinnati and Chicago adopted him, and finally solved the financial problem of his famous orchestra. He has died in harness, as he would have chosen, and with his place in art and share in the evolution of a better American culture honorably recognized, and the great work of his planting in full bearing."

FROM "THE SPRINGFIELD REPUBLICAN"

"Theodore Thomas, the greatest of American orchestral conductors, one of the greatest of American
musicians,— playing, as he did, on thirty or fifty or a
hundred instruments at once with all the accumulated
spiritual and mental power and all the exquisite physical
skill of nerves and muscles which their performers had
attained,— Thomas has died, just at the entrance of his
seventieth year. It is a great loss to music in the future,
more especially in Chicago, the centre of that culture for
the West, and where at least he had gained the great
aim of his life, the endowment and home possession of
a great orchestra, in which he could carry out all his
purposes and ideals without fear of deficits in the season's
income. The disappointment is no longer personal to
him, it is true —'far has he gone from wish or fear '— but
who shall seize and wield his baton hereafter must trouble
Chicago not a little. Thomas was in himself Berlin
or Vienna, Leipsic or Paris; where he was the greatest
orchestral results were produced — the greatest and the
finest. He had no fellow in America, not even in the
best men that have ruled Boston's symphony orchestra,
or that of the Philharmonic Society of New York. Not
even Anton Seidl endangered his supremacy in this line."

FROM "THE PHILADELPHIA LEDGER"

"The most conspicuous figure in the modern history
of music in America has passed away in the death of
Theodore Thomas, who completed, with the opening of
this season, an active career of forty years as an orchestral
conductor of the highest authority. It is not too much
to say that he created, in this country, by long and

laborious effort, the popular taste for orchestral music that now finds gratifying expression in the support of great orchestras in many principal cities. Though younger men have taken up the work, none has disputed Thomas's leadership, and the receptive mind and broad appreciation which early put him at the head of the modern movement in the United States were maintained to the very end of his strenuous and useful life.

"Though born in Germany, and retaining many German traits, his whole life, from childhood, was passed in America, and was devoted to the service of the American people. His reputation as a violinist was earned as a boy, and increased in early manhood, but it has been almost forgotten in his larger fame as a master of the orchestra. He was the first man here to build up a complete orchestra upon modern lines, as a permanent organization, and to weld it into that absolute unity that made it an instrument obedient to the conductor's mind. The work was so new in this country, and the public to be addressed was at first so small, that it required all of Thomas's stolid temperament and uncompromising will, and the obstacles he met would have disheartened almost any other man; but Thomas never wavered, even in the face of repeated defeats, though from time to time compelled to change his base. Unmoved by opposition or by financial loss, he worked on, raising his standard always higher and higher, and it is gratifying to know that in Chicago, where he had recently made his home, he had at last placed his orchestra on a substantial basis, in a hall of its own, that will remain as a monument.

"A not less durable monument he has built for himself in the grateful memory of the many who owe to him no small measure of their own awakening to the boundless

resources of the orchestra, and of their early acquaintance with that musical development which is the distinctive manifestation of the modern æsthetic sense. He
wrought a great work, in whose results we are all in some
degree the sharers, and though he had come to his three
score years and ten, his firm and forceful personality has
left an impression on the musical life of the country that
the lapse of years cannot efface."

### FROM "THE CHICAGO TRIBUNE"

"One of the few really great orchestral conductors
of the world, and the foremost leader of musical progress
in the United States, has passed away, after more than
fifty years of honorable, dignified, consistent, and un-
commercial service. He was a musician with great gifts,
which he never degraded, and with which he never trifled.
Music was never an amusement to him, but the highest
expression of æsthetic possibility, and his work for it
was always of an educational character.

"While yet a youth he conceived a far-reaching purpose, and he labored for it until he reached the scriptural
limit of age, never lowering the standard he set, and never
doubting that he should live to see its fruition. That
purpose was to make the best and highest music popular
by the best and highest performance possible of it, and
by insistent repetition if necessary. For such a great
work he was magnificently equipped. He brought to
it profound musical scholarship, exceptional general
culture, catholicity of taste, rare technical skill, and inherent qualities of leadership, which made his men
devotedly attached to him, while they submitted to his
stern discipline.

"His life work was singularly complete. It reached

half a century, and in that period is comprised a successful growth, with a future promise such as few musical leaders have ever achieved. He lived to see the accomplishment of his purpose, and to receive his reward in such a popular gift as no other musician has received, as no other city has attempted to make. Grand in his ideals, unswervingly honest and honorable in his career, splendid in musical gift, and noble in manliness of character, with a great, loving heart behind his austere seeming, he has gone, and thousands will mourn for him. Who can take the place of Theodore Thomas?"

FROM "THE CHICAGO RECORD-HERALD"

"Not only will Theodore Thomas be celebrated as the founder of the Chicago Orchestra, and as the educator of at least two generations of music-lovers, but he will live in musical history as one of the world's great conductors. His catholicity and sympathy were as remarkable as his grasp and profundity. Some conductors, like the great Seidl, for example, are admirable in Wagnerian and other essentially modern music. Some are at home only in the classical compositions. Some are purely emotional, others are distinguished for precision and technical perfection. Theodore Thomas had preferences, and very decided ones, but no limitations. While it is well known that Beethoven was to him the Alpha and Omega of symphonic music, he never allowed this conviction to mar in the faintest degree his treatment of other composers. He was as good in Brahms and Liszt and Tschaikowsky as he was in Beethoven and Mozart.

"He was a true and masterly interpreter of music. He understood the spirit of a composition, 'the tone of time' in it, the national genius when it was in any manner colored thereby, the deepest meaning of the composer. He was criticised for his readings of Bach, but the more one studies the life, thought, environment of that master, the more one appreciates the legitimacy of Mr. Thomas's interpretation of him. Outwardly stern and impassive, Mr. Thomas had a rare instinct for the sensuous beauty, the passion and emotional significance of music. He was always vital, never perfunctory or 'academic' in his work.''

### FROM "THE ST. PAUL DISPATCH"

"American music seems dead with Thomas. For he made it all that it is, built it slowly, line on line, phrase after phrase, wrote its signature in the C major of sanity and clarity, experienced all its accidentals, its capricious modulations, its movements from lento to presto, formed it into a mighty chorus, where the main theme is being repeated from the four corners of the land — but now, alas, never to be written da capo. What music in America is, and why it is, every man who comprehends music may answer — Thomas. What it may be to-morrow no man dares answer. For though there are good men and capable, there is not another Thomas.

"Thomas was not an American. Had he been there would have been less American music, or of a lesser sort. He came hither in the middle of the fourth decade, and America itself scarce existed then, so chaotic, so diverse, were its endeavors, its Puritan element so barren of art, its Cavalier so tinkling. Thomas came as a mere boy, not more than ten years old, but it was because of this youth, and because music was great within him, and because he made his mastery equal his opportunity, that he is the great American in music, and American music is potentially great. What those dreary middle years of the century meant to him we may learn from the forthcoming autobiography, but they were not more uncertain than was American life itself. Yet this was touched with an idealism, without which Theodore Thomas could not have wrought so masterfully. And, moreover, they were malleable years. The orchestral conductor, as he moved restlessly from place to place, seeking his own, must often have doubted his mission, must nearly always have doubted his mission field. But he won, not the ease in musical Zion which Weingartner finds in Berlin, Nikisch in Leipzic, or Lamoureux and Colonne in Paris, but the consciousness of tremendous accomplishment, which these men can never know, the foundation and superstructure of the music of a nation. And it is typical that the last thirteen years of this sixty years in America should be lived in Chicago, where, perhaps, after all, the truest appreciation and the least prejudice may be found, without which art cannot be lasting."

### FROM "THE CHICAGO CHRONICLE"

"It is forty years since Mr. Thomas gave to Americans the first adequate testimony they ever had of the possibilities of orchestral music. Ten years earlier some of them had heard the big orchestra or band of M. Jullien; but that was more sensational than artistic. Theodore Thomas, foremost of all men, opened to Americans as a whole their first appreciation of the union in orchestra music of the profoundest science with the utmost refinement and polish in art.

"Thomas antedated all others in this regard, though in Boston the conditions existed which later blossomed in the Boston orchestra, but Mr. Thomas's work owed nothing to that. It was original and independent in him and in his devotion to the highest and purest in music, both as science and as art, he never wavered for a moment in all the long battle of forty years.

"For the inspiration of a like devotion in others, and the appreciation by them of the rewards it may win, thereby widening and deepening and elevating the hold of music on the public love and taste, Mr. Thomas has done more than all his fellow-laborers. They can hardly be called his rivals, because he never so regarded them, but only as co-laborers."

FROM "THE NORTHWESTERN CHRISTIAN ADVOCATE," CHICAGO

"Mr. Thomas's claim to public recognition and gratitude is many sided. He was a reformer; and he gave the world a striking example of the spirit and method of the true reformer. He sedulously effaced himself; he said little, wrote nothing, and was the despair of the newspaper man. He accepted the disapproval of his audiences with the same imperturbability that he accepted their approval; apparently he was never conscious of anything personal to himself in either. He was a man of one work. He doubtless might have been a great performer, or a great composer, or a great impresario; he had it in him to achieve greatness in many ways. But he decided to do one thing, in its way the most important thing of all; he decided to educate the musical taste of the people of this country, so that the riches of their inheritance in the greatest masters of music might become accessible to them. He had a sound and worthy conviction that any people might be brought to appreciate what was best in music if they had it properly presented

and presented often enough. It was simply a matter of
training. Never was mother more patient with unknow-
ing and wilful child than Mr. Thomas with his mammoth
baby-public. The task before him was tremendous.
First, he had to create an orchestra and mould musicians
to his ideals — not so easy a matter as it seems on paper;
then he had to woo a public which could not be compelled. He played Bach; the people cried for Strauss
waltzes; he gave them Strauss and more Bach. He
played Wagner; and the public, unintelligent and bored,
clamored for more Strauss. Strauss was conceded, but
Wagner followed. He played Beethoven, and his public
yawned; he aroused them with Strauss again, and fed them
more Beethoven. For forty years Mr. Thomas went on
with this work, never complaining, never scolding, but
never openly discouraged, and never yielding. It would be
too much to say that even now the average concert goer
is exuberant over a programme exclusively 'classical';
but it is not too much to say that there is not a man or
woman, boy or girl, that has any musical taste whatever,
who has not been made to feel that in these classics
the heaven of music lies. For this temper, so bracing
and hopeful in itself, so full of promise for the future
of American music, the nation is debtor, in larger degree
than to any other one man, to Mr. Thomas."

FROM "THE DIAL," CHICAGO

"It is not easy to adjust our minds to the fact that
Theodore Thomas is dead. Those who, like the present
writer, have heard something like five hundred concerts
given under his leadership during the past thirty years,
who owe to him practically their whole acquaintance
with orchestral music, must be simply dazed by their

loss. To such, he has stood for all these years as the beginning and the end of music, almost as their sole means of access to its fountain of inspiration. The contrast between those who have had the inestimable opportunity of long continued contact with his work and those who have not is like the contrast between persons who have all their lives had the use of a comprehensive collection of English poetry and the persons who have had within reach only some 'Library of Poetry and Song,' or 'Golden Treasury' of excerpts. It is only by thus transferring the case to its literary parallel that it is possible to realize what such a loss means, or to imagine how much poorer life would have been without his labors for its enrichment. There are in this country — there are in Chicago alone — many thousands of men and women who have enjoyed a liberal education in music through his agency, and who could not without that agency have had anything but a casual and fragmentary acquaintance with the art which for the past two centuries — from Bach to Brahms — has contributed at least as largely as any other art to the upbuilding of the spiritual life.

"Mr. Thomas was in his seventieth year when he died, and sixty of his years were spent in the country of his adoption. It is easily within bounds to say that no other musician during those years has done so much as he for the development of musical taste in the United States. And the secret of his achievement — if we may call it a secret — is found in his steadfast devotion to the highest ideals of his art. His rugged and uncompromising temper, in all questions directly concerning his art, often made him enemies, but of a kind for which his

followers loved him all the more.  It is barely ten years
since, in the city which he had honored by choosing it
for his permanent home, he was made the victim of a
vicious and virulent attack, accompanied by every imagi-
nable form of mean and malicious insinuation, solely
because he refused to lower his standards for the sake of
a cheap popularity, or to prostitute his art to commercial
considerations.  And even after the fury of that outburst
was past, and those responsible for it had been revealed
in all their contemptible insignificance, there were still
raised against him from time to time the voices of those
who should have been better advised, urging that he make
concessions to the ignorant humor of the public, and
give them the music for which they clamored, instead of
the music which he knew that they ought to hear.

"To all these appeals Mr. Thomas turned a deaf ear,
and continued in his imperturbable course.  And if we
accord him all honor for this attitude, we must permit
the honor to be shared with the men upon whose invitation he had come to Chicago in 1891, and who gave him
unfailing support to the end.  It was a loyal body of
public-spirited citizens — fifty at first, the number afterwards dwindling to much less than that — who made
with him in the beginning the solemn compact that only
artistic considerations should prevail in the management
of the enterprise, that the question of box-office receipts
should never be allowed to modify a standard of excellence
which art alone should dictate.  How well that promise
was kept, and at how great a personal sacrifice on the
part of those who kept it, is a matter of history."

### FROM THE CHICAGO AUDITORIUM ASSOCIATION

[Extract from resolutions adopted by the directors of the Chicago Auditorium Association, on motion of Ferdinand W. Peck.]

"Theodore Thomas was the great missionary — in our country — of the 'music of the brain'— a music which not only appeals to the soft emotions of the human heart, but also elevates, refines, ennobles, inspires, stirs, and impassions the mysterious weft of the human mind. With him music was an art and a science — art in its highest, most dignified form. He was the great music teacher, not of a city, or of the East, or of the West, or the South, or the North; he was the great music teacher of a nation. In this cause he lived and labored and suffered and triumphed like a true hero. And to-day not only this city, in which he closed his magnificent career, but this nation mourns his loss as deeply, as sincerely, as it ever mourned the death of one of its illustrious sons. His life is gone, but his work lives."

### FROM PROMINENT MUSICIANS

"Theodore Thomas was the pioneer of music in America. We younger composers must always be especially grateful to him because he often brought out our works in the United States before they were presented here. His memory will never be forgotten."

FELIX WEINGARTNER.

"Not only America but we all owe Theodore Thomas enormous thanks. Without his indefatigable pioneer work we musicians of the Old World could never have had such success in the United States."

ARTHUR NIKISCH,
*Conductor Berlin Philharmonic Orchestra.*

"I confess the death of Theodore Thomas shocked me in the highest degree. Art loses in him a musician of the rarest purity and strength of character. I myself mourn the deceased great master as a faithful friend, whose memory I shall always honor. What Thomas signified for musical development in America is universally known. What we Germans owe him shall be held in everlasting remembrance."

RICHARD STRAUSS.

"America has lost one of the greatest musical leaders this or any other country ever had."

EMIL PAUR,
*Conductor Pittsburg Orchestra.*

"It is impossible to exaggerate the great loss the death of Mr. Thomas means to the musical world. His position was unchallenged; the greatest orchestra conductor in the world. He had no equal. There is none to take his place." WILHELM GERICKE,
*Conductor Boston Orchestra.*

"It was in 1855 I met Theodore Thomas, and the affectionate friendship we then formed has continued through the half-century that has elapsed. He was a very great conductor, the greatest we have ever had in America; great not only in the Beethoven symphonies and other classics, but also in Liszt, Wagner, and the extreme moderns."

WILLIAM MASON.

"To Mr. Thomas is unquestionably due the greatest credit for his consistent and heroic work in advancing the cause of good music in this country."

FRANK D. VAN DER STUCKEN,
*Conductor Cincinnati Orchestra.*

"It is the death of a man who never swerved from his lofty artistic purpose, no matter what the difficulties met with or personal sacrifice demanded. No discouragement could make him falter, or trials cause him to lower the art standard he had set for himself and his musicians. He did more for musical art in America than any man ever did or ever will accomplish. 'We ne'er shall look upon his like again.'"

HEINRICH CONRIED,
*Director Metropolitan Opera House Co., N. Y.*

SEATTLE, January 5, 1905.
MRS. THEODORE THOMAS:

The entire musical world joins you and your family in deepest sorrow over your terrible bereavement. The passing away of your illustrious husband is an irreparable loss to our art, for scarcely any man in any land has done so much for the musical education of the people as did Theodore Thomas in this great country. The purity of his character, firmness of his principles, nobility of his ideals, together with the magnitude of his achievements, will assure him everlasting glory in the history of artistic culture. Personally, I deplore from the bottom of my soul, the loss of one of my very dearest and most beloved friends. To you, madame, who have been the devoted companion of the great departed, who have given him so much of happiness, we send the homage of our profound affliction and mournful sympathy.

I. J. PADEREWSKI.

## EARLY MUSIC IN CHICAGO

Mr. Thomas and his two orchestras were such prominent factors in the musical progress of Chicago, by reason of his many visits to that city, his extraordinary series of summer night concerts, and his fourteen seasons as leader of the Chicago Orchestra, that some reference to its musical history should be made in any volume dealing with his life. It was his home in his closing years, the city where his greatest successes were made, and where the ambition of his life was gratified. Some of the events leading up to his first appearance there in 1869, and of those preceding his organization of the Chicago Orchestra in 1891, should form part of a memorial of his life.

Julius Dyhrenfurth, a German amateur violinist, was the father of the orchestra in Chicago. He came to this country in 1837, and made some tours with Joseph Hermann, a pianist, in Ohio, Pennsylvania, and northern Virginia, but returned to Europe in 1841. Six years later he landed again in New York, and went to Chicago. He purchased a farm in the outskirts of the city, and made it a kind of retreat for expatriated Germans. Curiously enough nearly all of them were musicians. They repaid him in music for their subsistence, and at last he organized them into the nucleus of what was Chicago's first orchestra. Mr. Dyhrenfurth christened it the "Philharmonic Society," and announced a series of eight concerts, at the new Tremont Hall, the programmes to consist of "orchestral pieces, choruses combined with orchestra, vocal and instrumental numbers, etc." The first concert was given October 24, 1850, with the following programme:

1.—Potpourri, "Fille du Régiment"  .    .    . Orchestra
2.—Song, with vocal quartette accompaniment  .    Palme
3.—Violoncello solo    .    .    .    . Carlino Lassen
4.—Comic song and chorus    .    .    .    Weinmann
5.—Chicago waltz, for orchestra, composed for the
        occasion    .    .    .    .    .    . Lassen
6.—Vocal trio    .    . Davis, Lumbard, and Dunham
7.—Medley of negro airs, arranged by    . Dyhrenfurth
8.—Polka—French song—'cello accompaniment    Lassen
9.—French grand chorus, with full orchestral ac-
        companiment, from "Preciosa," arranged by Weinmann

Up to 1851 the Philharmonic efforts were of a desultory nature, and depended for their success upon the
labors of a single individual.   During the fall of the next
year, however, there was a more general effort to achieve
something of importance, and in November, 1852, a
Philharmonic Society was organized for the practice both
of vocal and instrumental music, with G. P. Abell for
conductor.   On the 22d of February, 1853, the Legislature
incorporated the Society by an act entitled "An Act to
encourage the Science of Fiddling."   With this undignified
christening, the Society sprang into complete existence,
with Christopher Plagge for conductor.   Carl Bergmann
succeeded Plagge, as I have related elsewhere, but resigned after giving two concerts, and the Society went to
pieces.   It was reconstructed in 1856, and the conductorship was assigned to Professor C. W. Webster, whose
term was barely longer than that of Bergmann.

These short-lived organizations, however, were gradually preparing the way for a full grand orchestra.   A
very decided impulse was given to the good work by the
concerts of the famous Germania Orchestra in June,
1853.   At one of their concerts, a symphony (Beethoven's

Second) was given entire for the first time in Chicago, and, of course, was not appreciated, for the symphonic days were yet afar off. Nevertheless, the Germania Orchestra did a great work in making the people acquainted with orchestral music, and the possibilities of a full orchestra. Gradually the material shaped itself for a local orchestra. In 1854, the Light Guard Band, and in 1856, the Great Western Band, were organized under Messrs. Vaas and Burkhart. All that was needed was the leader to organize this material, and drill and discipline it. The leader soon appeared. The Germania Orchestra disbanded shortly after its season in Chicago, and its members were widely scattered. Among those who came to Chicago was Henry Ahner, the cornet player. He at once availed himself of the material which was offered him in the organizations of the Light Guard and Great Western Bands, and carefully developed it into an orchestra of about thirty pieces. On the 29th of November, 1856, he commenced a series of Saturday afternoon concerts at Metropolitan Hall, five in number, assisted by Henry Perabeau, the pianist, and Louis Dochez (De Passio), the barytone, but the season was a financial failure. Nothing daunted, he at once made his arrangements for a second series of five concerts, which commenced January 24, 1857. The programmes were improved in character, and for the first time concert goers heard one of the overtures to "Fidelio," the "Midsummer Night's Dream" music of Mendelssohn, a movement from Mozart's D major symphony, and arias from the "Magic Flute" and "Der Freischütz." The second series, however, proved to be a financial failure, like the first. He inaugurated a third series, March 6, with a musical festival, in which his orchestra was increased to sixty pieces, for the performance of Beethoven's First Symphony. Like the performance of the Second Symphony, however, three years before, it was not appreciated. This series ended like the other two, in failure. He commenced his fourth series April 4, but it was the same old story. On the 7th of November, 1857, he began a fifth series of afternoon concerts, which closed December 5 with the same melancholy result. He gave five concerts of the sixth series, the last one January 6, 1858, and they left him penniless and almost friendless.

Mr. Ahner's plan of Saturday afternoon concerts was not allowed to drop. It was resumed on the 18th of February of the same year by Julius Unger, who also had been a member of the Germania Orchestra — a man of coarser, harder type, whom no amount of failure could ever crush. His first series of concerts was five in number, closing March 26. The first blow which he received came from an orchestra brought here by Ullmann in October, 1856, to accompany the *début* of Carl Formes, which included Theodore Thomas and Mosenthal (first violins), Carl Bergmann ('cello), Herzog (contra-bass), Meyer (oboe), Schmitz (French horn), Lacroix (trumpet), and Letsch (trombone), with Carl Anschütz for leader. Shortly afterwards came the first Italian opera troupe, with Parodi, Colson, Wilhorst, Amalia Patti, Brignoli, Amodio (the elder), and Junca; in the splendors of that season Unger went out of sight and disappeared, no one knew where, leaving behind him nothing but some unhappy creditors.

But all this time events were shaping themselves for a revival of the Philharmonic interest. On the 18th, 19th, and 20th of June, 1857, the Northwestern Sängerbund held its annual festival, and Hans Balatka, of Milwaukee,

came to lead its concerts. Three years later he came
to Chicago to reside. On the 9th of October, 1860,
Messrs. E. I. Tinkham, Edward Stickney, U. H. Crosby,
Samuel Johnston, J. V. LeMoyne, and a few others, met
and organized the new Philharmonic Society. They
called Mr. Balatka to the conductorship, and he accepted.
The first concert was given at Bryan's Hall, November 19,
1860, with the following programme:

1.—Symphony, No. 2, D major, op. 36 .   .   . Beethoven
2.—Quintet and chorus from "Martha"   .  .   Flotow
3.—Overture to "Merry Wives of Windsor"  .  .   Nicolai
4.—Sextet from "Lucia"   .   .   .   . Donizetti
5.—Solo for violin (fantaisie dedicated to Paganini) . De Bériot
                 Mr. Emil Weinberg.
6.—Chorus from "Tannhäuser"  .   .   .   . Wagner

The existence of a Wagner cult in Chicago, even at
that early day, is shown by the following note on the
programme:

"N. B.—In order that those who desire to listen to the last
piece on the programme may not be disturbed by those who
prefer to leave at that time, an intermission of a few minutes
will be made previous to the last chorus, after which those present are politely requested to remain in their seats until the end
of the performance."

I remember that scarcely a person left the hall.

Before many of these concerts had been given they
became the rage. So immense were the crowds, that
people often gathered in the entrance of the hall an hour
before the doors opened, in order to secure seats. Not even
the opera attracted such brilliant and fashionable audiences
and Balatka soon found himself famous, and the musical
lion of the city. The concerts, as I have said, commenced

November 19, 1860, and closed April 3, 1868, at which time the society died insolvent, having given during the eight years fifty concerts.  It accomplished an important work in the education of the people and in preparing them for the new leader soon to come, who was to make Chicago a musical center.  Mr. Balatka gave a few concerts in 1869, and then abandoned the field, the Thomas Orchestra having arrived in the same year.  In 1888, after the disbandment of the Thomas Orchestra, the Chicago Symphony Society was organized, with Louis Wahl as President and Mr. Balatka, conductor.  An orchestra of sixty members was secured, and an excellent series of programmes was prepared, but the scheme failed of success, and soon was abandoned.  To these three men, however, Ahner, Unger, and Balatka, is due the credit of preparing the way for the greater skill and higher interpretative ability of Mr. Thomas and the greater perfection of his instrumental force.  They at least introduced the higher music to Chicago, and one of them, Balatka, acquainted his audiences with every one of the Beethoven symphonies, as well as with many of Mozart's, Haydn's, Mendelssohn's, and others.

There was still another organization which did a great work for good music, even before the Philharmonic Society began its successful career.  It was a quartette — Paul Becker, pianist; Henry de Clerque, violinist; A. Buderbach, second violinist, and A. Melms, violoncellist, which gave two series of chamber concerts in the Briggs House in 1860–61.  Here is one of the earliest programmes:

1.—Quintet, op. 44, in E flat major . . Schumann
    Becker, DeClerque, Müller, Grote and Melms.
2.—"Wanderer's Night Song" . . Mendelssohn
    Gentlemen of the Mendelssohn Society.[1]
3.—"Fantaisie Caprice" . . . . . Vieuxtemps
    Mr. De Clerque.
4.—"Oh! Mighty Magic," from "The Pardon of
    Ploërmel" . . . . . . Meyerbeer
    Mr. De Passio.
5.—Quartet, op. 18, No. 4, C minor . . Beethoven
    De Clerque, Müller, Grote, and Melms.

Such programmes as these, be it remembered, were played in Chicago only five years after the famous Mason-Thomas concerts had been started in New York. They included such numbers as Beethoven's quartet, op. 16, sonata for piano and 'cello, op. 7, quartet, op. 18, No. 5, A major, sonata for piano and 'cello, op. 17, trio, op. 97, quartet, No. 4, C minor, trio, op. 70, No. 1, D minor; scherzo from Brahms's trio, op. 8; Mendelssohn's trio, op. 49, D minor; Schumann's quintet, op. 44, E flat major, and Mayseder's "Variations Concertantes," for piano, violin, alto, and 'cello. The audiences were not large, but there were those among them who were destined to be of great service to Mr. Thomas ten years later. The players are now mostly forgotten, but they were earnest, honest musicians with high standards, and were making the same fight at the same time for good music in the West that the Mason-Thomas combination was making in the East.

A year after this time (1860), Mr. Thomas severed his connection with the opera and began the establishment of his own orchestra, and a year or two later he announced

[1] The Mendelssohn Society, a mixed chorus, was led by Mr. A. W. Dohn.

his first series of Symphony Soirees at Irving Hall. Nine years later he came to Chicago under circumstances and with results already described. From 1869 until 1891, when Chicago secured the services of Mr. Thomas and induced him to leave New York, the city was literally without an orchestra of its own that could be designated as *the* Chicago Orchestra.

To complete the story of musical effort and progress in Chicago with which Mr. Thomas was largely concerned, for his influence reached out in all directions, some reference should be made to vocal music and musical societies. Of the latter, those which exerted the widest influence during the ante-fire period were the Musical Union, the Oratorio Society, the Mendelssohn Society, and the Germania Männerchor.

The Chicago Musical Union was organized January 31, 1857, with Mr. C. M. Cady as conductor, and for many years it held a very important position among the musical institutions of the city. Its first concert was given on the 7th of the following April. As a matter of curiosity I append the programme:

1.—Overture to "Semiramis," by . . . . Orchestra
2.—"The Lord is Great," by . . . . Society
3.—"Oh! Steal not the Ray" (tenor solo), by . A. B. Tobey
4.—"Prayer," from "Moses in Egypt," by Mrs. C. Blakely
    Fanny S. Collins, A. Leonard, and J. Q. Thompson.
5.—Cornet solo, by . . . . . Henry Ahner
6.—Solo and Chorus, "Marseillaise," by J. Q. Thompson
    and Society.
7.—Chorus, "Crowned with the Tempest," by . . Society
8.—"The Skylark," by . . . Mrs. C. Blakely
9.—Duo from "Norma," for piano, by Franz and Louis Staab
10.—Glee, "O, Give Me Music," by the Misses Kate and
    Mary Jones and Messrs. Leonard and Lumbard.
11.—Chorus from "Mozart's Twelfth Mass," by the Society

The Society disbanded in 1865; during the eight years of its existence it did a great work for music, especially in the introduction of oratorios.

In December, 1858, one ot the best societies ever established in Chicago was organized under the leadership of Mr. A. W. Dohn, with Mr. Harry Johnson, President. It was started originally as a male chorus, but eventually ladies were admitted to membership. For a time it gave no public concerts, but devoted itself to hard and faithful study of music under its excellent leader. Its first public appearance was made at the third concert given by the Laborde-Formes troupe, March 26, 1859. It at once made a reputation, especially among musicians and musical connoisseurs, which it diligently preserved many years, by never appearing in public until it had something to sing, and until it was ready to do that something well. Its subsequent public performances were as follows: March 23, 1860, Mendelssohn's "The Wanderer's Night Song," at one of the memorable Briggs House classical concerts; April 30, 1860, dedicated Kingsbury Hall (afterwards Wood's Museum), with the performance of Sir Sterndale Bennett's "May Queen" and Titl's "Consecration of Solomon's Temple"; Mendelssohn's "Walpurgis Night," at the Sherman House in the spring of 1862. The Society also sang at the funeral of one of its members, Mr. Holt; and the last time it appeared in public was at the funeral of President Lincoln, when it sang some chorals from Mendelssohn's "St. Paul."

The Chicago Oratorio Society was organized early in 1869. Mr. George L. Dunlap was the first President; E. I. Tinkham, Vice-president; Wm. Sprague, Treasurer, and Hans Balatka, conductor. It gave its first perform-

ance May 28, 1869, upon which occasion the "Creation"
was given with the following cast:

| | |
|---|---|
| Gabriel and Eve . . . | Mme. Parepa-Rosa |
| Uriel . . . . . . | Mr. Nordblom |
| Raphael and Adam . . . . | Mr. Rudolphsen |

In the great fire it lost all its property. The Handel
and Haydn Society, of Boston, donated it six hundred
volumes of music, and these were again lost by fire, and
the Society not long afterwards gave up its work. Oratorio was never greatly valued in Chicago.

The history of the German musical societies of Chi-
cago is an interesting one. The first in Chicago was the
Männergesang-Verein, which was organized in 1852, with
Mr. Charles Sonne, as President, and Mr. Emil Rein,
conductor. In 1855 a split occurred in the Society, and
a number of the members seceded, and organized the
Freie Sängerbund, under the leadership of Henry Ahner.
Mr. Unger succeeded Mr. Rein as the conductor of the
Männergesang-Verein, but the secession was fatal to it,
and it expired in 1859.

The Germania Männerchor was organized in 1865
by Mr. Otto Lob, who called together a male chorus for
the purpose of musical participation in the funeral ob-
sequies of President Lincoln. Out of this temporary
organization was born, April 28, 1865, the Germania
Männerchor. Mr. Henry Claussennius, the Prussian
Consul, was elected President, and Mr. Lob, conductor.
For a time matters went on smoothly and prosperously,
but at last the *Meerstille* was ruffled by a very stirring
breeze. In February, 1866, the name of Hans Balatka
was proposed for membership, and by a unanimous vote
of the Society he was made an honorary member. At a

subsequent meeting.  Mr. Lob insisted that the resolution by which Mr. Balatka had been made an honorary member should be cancelled, and threatened to resign.  Furious discussions ensued at subsequent meetings, until April of the same year, when a majority of the members, eighteen in number, withdrew and organized the Concordia Männerchor, Mr. F. A. Hoffman, President, and Mr. Lob, conductor.  The Germania Männerchor was then reorganized, with Mr. Claussennius for President, and Mr. Balatka for conductor.

The rivalry between these societies was musically profitable to the public.  The Germania Männerchor gave a remarkable performance of "Der Freischütz," in which Mrs. Clara Huck and Messrs. Koch and Schultze took the leading parts.  Its success stimulated the Concordia Männerchor to give the "Magic Flute," Mrs. Huck, Clara Lang, Mrs. Goldsticker, and Messrs. Foltz, Bischoff, and Hofmann being cast in the leading parts.  The Germania, not to be outdone, performed "Stradella," with an ensemble, especially in the carnival scene, surpassing anything ever presented by the professional troupes.  Internal troubles, however, soon arose in the Germania, eventually leading to Mr. Balatka's resignation.  In July, 1871, the Chicago Liederkranz was organized with Mr. Edmund Jussen as President; Arno Voss, Vice-president, and Mr. Balatka, conductor, but its existence was brief.  One of the results of the great fire of that year, was the union of the Germania and Concordia Männerchors in a large and flourishing society.

In 1872 the Apollo Musical Club was organized as a Männerchor, with the following officers: President, George P. Upton; Vice-president, William Sprague; Secretary, C. C. Curtiss; Treasurer, Frank Bowen;

Librarian, W. C. Coffin; conductor, A. W. Dohn. Its first season was a great popular success. In 1873 the Club gave a series of concerts in connection with the Thomas orchestra, and in 1874 it had the honor of producing Schumann's "Paradise and the Peri" for the first time in this country, with the accompaniment of the orchestra. At the close of 1874 Mr. Dohn resigned, and Carl Bergstein became conductor. He held the position for a short time only, and was succeeded by Mr. William L. Tomlins, who organized a mixed chorus, and led the Club with success for many years. It is still prospering under the direction of Mr. Harrison Wild, and is the inseparable associate of the Chicago Orchestra. It has done splendid service for choral music in Chicago, and is now virtually master of the field. Its only competitor, the Beethoven Society, retired some years ago, after eleven years of excellent work under the leadership of Mr. Carl Wolfsohn, almost the only one now left of Mr. Thomas's early associates in music. Mr. Wolfsohn, through his labors with this Society and his memorable recitals and chamber concerts, has exerted a power in music that can hardly be overestimated. He was a loyal friend to Mr. Thomas from the days when, as young men, they were associated in chamber concerts in Philadelphia, and he was one of the first to come forward with assistance in assuring the finances of the orchestra in 1891. In all of the choral work in Chicago since 1869, Mr. Thomas's influence has been felt, both in the style of performance and the standard of music.

EDITOR.

# INDEX

# EDITOR'S PREFACE

MR. THOMAS placed at my disposal for use in the preparation of this volume his entire collection of concert and festival programmes from the year 1855,— when, in coöperation with Mr. William Mason, the pianist, he inaugurated the Mason-Thomas chamber concerts in New York,— until the year 1905, which has witnessed the close of the fourteenth season of the Chicago Orchestra, and its first season as an endowed, permanent organization in its own hall.

These programmes, such was the industry and devotion of their maker, number nearly ten thousand. It would have been manifestly inconvenient to present the entire set in one volume, and besides, it would have involved considerable repetition, as many of the programmes for tours in the spring and summer are the same as those performed in the larger cities in autumn and winter, and several others are programmes of public rehearsals preceding the regular weekly concerts.

Fourteen of the programme groups, representing some of the most important concerts, are presented complete; in other cases, those have been selected which help to preserve the value of the whole for historical reference. In making a choice I have also sought to demonstrate by comparison the progress of popular education in the higher music, as well as the steady elevation of the popular taste and enjoyment of the best music of all kinds. In editing these programmes I have followed the lingual and orthographical text of the originals, making no changes except in the case of obvious typographical errors.

It adds special value as well as authority to this volume that Mr. Thomas consented to introduce the programmes with an exposition of his system of programme-making. His universally acknowledged skill in this direction, as well as his concise and illuminating reference to the two "pillars"— Beethoven and Wagner — and the important purpose they have subserved in the general plan of structure, invest this part of his introduction with extraordinary interest. Mr. Thomas's dislike to encores is also well known from long experience and many stoutly contested struggles with over-enthusiastic and importunate audiences. He furnishes an explanation of his opposition to this prevalent and sometimes pernicious habit which should be satisfactory to any reasonable concert-goer. He also makes some timely suggestions to the habitual late-comers, and closes his introduction with an extremely interesting short essay upon the modern orchestra technique, which should attract general attention in the musical world.

This extraordinary array of programmes stands for what Mr. Thomas accomplished in popular musical education by untiring industry, masterly skill, and a single-minded devotion to his art, which was never disturbed by ill fortune or influenced by commercialism. How he accomplished this, what obstacles he overcame, what battles he fought with prejudice and ignorance, how steadily and persistently he strove to reach his high ideal, is shown in the first volume of this work. This volume is filled with the evidences of accomplishment, which makes history, and with the memories of success, which are the most satisfactory awards of fame.

G. P. U.

*Chicago, December 15, 1904.*

[This preface was in type before Mr. Thomas's death, which occurred January 4, 1905. His introduction, which was written at Felsengarten, his New Hampshire summer home, in 1904, I have left without change.— EDR.]

# INTRODUCTION

THE following pages have been written in response to a request for an account of the method I use in arranging my programmes.

In earlier years they always included a Beethoven number; first, because Beethoven is the nearest to us in spirit; second, because he expresses **Programme-** more than any other composer; and **Making** third, because he has reached the highest pinnacle in instrumental music, which became through him a language. Thus Beethoven answers a double purpose; he gives delight to the educated, and teaches the uneducated. His place was always in the first part of the programme.

I have always believed in climaxes, also in giving people the most recent musical productions, and Wagner is the composer who satisfies both these essentials. Like Beethoven, he also answers a double purpose. He represents the modern spirit, and his effective scoring makes the desired climax. Wagner excites his hearers, especially the younger generation, and interests the less musical.

In this way Beethoven and Wagner became the pillars, so to speak, of my programmes. The effect of these composers on the public was plainly apparent. So I placed them where they belonged, and then filled out the rest of the programme so as to keep within a certain limit of time, have each piece prepare for the one to follow, observe a steady *crescendo*, never allow an anticlimax, and "keep a trump" for the last. I knew exactly the character of the pieces I needed for filling up and completing the programme after I had selected my so-called pillars, and began to hunt for them, but often I failed to find them. As I could not compose them, I finally had to give up the search in such cases, and change my sketch.

The real trouble, however, was the one-sidedness of the public taste, which made it difficult in this scheme to meet the popular demand to any considerable extent and still preserve the unity of the programme. Two numbers served this purpose well for many years — the "Träumerei" by Schumann, and the "Blue Danube Waltz" by Johann Strauss. While I was in Europe, in the spring of 1867, Mr. George Matzka had arranged the "Träumerei" for small orchestra at the request of some of the friends and patrons of the Summer Night Concerts at Terrace Garden, New York. He added as a trio the well-known Romanza. For the following winter season I rearranged the "Träumerei" for strings only, without the double basses, retained the trio, and then repeated the "Träumerei," but this time with muted strings, making an effective *diminuendo* at the end, finishing with a *piano, pianissimo, pianisissimo, à la* Ole Bull. This was altogether a new effect. The tone colors created sufficient sensation to prove an attraction, but we remained in our places after having reached the softest point of "*pianisissimo*," while Ole Bull, in his performance of the "Arkansas Traveller," would move slowly backward on the stage as he played softer and softer, and finally only continue the movement of his bow, without touching the strings, leaving the listener to the illusions of his imagination. About this time I brought over with me from Vienna, where I had enjoyed hearing them as given by the composers, "The Blue Danube Waltz" and many other dances, by the brothers Johann and Joseph Strauss, and the playing of these never failed to make a popular sensation in the concert-room.

The greatest difficulty I have found in arranging programmes, until very recent times, has been to interest the audience in other masters besides Beethoven and Wagner, and thereby enlarge the *repertoire* of the public and broaden its conceptions. I have never wished to pose as an educator or a philanthropist, except in so far as I might help the public to get beyond certain so-called "popular music" — which represents nothing more than sweet sentimentalism and rhythm, on the level of the dime novel. Nor has it been a fad of mine, as some people have imagined, to persevere for half a century and insist upon preserving the unity of a programme. If anything, it has been a fixed principle, and the determination to be associated with something worthy and to represent something to which a man need not be ashamed of devoting his life, which have actuated me. The practical question of "bread and butter" for the orchestra player also entered into the problem. If the only aim of a musician were to amuse the people, the sublimest of all the arts would soon be lost to humanity.

And here I think it is apropos to speak of the encore habit. While judicious applause is stimu-

**The Encore Habit**

lating, and an occasional repetition of a short piece is excusable, the constant demand for the repetition of numbers, or parts of them, must be characterized as greedy and in bad taste. It is still worse to interpolate something else.

The effect of a repetition is never so good as that of the first performance. In the case of master works it creates an anticlimax. Ordinary respect for the composers should restrain any one from assisting in a demonstration to force such an encore. A mastermind in music, as in any other sphere of creation, closely calculates the effect he wishes to make. If he did not succeed in making it, he would not be a master. Therefore, to prolong a composition by repetition defeats its creator's purpose, as it produces a different effect from that which he intended. There are practical reasons against encores, also. They place the last numbers on the programme at a disadvantage, prolong it to an unreasonable length, and tire the listener. In a programme consisting principally of marches and dances, it makes little difference whether encores are given or not, since, with the exception that one may be more brilliantly scored than another, the aim and character of all the pieces are similar. But a programme consisting of works representing varied emotions is arranged with proper regard to the relationship between the numbers. Consequently, such a programme must be made with a view to the exclusion of encores.

Again, the public are not of one mind. To what pleases one, another may be utterly indifferent; but each wishes his own favorite repeated, and thinks that he is entitled to it. Consequently, as a matter of mutual justice, when one begins to applaud, the rest assist. It is tantamount to saying, "I have had my piece repeated; it is but fair you should have yours." The inevitable effect is to give any programme a miscellaneous character.

Lastly, it certainly is not the actual time an encore takes to which executants object, for every player is willing to give this, but the modern composer has no consideration for the executant in obtaining his effects, and some pieces are so fatiguing that an immediate effective repetition is impossible. Sometimes, also, it is unadvisable as well as overburdening, in view of the rest of the programme, which may also be fatiguing.

The foregoing pages present a sketch of the general plan on which I have always made my programmes. In arranging a symphony programme today, we do not any longer need the outward attractions which formed my so-called "pillars" in earlier times. The symphony audience is now beyond that.

Its horizon has broadened, and it recognizes the
necessity of the lesser lights in the solar system of
music, in order to measure the value of the greater.
The craving for excitement of the nerves has given
place to intellectual enjoyment, and a programme
arranged from works by Bach and Mozart and ending with Beethoven is enjoyed as much as, at times,
a combination of Wagner, Tschaikowsky, and
Strauss. The symphony chosen — either by rotation
or advisability — decides the character of the programme. The time allowed for the performance,
and the selection of works in keeping with that
symphony, do the rest.

I admit, at the outset, that this is a delicate subject for discussion, so before we go any further let us
**A Word to** understand the point in question. Some
**Habitual** people have not learned to think about
**Late-Comers** art matters, and probably never will,
while others are "born late." It will be difficult to
convince the average amusement seeker, who shows
no consideration for his neighbor because he is a
stranger, that he has no right to come to a theatre
or concert when he pleases because he has paid for
his ticket.

But, can a greater injustice be perpetrated on
others who perhaps have made considerable sacrifice to be punctual, and have prepared themselves to
enter into the spirit of the music to be performed,
than suddenly and rudely to be aroused from a musical exaltation, in which they are oblivious of their

surroundings, by persons who oblige them to rise and let them squeeze by to their seats, and who perhaps even talk, after they are seated, about something not at all in harmony with the music or the occasion? Why, everybody understands that it is not only rude to be late to a dinner party, but that the seating of the late-comer creates such a disturbance of the atmosphere that it is difficult to establish unity of feeling again for that evening. How much more fatal is it to the unity of a concert!

Even though the late-comers to a concert wait until there is a pause, the disturbance is almost the same. If a symphony opens the programme, the movements are related to each other. In a programme without a symphony the pieces are selected with a view to the effect which each has upon its next neighbor, and this effect is nullified by any disturbance in the audience. The proportion of late-comers, as a rule, is so small that a thinking person should feel embarrassed to belong to that class. A person who is accidentally delayed ought to wait until the intermission before taking his seat, or, in any event, if a symphony is being played, until it is finished.

We do not all enjoy the same things, nor even the same music, with equal intensity; but the music-lover is more absorbed by his music than by anything else, and is more sensitive to disturbance. I never open a programme with a Beethoven symphony if I can help it, simply on account of late-comers, although this often leads to undue length in the programme. The late-comers not only disturb

the audience, but the executants also become irri-
tated. How, then, can they do justice to the task
before them, or be in the proper mood for it, when
their minds are not concentrated upon their work?
This, of course, also affects the conductor, and
mostly in his interpretation. The late-comers who
own boxes can easily avoid disturbing others by re-
fraining from talking. I must be excused from
giving an opinion on this species of disturbance, for
my gift of emphatic language is not adequate to the
subject.

If I have given my opinion freely on these matters it is because the public sin in this way from
thoughtlessness rather than from intention, and generally without realizing the injustice of which they are
guilty. I have also been encouraged by the following incident to believe that the majority of people
would be more considerate in this matter if their
attention were called to the importance of it. Some
years ago I gave a "Historical Beethoven Programme," and it had to begin with the Eroica Symphony. I was not willing to have the whole effect
of the symphony marred and perhaps ruined by late-
comers taking their seats between its movements,
so I made a public appeal in advance in a notice
explaining the situation, requesting patrons to be
on time, and stating that the doors would not be
opened to admit late-comers until the symphony was
finished. We had no difficulty, and the audience
were promptly in their seats. The few late-comers
who had not seen the preliminary notice were satis-

fied after an explanation by our tactful manager, and waited at the rear until the symphony was ended.

There is no class of men in the world which suffers so much from fatigue as our American business men. **Some Practical Effects of Music** The fatigue alluded to is that caused by applying certain faculties for an undue length of time to any one thing. Nor is there anywhere a class as much in need of a healthful and elevating recreation that will necessitate the use of other faculties, and by stimulating the latter rest the former, and thus create a healthy harmony in the system. To listen to music is restful to the human being, because faculties are called into action and appealed to other than those he ordinarily uses, and also because it absorbs all his attention and frees him from his worldly cares. Instrumental music is especially restful, because it appeals to his imagination and intellect, and permits his own interpretation to the extent of his experience, whereas in vocal music the interpretation is bound by the text. I speak now of master works, and not of sentimental rhythmical trifles. A prominent physician — not musically inclined — one evening attended one of my concerts. During the intermission he came to see me. "What are you doing here?" I asked, and he replied that he had a very serious and difficult case and had not been to bed for two nights, and his mind was distracted over it. "I came here," he added, "to listen to your music, and I thank you

for it. I feel better, and rested, and now I see my
case clearly." Let the medical men try this. I
could give many similar instances of editors, lawyers,
and other men whose business was of an annoying
and taxing nature, who have told me that, although
they were not musical in the strict sense of the term,
they found rest and relaxation in listening to our
orchestral concerts. One reason why I came to
Chicago was because I understood the excitement
and nervous strain that every one, more or less, suffered from who lived there, and realized the consequent need of establishing a permanent musical
institution in such a community.

Since Wagner's works have been given on the
operatic stage in America, I have left off from my
**The Modern** concert programmes many of the excerpts
**Orchestra** from them which I formerly played; in
**Technique** fact, as many as the public would allow.
The necessity for calling attention to his works no
longer exists, nor does he suffer from being neglected,
and besides, much of his music is not suitable or
legitimate for concert purposes.

Wagner always aims at a climax, and at times uses
means which are too realistic for the concert stage
but perfectly legitimate for the operatic stage, for
which they were intended. He often employs the
same methods as the impressionist painters.
Their pictures are effective only at a certain distance. In like manner Wagner's music is effective
only at a certain distance, and only under cer-

tain conditions. While the brain is engaged with
the dramatic action, the eye can take in scenery,
color, etc., and still not hinder the ear from taking
in the tone-flood prepared by the composer and
justified by the situation, so as to saturate the
whole human system. All may be in keeping with
the dramatic action, and yet be at the expense of
music and without soul. The difference between
the music of the concert-room and that of the
operatic stage is not sufficiently understood and
observed to-day.

When Wagner's music was first introduced,
many a conductor ruined it, and himself as its interpreter, by taking the tempo as the technique would
indicate, allowing time for rapid passages and expression marks, as should be done in concert
music. Wagner, however, does not depend upon
individual efforts, but rather upon combinations and
massing, rapid passages for the strings, for instance, which a single player cannot perform. A
number of violins, say sixteen first and sixteen second,
which is the number Wagner demands for his scores,
will make an effect in which everything is distinct.
The intervals which one man drops another will
play, as no two players will drop the same interval,
and so the general effect is satisfactory. This, taken
as a principle, may answer for an opera orchestra,
but it would never do for a concert orchestra. De-
terioration would be the speedy result.

And yet the Wagner technique has something very
fascinating about it, and one learns the music readily

by heart. There is something spontaneous and melodious about its figures,— symmetrical, I might say,— and the fingers seem to run without effort if one has the passage in his head. I remember, in 1872, when I engaged Mr. Lockwood, who was London's best harpist and a very able player and conscientious man, he had never seen the music of "Tristan," or anything from "the Ring," and he nearly went crazy over it the first few weeks. But he set to work and practised it so industriously that he soon mastered the music, and it became easy to him. I suppose it had impressed itself upon his memory. I may relate another instance. One day in the early seventies I received "Wotan's Farewell," and the "Magic Fire" scene, from the "Walküre" (in manuscript), from Europe, while we were travelling. We had but a short journey to make in the morning before reaching the next place, so I called a rehearsal for the strings in the afternoon, and began at once with the Fire motive, asking the first stand to play alone. The two concertmeisters, well known virtuosos, began, but found the music very difficult. After working on it for about an hour and a half with the first stands of the first and second violins, I realized that it was getting late, so I exclaimed, "You see what is before you, and you had better study this privately before we have another rehearsal. But let us all try it together once, and hear how it sounds." Meanwhile, of course, the other stands had read the music while the first and second violins were playing, and were to some extent familiar with it. We tried it together, and it sounded so well, and the figures were so distinct, that we all left the hall in very merry mood, and from that day to this I have never rehearsed those string parts again.

I had the same experience with the "Ride of the Valkyries." The score and parts arrived one morning during a rehearsal. The package was brought to me, and I explained to the orchestra what it contained. We were all eager to try it, so I had the parts put on the stands. We started, but it was not long before the first violins stopped, so I gave a sign, and the rest of the orchestra came to a stop also. The concertmeister then said, "Mr. Thomas, it is impossible to play this music in that tempo." Now, he knew perfectly well that I was also a violinist, and he knew what was possible and what was not, but he did not know what I was after, and that I cared more for the spirit of the music than the technique. So I said, "Try it; it sounds all right. I shall take the same tempo, and you can play as many notes of each passage as you can. Begin a passage in time, and end in time." We started again, and the result was the same as with the "Magic Fire Scene."

An interesting incident occurred somewhat later, when Rubinstein and Wieniawski were both concertizing with us. One evening we had the "Ride of the Valkyries" on our programme. At the end of the first part, after we had all left the stage, a sudden tumult arose. I listened and heard voices saying, "You can't play it, either," and "Let's hear you play it," etc. Looking for what it all meant, I saw some of the players addressing Wieniawski. Meanwhile some one had gone for the music and placed it on a table in the centre of the large room. Wieniawski went to the table and began to play, the whole orchestra standing around him. The scene was so comical, and such a noise was kept up, that I do not remember whether he succeeded in playing it or not. I am inclined to believe he did not, but that makes little difference, for Wieniawski was one of the greatest violinists of all ages.

I think these incidents sufficiently illustrate what I mean by saying that this kind of technique is not legitimate for the concert-hall, where accurate execution, tone quality, and expression are the first requisites, and are of more importance than descriptive music.

Descriptive music was written by Bach, and it was attempted long before him even, but it is safe to say that it was not successful until Beethoven wrote his Pastoral Symphony. The expansions and innovations of Berlioz, Liszt, and Wagner, were the natural evolutions of their time. Beethoven was not understood by Berlioz, and possibly the greatest influence Beethoven had over him was in his use of nuances, *sfz*, *ppp*, etc. Berlioz recognized and adopted the outward innovation which Beethoven achieved in his "Eroica" by expression marks, contrast, and passion, but the soul or spirit expressing the deepest humanity he hardly understood. He expanded his score, and tried to replace soul by adopting a text which should interest the listener and to cover up the lack of musical expression with material effects. This is the much-debated programme music. Beethoven's music in the Pastoral Symphony is easily understood by everyone, but that of Berlioz, even with an underlying text, is not. In other words, his music and text do not harmonize, though his works were interesting for a time.

Liszt, with his great heart and human impulses, must have been a skilful interpreter of Beethoven on the piano, but hardly with the orchestra. His own orchestral scores show too plainly that he never entered into the secrets of that world. He also looked for new paths, for the same reasons as Berlioz, and succeeded in making valuable suggestions, but he was never able to reach the heights to which he so ambitiously aspired.

Wagner understood Beethoven principally from the intellectual side, and adopted and expanded everything, but also without soul. His text and music, however, blended. He made a great impression on the world by his combination of intellect and passion, or sensuousness. He touched greatness in "Siegfried's Death March," but even in this chiefly by his intellect. Wagner did not care for humanity, but in his later life he became sentimental, as is shown in his "Parsifal"—though the Flower Maiden scene shows that he remained sensuous to the last.

Liszt and Wagner both suffered much in the nineteenth century from lack of appreciation, in consequence of the small size of halls and theatres at that time. Their expanded scores were too noisy for the halls and theatres of their day, nor could the balance of the strings with the other choirs be observed. All this has greatly changed. The spirit of expansion soon prevailed generally, and larger auditoriums were built. I myself visited three new large modern opera houses — those of Paris, Vienna, and Leipsic — in one year (1867). Orchestras have been enlarged and larger concert-halls built, until at last the reverse conditions prevail. The modern music is heard to advantage, but in the meantime in these large places Mozart and Beethoven have ceased to be effective.

Wagner and his followers have nearly doubled the size of the string choir of the orchestra, as well as of the wood wind, and even the brass, partly for color and partly to obtain the independence of each choir, as well as volume for the large modern halls. While the classic writers knew only the primary colors, the moderns generally use all the mixtures of the palette, and although by this means they gain in color and volume, they sacrifice individuality, which is the expression of the soul.

The Ninth Symphony, for instance, I have decided not to give again in the immense halls in which I have had to play of late years in Chicago, New York, and Cincinnati. It is an injustice both to the work and the audience. The impression made by this work, and the excitement caused at the first Festival in Cincinnati, where we gave it in a wooden hall of moderate size, called the Sängerfest Halle, we have never been able to repeat in the new hall of larger dimensions. When I speak of a large hall, I mean large in the European sense of the term. Our monster American halls and theatres are fit only for mass meetings and horse shows. Orchestral music of every school is ineffective in them.

Wagner calls his trilogy, "Der Ring der Nibelungen," a "Bühnenfestspiel."[1] He intended that it should be given only on exceptional occasions and under certain conditions and moods. He ought to have understood the aggressive spirit of the nineteenth century (which is often misnamed progress) better. When a young composer to-day writes an accompaniment to a song or lullaby, he will try to use the same force as that of the Festspiel orchestra, to show that he also has the ability. We must now always have the "biggest"—and not only that, but "one more," and enlarge upon the past, whether it shows progress or not. Many things thus take on a different aspect; but change is not necessarily progress.

No doubt orchestra technique was advanced by Wagner; but the demands of Richard Strauss upon the orchestra are much greater, even, than those of Wagner, and he consciously writes practical impossibilities. In fact, he revels and delights in doing so. Now, the question is this: Should the composer not observe a certain standard and average technique for the orchestra, compatible with progress and practice, as in other relations of life — self-control and

---

[1] Festival Stage Play.

good manners, so to speak? A burning question remains, which every sincere musician ought to observe,— purity of style.

Our art is old enough now to warrant the representation of every period, as far as possible under its own conditions, by using the same instruments as those for which the composer conceived his work. We are in need of a music museum, so to speak, and I believe it will be organized some day, perhaps in connection with a great national school, in which the various periods will be adequately represented, in halls of different sizes, and with orchestras selected for the purpose. Beginnings have already been made in this direction in Munich, for instance, which has a suitable building for Wagner's music-dramas, and also a small building for the operas of Mozart. For the last few years I have given works of Bach which allow massing — both instrumental and choral — with an orchestra, which not only balanced the chorus, but in which, also, the same proportion between the wood-wind and string choirs was observed as in the orchestra for which he wrote. By thus massing all the choirs, I used the method of the modern orchestra palette for the three so-called trumpet parts, and by a discreet rewriting of these parts for four D cornets for the first and second, and two trumpets in A for the third, and duplicating these with four D and two A clarinets — according to compass — I obtained a characteristic color of the trumpet parts, and at the same time made them powerful enough to blend with sixteen first violins, twelve

flutes, twelve oboes, etc. This combination also
enabled the players to give the original ornamenta-
tions of the composer, which one might call to-day
a secret language, and which were fully written out
in all the parts. The effect of Bach's music played
by an orchestra thus proportioned is entirely different
from that which is produced when played by the
orchestra ordinarily used in modern times.

# WORKS INTRODUCED INTO THIS COUNTRY BY MR. THOMAS

[The following record of works rendered by Mr. Thomas for the first time in this country, showing locality and date of performance, has been prepared with scrupulous care, Mr. Thomas himself, Mr. Frederick Stock, assistant conductor of the Chicago Orchestra, Mr. Theodore McNicol, its librarian, and the editor of this work having coöperated in its compilation. It may be relied upon as correct, and therefore cannot but prove of important historical value to the musical student, while at the same time it will interest the general musical public as a proof of his wide research, catholic taste, and artistic enterprise.—EDR.]

ABERT.
  Symphony No. 1, D major, "Columbus," op. 31, Brooklyn, October 27, 1866.

D'ALBERT.
  Prelude to "The Ruby," Chicago, January 3, 1896.
  Overture, "Der Improvisator," Chicago, October 14, 1901.
  Vorspiel, "Kain," Chicago, January 30, 1903.

AUBER.
  "Grand Inauguration March," New York, September 18, 1862.

BACH (Johann Sebastian).
  Toccata in F (Esser arrangement), New York, January 13, 1865.
  Passacaglio (Esser arrangement), New York, April 8, 1865.
  Suite No. 3, in D, New York, October 26, 1867.
  Eight-part Chorus, "I Wrestle and Pray," New York, March 13, 1869.

Suite in B minor, New York, November 27, 1874.

Magnificat in D, Cincinnati, May 13, 1875.

Suite No. 1, in C, New York, March 25, 1876.

Prelude, adagio, gavotte, and rondo (Bachrich arrangement), New York, January 24, 1880.

Ciaconna (arranged by Raff), Philadelphia, February 24, 1887.

Fugue in A minor (Hellmesberger Edition), New York, December 6, 1887.

Gavotte, sicilienne, and bourrée (string orchestra), New York, April 14, 1888.

Bourrée, gavotte, réjouissance, Suite No. 4, Chicago, November 1, 1901.

BACH (Carl Philipp Emanuel).

Symphony in D major, New York, September 18, 1862.

BALAKIREW.

Symphonic poem, "Thamar," Chicago, October 23, 1896.

BARGIEL.

Overture, "Prometheus," Brooklyn, October 28, 1865.

Symphony in C, op. 30, New York, January 13, 1866.

"Trois Danses Allemandes," op. 24, New York, August 6, 1869.

Intermezzo, Chicago, July 28, 1887.

BEETHOVEN.

Concerto No. 2, for piano, Brooklyn, January 21, 1865.

Concerto for piano, violin, and violoncello, New York, February 18, 1865.

Concerto for piano, No. 3, Brooklyn, December 8, 1865.

Choral fantasia (complete), New York, January 13, 1866.

Symphony No. 9, in D minor, op. 125, Brooklyn, April 14, 1866.

Overture in C, op. 115, New York, December 2, 1866.

Music to "Prometheus," New York, December 15, 1867.

Twelve minuets, New York, August 6, 1874.

Serenade, op. 8, New York, July 13, 1875.

Rondino, for two oboes, two clarinets, two bassoons, and two horns, Chicago, July 14, 1885.

Cavatina, from String Quartet, op. 130, Brooklyn, October 26, 1886.

Grand Fugue, op. 133, New York, March 29, 1888.

"Ritter Ballet," New York, January 17, 1889.

### BENNETT.
Symphony in G minor, New York, September 7, 1875.

### BERLIOZ.
Overture, "Corsair," New York, March 7, 1863.

Symphony, "Harold in Italy," New York, May 9, 1863.

Second part from dramatic symphony, "Romeo and Juliet," New York, December 3, 1864.

Overture, "Benvenuto Cellini," Brooklyn, November 9, 1867.

"Tristia," op. 18, New York, February 5, 1885.

### BIZET.
Egyptian dance from "Djamileh," Chicago, April 24, 1896.

### BOËLLMANN.
Variations symphoniques, for violoncello, Chicago, November 14, 1902.

### BORODIN.
"Sketch of the Steppes," Brooklyn, March 23, 1886.

### BÜLOW.
Ballad, "The Minstrel's Curse," op. 16, New York, February 15, 1868.

### BUNGERT.
Symphonic poem, "Auf der Wartburg," New York, February 28, 1888.

### BRAHMS.
Serenade in D, op. 11, New York, May 29, 1873.

Variations on theme by Haydn, Brooklyn, April 11, 1874.

Theme and variations, from Sextet, op. 18, Brooklyn, December 19, 1874.

Hungarian dances, New York, February 6, 1875.

"Tragic" Overture, New York, November 12, 1881.

"Academic" Overture, New York, November 29, 1881.

Rhapsody, op. 53, New York, January 6, 1883.

Third Symphony, F major, op. 90, New York, November 15, 1884.

Second Symphony, D major, op. 73, New York, October 3, 1878.

BRISTOW.

Overture, "Great Republic," Brooklyn, May 10, 1879.

BROUELET.

Suite, "Scènes Fantasistes," Chicago, July 19, 1890.

BRUCH.

Symphony in E flat, op. 28, New York, March 13, 1869.

"Honors of War to Patroclus," from "Achilleus," New York, April 1, 1886.

BRUCKNER.

Symphony, No. 7, E major, Chicago, July 29, 1886.

"Te Deum," Cincinnati, May 26, 1892.

Symphony, No. 4, "Romantic," E flat, Chicago, January 28, 1897.

BRUNEAU.

Symphonic poem, "La Belle aux Bois Dormant," Chicago, November 7, 1903.

Entr'acte symphonique, "Messidor," Chicago, February 24, 1903.

BUCK.

"Centennial Meditation of Columbia," Philadelphia, May 11, 1876.

CATEL.
Overture, "Semiramide," New York, December 12, 1868.

CHADWICK.
"Columbus Ode," Chicago, May 26, 1892.
"Pastoral Prelude," Chicago, January 25, 1895.

CHAMINADE.
"Concertstück," Chicago, February 8, 1895.

CHANSSON.
Symphonic poem, "Viviane," Chicago, October 21, 1898.

CHARPENTIER.
Suite, "Impressions of Italy," Chicago, November 25, 1893.

CHERUBINI.
Introduction to Act III, from "Medea," New York, October 26, 1867.
Entr'acte and ballet music, "Ali Baba," Brooklyn, January 16, 1879.

COLERIDGE–TAYLOR.
Ballad in D minor, Chicago, February 13, 1903.

CONVERSE.
"Festival Overture," Brooklyn, January 25, 1868.

COWEN.
Scandinavian Symphony, New York, November 11, 1882.
Welsh Symphony, No. 4, B flat minor, New York, April 11, 1885.
Symphony, No. 5, New York, February 28, 1888.
Overture, "The Butterfly's Ball," Chicago, October 28, 1902.

CUI.
"Tarantella," New York, October 28, 1886.

DAVID (Ferdinand).
"Festival March," New York, July 30, 1874.

DELIBES.
Ballet, "Sylvia," New York, March 24, 1886.
"Scène de Bal," New York, April 30, 1886.
Ballet, "Coppelia," New York, January 15, 1887.

DOHNANYI.
Symphony in D minor, Chicago, January 16, 1904.

DUKAS.
Scherzo, "L'Apprenti Sorcier," Chicago, January 13, 1899.

DUPARC.
Symphonic poem, "Lenore," Chicago, November 13, 1896.

DVORAK.
"Slavonic Rhapsody," No. 3, op. 45, Cincinnati, February 4, 1880.
Symphony in D, op. 60, No. 1, New York, January 6, 1883.
"Scherzo Capriccioso," Brooklyn, November 8, 1884.
Overture, "Husitzka," New York, November 15, 1884.
Symphony, D minor, op. 70, No. 2, New York, January 9, 1886.
Cantata, "Spectre's Bride," op. 69, Brooklyn, March 20, 1886.
"Légende," New York, March 1, 1887.
Suite, op. 39, New York, March 31, 1887.
"Slavonic Dances," op. 72, Second Series, New York, November 12, 1887.
"Symphonic Variations," op. 78, Chicago, July 19, 1888.
Tone poem, "The Golden Spinning Wheel," Chicago, January 1, 1897,
Symphonic poem, "The Wild Dove," Chicago, October 20, 1899.
Overture, "Mein Heim," Chicago, November 15, 1901.

ELGAR.
Concert overture, "Cockaigne," "In London Town," Chicago, March 15, 1901.
"Variations," op. 36, Chicago, January 3, 1902.
Military Marches, "Pomp and Circumstance," Chicago, November 28, 1902.
Incidental music and funeral march from "Grania and Diarmid," Chicago, November 7, 1903.
Concert overture, "Froissart," op. 19, Chicago, January 20, 1905.

FUCHS (Robert).
Symphony in C major, New York, December 10, 1885.

FRANCHETTI.
Prelude to "Asrael," New York, January 24, 1888.

FRANCK (César).
Symphonic poem, "Les Éolides," Chicago, November 8, 1895.
Symphonic poem, "Le Chasseur Maudit," Chicago, February 8, 1898.

GADBY.
Orchestral scene, "The Forest of Arden," New York, October 26, 1886.

GADE.
"Spring Fantasia," op. 23, New York, January 16, 1869.
"Noveletten," op. 53, New York, January 4, 1877.

GERMAN.
Three Dances, "Henry VIII.,'" Chicago, October 25, 1895.

GERNSHEIM.
"Tarantella," from Symphony in F, Brooklyn, March 23, 1886.

GLAZOUNOW.
"Oriental Rhapsody," Chicago, November 13, 1896.
Second Concert Waltz, Chicago, October 29, 1897.

Symphony, No. 6, in C minor, Chicago, October 19, 1900.

Tableaux musicales, "Le Printemps," Chicago, November 4, 1897.

"Ruses d'Amor," op. 6, Chicago, March 15, 1901.

Overture, "Solennelle," Chicago, December 6, 1901.

Suite, "Moyen Âge," op. 79, Chicago, January 23, 1904.

GLEASON.

Symphonic poem, "Edris," Chicago, April 17, 1895.

GLINKA.

Overture, "Rouslane et Ludmila," New York, July 10, 1873.

GLUCK.

Overture, "Paris and Helen," New York, January 8, 1875.

GOETZ.

Concerto, B flat, for violin, New York, April 15, 1882.

Opera, "The Taming of the Shrew," New York, January 14, 1886.

GOLDMARK.

"Wedding March and Variations," from "Country Wedding," op. 26, Brooklyn, February 16, 1878.

Overture, "Penthesilea," op. 31, Cincinnati, December 3, 1879.

Symphony, No. 2, in E flat, op. 35, New York, November 17, 1888.

Overture, "Spring," op. 36, New York, March 9, 1890.

Overture, "Prometheus Bound," op. 38, New York, December 6, 1890.

Overture, "Sappho," op. 44, Cincinnati, May 23, 1894.

"Scherzo," op. 45, Chicago, December 28, 1894.

GOUNOD.

Ballet music, "Queen of Sheba," New York, July 1, 1867.

Larghetto and scherzo from Second Symphony, New York, June 27, 1871.

Overture, "Le Médecin Malgré Lui," New York, May 14, 1874.

Overture, "Mireille," New York, May 20, 1874.

Oratorio, "Redemption," New York, December 6, 1882.

Oratorio, "Mors et Vita," St. Louis, October 30, 1885.

GRÄDNER.

"Eine Lustspiel Ouvertüre," op. 28, New York, December 24, 1887.

GRIEG.

Concert overture, "In Autumn," New York, November 24, 1888.

Suite No. 1, "Peer Gynt," op. 46, New York, January 24, 1889.

"Symphonic Dances," op. 64, Chicago, January 17, 1899.

GRIMM.

Suite in canon form, op. 10, New York, December 30, 1866.

Second Suite in canon form, op. 16, New York, May 22, 1873.

GUIRAUD.

"Carnival," Chicago, July 20, 1877.

HALVERSON.

"Boyard's March," Chicago, December 13, 1895.

HAMERIK.

"Nordish Suite," op. 22, New York, September 3, 1873.

"Christian Trilogie," Baltimore, May 1, 1884.

HANDEL.

"Royal Fireworks Music," New York, October 21, 1868.

Concerto in F, for string orchestra, Chicago, April 17, 1896.

## VON HAUSEGGER

Symphonic poem, "Barbarossa," Chicago, October 31, 1902,

## HAYDN.

Theme and variations, "Kaiser Franz Hymn," Brooklyn, November 9, 1867.

"Oxford Symphony," New York, March 4, 1875.

"Surprise Symphony," G major, Brooklyn, January 20, 1881.

## HILLER.

"Dramatic Fantasia," New York, May 21, 1874.

## HLARAC.

"Chopin Suite," New York, March 3, 1888.

## HOFFMAN.

"Hungarian Suite," New York, May 14, 1874.

## HOFMANN.

"Frithjof Symphony," New York, February 6, 1875.

"Pictures from the North," Chicago, July 11, 1877.

"Overture to a Drama," Chicago, July 12, 1882.

## HOHNSTOCK.

Overture, "Hail, Columbia," Brooklyn, March 4, 1865.

## HORNEMANN.

Fairy Overture, "Aladdin," New York, July 16, 1871.

## HUBER.

"Tell Symphony," New York, February 11, 1882.

"Römischer Karneval," Chicago, July 21, 1887.

## HUMPERDINCK.

Dream music from "Hänsel und Gretel," Chicago, November 15, 1895.

Tone picture from "Dornröschen," Chicago, October 14, 1902.

## D'INDY

"Wallenstein's Camp," from "Wallenstein Trilogie," Chicago, October 19, 1900.

"La Forêt Enchantée," Chicago, December 6, 1901.
Introduction symphonique to "L'Étranger," Chicago,
October 31, 1903.

JADASSOHN.
Serenade in canon form, New York, September 11,
1873.

JÄRNEFELT.
Symphonic poem, "Korsholm," Chicago, November
21, 1902.

JENSEN.
"Wedding Music," op. 45, Jersey City, January 21,
1886.

JOACHIM.
March No. 1, in C, New York, June 27, 1871.
March No. 2, in D, New York, July 21, 1871.
Hungarian Concerto, Brooklyn, January 10, 1874.
Concerto for violin, G major, New York, January 10,
1891.

KAUN.
"Festival March and Hymn," Chicago, January 7,
1898.
Symphony in D minor, op. 22, Chicago, January 14,
1898.
Overture, "Der Maler von Antwerpen," Chicago,
February 3, 1899.
1. Symphonic poem, "Minnehaha," Chicago, February 6, 1903.
2. Symphonic poem, "Hiawatha," Chicago, February 6, 1903.

KLEIN.
"Liebeslied," New York, April 14, 1888.
"Hochzeits Klänge," New York, April 14, 1888.

KRUG (Arnold).
Prologue to "Othello," New York, November 14,
1885.

KÜCKEN.

Quadrille, "Nuss Knacker," New York, June 20, 1872.

LACHNER.

Suite in D minor, op. 113, New York, December 3, 1864.

LAMOND.

Overture, "From the Highland," Chicago, December 28, 1893.

LAZZARI.

Prelude, "Armor," Chicago, March 3, 1899.

LISZT.

Symphonic poem, "Mazeppa," New York, November 11, 1865.

Concerto for piano, No. 1, in E flat, New York, December 2, 1865.

Mephisto Waltz (after Lenau), Brooklyn, December 8, 1866.

March, "Vom Fels zum Meer," New York, July 5, 1867.

Symphonic poem, "The Ideal" (after Schiller), New York, January 11, 1868.

Symphonic poem, "Prometheus," New York, April 3, 1869.

"Goethe March," New York, May 9, 1870.

Symphonic poem, "Orpheus," New York, June 20, 1872.

Symphonic poem, "Héroïde Funèbre," New York, August 8, 1872.

"Rhapsodie Hongroise," No. 1, New York, May 27, 1875.

"Rhapsodie Hongroise," No. 6 "Pesther Carneval." New York, June 22, 1875.

"Second Mephisto Waltz," Chicago, July 18, 1882.

Concerto, "Pathétique," New York, March 16, 1886.

MACCUNN.

Concert Overture, "Land of the Mountain and the Flood," Chicago, November 11, 1892.

MACKENZIE.
   Scotch Rhapsody, "Burns," op. 24, Brooklyn, November 3, 1883.
   Oratorio, "Rose of Sharon," New York, April 16, 1885.
   Overture, "Twelfth Night," op. 40, New York, March 9, 1889.
   "Benedictus," New York, March 14, 1889.
   Nautical Overture, "Britannia," Chicago, January 25, 1895.
   Three dances from "Little Minister," Chicago, October 21, 1898.

MASCAGNI.
   Intermezzo, "L'Amico Fritz," Chicago, October 21, 1892.

MASSENET.
   "Scènes Pittoresque," New York, July 29, 1874.
   "Variations," op. 13, Chicago, July 20, 1877.
   March, "Héroïque," New York, October 26, 1886.
   "La Vierge," for string orchestra, New York, October 28, 1886.
   Suite, "Esclarmonde," Chicago, April 15, 1891.
   Ballet Music, "Thaïs," Chicago, November 15, 1895.

MEHUL.
   Overture, "Horatius Cocles," Chicago, July 5, 1877.

MENDELSSOHN.
   "Trumpet Overture," Brooklyn, November 9, 1867.
   "March," op. 108, New York, May 21, 1869.
   Overture, "Wedding of Comacho," Chicago, May 1, 1875.

MEYERBEER.
   "Inauguration March," New York, June 25, 1874.

MOLIQUE.
   Concerto for violoncello, op. 45, Brooklyn, April 13, 1867.

MOSCHELES.
>Quartet for pianos, "Les Contrastes," New York, May 13, 1862.

MOSZKOWSKI.
>Suite, No. 1, op. 39, New York, March 22, 1887.
>Suite, No. 2, op. 47, New York, November 15, 1890.
>"Boabdil," Chicago, October 21, 1892.
>"Torchlight Dance," op. 51, Chicago, February 3, 1894.

MOZART.
>Symphony in G minor, Brooklyn, April 7, 1863.
>Symphony concertante, for violin and viola, New York, April 8, 1865.
>Symphony, No. 3, in D major, Brooklyn, January 20, 1866.
>Concerto for two pianos, in E flat, New York, February 10, 1866.
>Andante, variations, and menuetto (from the First Divertimento), New York, August 29, 1866.
>"Turkish March," New York, August 29, 1866.
>First, Second, and Third Motets, New York, December 12, 1868.
>Symphony in E flat, Brooklyn, April 17, 1875.
>Introduction and Fugue, for strings only, New York, August 5, 1875.
>Nocturno, from Serenade, op. 8, New York, April 1, 1881.
>Overture and ballet music, "Idomeneo," Chicago, July 11, 1882.

MÜLLER.
>"Festival March," New York, May 26, 1867.

NICODÉ.
>Symphonic Variations, New York, January 10, 1885.
>"Jubilee March," New York, October 28, 1886.

PAINE.
>"Centennial Hymn," Philadelphia, May 11, 1876.

"Columbus March and Hymn," Chicago, May 26, 1892.

PHELPS.
"Hiawatha Symphony," New York, May 10, 1880.

PRAEGER.
Symphonic poem, "Life, Love, Strife, and Victory," New York, April 14, 1888.

PRATT.
"Court Minuet," New York, March 23, 1886.

RAFF.
Symphony, "An das Vaterland," New York, February 18, 1865.
Suite in C, op. 101, New York, January 12, 1867.
Overture, "Dame Kobold," New York, August 1, 1872.
"Lenore Symphony," Boston, December 5, 1873.
Sixth Symphony, D minor, op. 189, New York, January 8, 1875.
"Sinfonietta," op. 188, for wind instruments, New York, June 24, 1875.
Suite No. 2, in F. op. 194, New York, February 26, 1876.
Suite for piano and orchestra, op. 200, New York, November 20, 1877.
"Die Jahreszeiten," for chorus, piano, and orchestra, Brooklyn, March 20, 1886.
"Festival March," New York, November 4, 1886.
Concerto for violoncello, op. 193, New York, March 17, 1888.

RAMEAU.
"Romaneska," Chicago, July 20, 1877.
Gavotte, tambourin, minuet et passepied, from "Castor et Pollux," New York, February 7, 1885.

REINECKE.
Overture, "King Manfred," after Uhland, New York, May 24, 1868.

"Festival Overture," New York, June 13, 1871.
"In Memoriam," New York, August 13, 1874.
Variationen über "Ein feste Burg ist unser Gott,"
New York, November 12, 1887.

REYER.
"Waking of the Valkyrie," from "Sigurd," New York,
December 8, 1888.

RHEINBERGER.
"Wallenstein's Camp," New York, August 10,
1871.
Overture, "Demetrius," New York, March 11,
1881.
"Passacaglio," op. 132, New York, April 14, 1888.
Concerto in G minor, for organ and orchestra, Chicago,
February 22, 1895.

RHEINHOLD.
Prelude, minuet, and fugue, op. 10, New York, Jan-
uary 24, 1879.
Concert overture, op. 32, New York, January 10, 1883.

RIETZ.
"Festival March," New York, July 9, 1867.

RIETZEL.
"Eine Volksthümliche Suite," New York, December
24, 1884.

RIMSKY-KORSAKOW.
Suite of characteristic dances, from "Miladi," Chicago,
January 8, 1897.
Symphonic poem, "Antar," Chicago, November 29,
1901.

RITTER.
Symphonic waltz, "Olafs Hochzeitsreigen," Chicago,
January 30, 1903.

ROENTGEN.
Ballad on a Norwegian Folksong, Chicago, December
11, 1896.

RUBINSTEIN.
"Faust," ein musikalisches Charakterbild, op. 68, New York, January 16, 1869.
Overture, "Dimitri Donskoi," New York, July 19, 1871.
"Don Quixote," Humoreske, op. 87, New York, May 30, 1872.
Ivan IV., Charakterbild, New York, January 24, 1874.
"Ouverture Triomphale," on a Russian hymn, New York, September 17, 1874.
Dramatic symphony, No. 4, D minor, op. 95, New York, March 4, 1875.
Fifth Symphony, New York, December 10, 1881.
Ballet music from opera "Nero," New York, July 16, 1881.
"Bal Costumé," first series, op. 183, Chicago, July 18, 1883.
"Vine" ballet, New York, February 7, 1885.
"Fantasia Eroica," Brooklyn, April 18, 1885.
Bal Costumé, second series, Chicago, July 5, 1886.
Oratorio, "Paradise Lost," Brooklyn, March 12, 1887.
Scenes from opera "Nero," New York, November 12, 1886.
Concerto No. 2, op. 95, for violoncello, New York, February 9, 1887.
Opera, "Nero," New York, March 14, 1887.
Overture, "Antony and Cleopatra," Brooklyn, January 17, 1891.
Second and third tableaux of "Moses," Cincinnati, May 25, 1894.

SAINT-SAËNS.
Symphonic poem, "Phaeton," op. 39, New York, October 9, 1876.
Tarentelle for flute and clarinet, op. 6, New York, June 24, 1873
"Marche Héroïque," op. 34, New York, May 21, 1874.
"Danse Macabre," op. 40, New York, Jan. 29, 1876.

Ballet music from "Samson and Delilah," St. Louis, March 15, 1877.
Suite, op. 49, Chicago, July 24, 1877.
"Suite Algérienne," op. 60, New York, April 1, 1881.
Ballet, "Henry VIII.," Chicago, July 20, 1886.
Concerto for piano, No. 3, op. 29, E flat, New York, November 12, 1885.
Third Symphony, C minor, op. 78, New York, February 19, 1887.
Symphony, No. 2, op. 55, Chicago, November 16, 1900.
Symphonic poem, "La Jeunesse d'Hercule," op. 50, Chicago, November 15, 1901.
Overture, "Les Barbares," Chicago, October 31, 1902.
"Coronation March," Chicago, January 30, 1903.
Symphonic poem, "Le Rouet d'Omphale," op. 31, New York, June 5, 1875.

SCHARWENKA (Philipp).
Fantasia, "Liebesnacht," op. 40, Chicago, July 21, 1887.
"Arkadische Suite," New York, January 28, 1888.
"Frühlingswogen," op. 87, Chicago, January 29, 1892.

SCHARWENKA (Xaver).
Concerto for piano, op. 56, No. 2, New York, February 1, 1883.
Symphony in C minor, op. 60, New York, December 12, 1885.
Concerto for piano, op. 32, No. 1, B minor, Chicago, March 24, 1893.

SCHOLZ.
Symphony in B flat, op. 60, New York, March 13, 1886.
Suite, "Wanderings," op. 74, Chicago, November 16, 1893.

SCHUBERT (Franz).
Fantasia, op. 15 (Liszt arrangement), New York, May 13, 1862.

"Reiter March," (Liszt arrangement) Brooklyn, October 27, 1866.
Entr'acte, "Rosamunde," New York, March 13, 1867.
Overture, "Rosamunde," New York, July 7, 1867.
"Unfinished" Symphony, B minor, New York, October 26, 1867.
"Twenty-third Psalm," New York, December 12, 1868.
Overture in Italian style, op. 170, New York, May 12, 1869,
March in B minor (Liszt arrangement), New York, August 17, 1871.
Overture, "Alfonso and Estrella," New York, June 11, 1874.
Impromptu in C minor, op. 90, New York, May 27, 1875.
Overture, "Teufel's Lustschloss," New York, May 28, 1875.
Octet, for string instruments, New York, August 10, 1875.
Symphony in C, No. 10, New York, August 20, 1875.
Divertissement à la Hongroise, op. 54, arranged by Erdmannsdörfer, New York, January 17, 1888.
Overture in E minor, New York, January 24, 1889.

SCHUMANN (Georg).
Symphonic variations, op. 24, for orchestra and organ, Chicago, October 20, 1900.
Variationen und döppelfuge, op. 30, Chicago, December 26, 1903.

SCHUMANN (Robert).
Overture, "Bride of Messina," New York, April 8, 1865.
Overture, "Genoveva," Brooklyn, April 13, 1867.
"Träumerei," New York, August 13, 1867.
"Gipsy Life," op. 29, New York, March 13, 1869.
"Paradise and the Peri," Chicago, February 18, 1874.
"Bilder aus Östen, op. 66, (orchestrated by Reinecke), New York, May 27, 1875.

"Concertstück," op. 92, New York, December 4, 1875.

"Marche Funèbre," from quintet, op. 44, (orchestrated by Godard), New York, November 4, 1886.

Fantasia for violin, op. 138, New York, March 28, 1889.

SCHYTTE.

"Pantomimes," op. 30, (orchestrated by Müller-Berghaus), Chicago, July 21, 1886.

SEIFERT.

"Festival March," New York, June 15, 1875.

SGAMBATI.

"Te Deum Laudamus," Chicago, December 28, 1893.

SHELLEY.

"Grand Sonata," for stringed instruments, New York, March 2, 1888.

SIBELIUS.

"Two Legends" from "Kalevala," Chicago, December 6, 1901.

Suite, "King Christian II.," Chicago, November 14, 1902.

Symphony, No. 2, D major, Chicago, January 2, 1904.

Tone poem, "Eine Sage," Chicago, April 30, 1904.

SINDING.

Symphony in D minor, Chicago, December 8, 1893.

"Rondo Infinito," Chicago, January 5, 1900.

"Épisodes Chevaleresques," Chicago, January 19, 1900.

SINGER.

Fantasia, for piano and orchestra, New York, April 3, 1869,

"Festival Ode," for chorus and orchestra, Cincinnati, May 14, 1848.

SIX RUSSIAN COMPOSERS.

Variations on a Russian theme, Chicago, October 24, 1903.

SMETANA.

Ouvertüre zur Oper, "Die verkaufte Braut," New York, November 12, 1887.

Symphonic poem, "Sarka," Chicago, October 25, 1895.

Symphonic poem, "Vysehrad," Chicago, April 24, 1896.

Symphonic poem, "Richard III.," Chicago, November 13, 1896.

STANFORD.

Serenade in G, New York, January 19, 1884.

STOCK.

Symphonic variations, Chicago, February 26, 1904.

STRAUSS (Johann).

"Blue Danube Waltz," New York, July 1, 1867.

Waltz, "From the Mountains," New York, July 7, 1867.

Waltz, "Bürgersinn," New York, July 14, 1867.

Polka Mazurka, "Lob der Frauen," New York, July 14, 1867.

Waltz, "Wein, Weib, und Gesang," New York, July 20, 1869.

Waltz, "Seid umschlungen Millionen!" Chicago, October 21, 1892.

STRAUSS (Richard).

Symphony in F minor, New York, December 13, 1884.

Symphonic fantasia, "Italy," Philadelphia, March 8, 1888.

Vorspiel, from opera "Guntram," Chicago, November 1, 1895.

Rondo, "Till Eulenspiegel's Merry Pranks," Chicago, November 15, 1895.

Tone poem, "Thus Spake Zarathustra," Chicago, February 5, 1897.

Tone poem, "Don Quixote," Chicago, January 6, 1899.

Tone poem, "Ein Heldenleben," Chicago, March 9, 1900.

Tone poem, "Macbeth," Chicago, October 25, 1901.
Love scene from "Feuersnot," Chicago, February 14, 1902.

SUK.

Ein Märchen, "Pohadka," Chicago, November 22, 1901.

SULLIVAN.

"Overture di Ballo," New York, May 20, 1873.
Overture, "Tempest," New York, July 16, 1874.
Cantata, "On Shore and Sea," Chicago, June 6, 1877.
Overture, "In Memoriam," Chicago, November 4, 1886.

SVENDSEN.

Symphony, No. 1, in D major, New York, June 12, 1873.
Symphonic Overture, "Sigurd Slembe," New York, September 18, 1873.
Fantasia, "Romeo and Juliet," op. 18, New York, March 11, 1881.
"Norwegian Artists' Carnival," New York, January 12, 1886.
"Festival Polonaise," New York, March 1, 1887.
Légende, "Zorahayda," op. 11, New York, March 14, 1889.

TSCHAIKOWSKY.

"Marche Slave," New York, November 2, 1886.
Suite No. 3, op. 55, New York, November 24, 1885.
Suite, "Mozartiana," New York, February 4, 1888.
Introduction and fugue, op. 43, New York, January 24, 1889.
Suite No. 1, Brooklyn, March 15, 1889.
Overture fantasia, "Hamlet," Brooklyn, February 14, 1891.
Suite, "Casse Noisette," op. 71, Chicago, October 22, 1892.
Suite du Ballet "La Belle au Bois Dormant," op. 66a, Chicago, October 19, 1900.

URSPRUCH.
Overture, "Der Sturm," Chicago, January 2, 1903.

VOLBACH.
"Es waren zwei Königskinder," Chicago, January 23, 1903.

VOLKMANN.
"Festival Overture," op. 50, Chicago, April 3, 1869.
Serenade in F, op. 63, New York, January 10, 1842.
Serenade in D minor, Brooklyn, January 10, 1874.
Concerto for violoncello, op. 33, Chicago, March 17, 1893.

WAGNER.
Overture, "Flying Dutchman," New York, May 13, 1862.
Vorspiel, "Die Meistersinger," New York, October 20, 1866.
"Kaiser March," New York, June 22, 1871.
"Huldigung's March," New York, September 8, 1871.
Introduction and final scene from "Tristan and Isolde," Boston, December 6, 1871.
"Ride of the Valkyries," New York September 17, 1872.
"Wotan's Departure," and "Magic Fire Scene," Philadelphia, January 8, 1875.
Introduction and Siegmund's Love Song from "Die Walküre," New York, September 14, 1875.
"Centennial March," Philadelphia, May 11, 1876.
"Siegfried Idyl," New York, February 28, 1878.
Vorspiel, "Parsifal," New York, November 11, 1882.
Flower Girl Scene from "Parsifal," Philadelphia, February 24, 1887.
"Dreams" (orchestrated by Theodore Thomas), New York, January 17, 1889.

WEBER.
"Invitation to the Dance" (Berlioz arrangement), New York, February 10, 1866.

Overture, "Abu Hassan," New York, May 14, 1874.
Symphony, No. 1, in C, New York, June 17, 1875.

WEIDIG.

Scherzo Capriccioso, op. 13, Chicago, January 5, 1900.

WIDOR.

"Chorale and Variations," for harp and orchestra, Chicago, November 28, 1902.

WOLF.

Symphonic poem, "Penthesilea," Chicago, April 23, 1904.
"Italian Serenade," Chicago, January 20, 1905.

ZELLNER.

Symphony, op. 7, New York, June 12, 1873.
"Melusine," op. 10, New York, August 21, 1874.

ZÖLLNER.

"Midnight at Sedan," Chicago, December 11, 1896.

# THE CHICAGO ORCHESTRA

The following is a list of the members of the Chicago Orchestra, which was directed for the last time by Theodore Thomas in the orchestra's new home, Orchestra Hall, December 24, 1904:

### FIRST VIOLINS.
Kramer, L., Principal.
Becker, L.
Krauss, A.
Seidel, R.
Marx, L.
Moerenhout, C.
Braun, H.
Tak, E.
Nuernberger, L.
Chapek, J.
Rhys, S.
Combel, A.
Bass, G.
Roehrborn, O.
Kruschwitz, E.

### SECOND VIOLINS.
Kuehn, B., Principal.
Hladky, F.
Hillmann, C.
Dasch, G.
Silberstein, J.
Woollett, W.
Novak, L.
Lampert, C.
Bichl, J.
Itte, F.
Fitzek, R.

### SECOND VIOLINS.
*(Continued.)*
Busse, A.
Singer, W.
Ulrich, A.
Rabe, H.

### VIOLAS.
Esser, F., Principal.
Stock, F.[1]
Meyer, G.
Haferburg, C.
Volk, F.
Hesselbach, O.
Fitzek, J.
Andauer, E.
Middelstaedt, F.
Strobach, C.

### VIOLONCELLOS.
Steindel, B., Principal.
Unger, W.
Brückner, C.
Ambrosius, R.
Corell, L.
Britt, H.
Klammsteiner, C.
Clusmann, E.
Kalas, J.
Felber, H.

[1] After the death of Mr. Thomas, Mr. Frederick Stock's name was withdrawn from the viola list, as it became necessary for him to perform his duties as Assistant Conductor until Mr. Thomas's successor was appointed.—EDR.

**BASSES.**

Beckel, J., Principal.
Klemm, L.
Parbs, H.
Glass, R.
Wolf, O.
Kramer, A.
Mayer, L.
Krausse, J.
Otte, F.

**HARPS.**

Tramonti, E.
Singer, W.

**ORGANIST.**

Middelschulte, W.

**FLUTES.**

Quensel, A.
Baumbach, C.

**PICCOLO.**

Ballmann, M.

**OBOES.**

Barthel, A.
Bour, F.

**ENGLISH HORNS.**

Starke, F.
Hesselbach, O.

**CLARINETS.**

Schreurs, J.
Gross, J.

**BASS CLARINET.**

Meyer, C.

**BASSOONS.**

Kruse, P.
Rabe, H.

**CONTRA-BASSOON.**

Friedrich, L.

**HORNS.**

de Maré, L.
Cras, R.
Frank, W.
Albrecht, C.

**TRUMPETS.**

Handke, P.
Llewellyn, J.

**CORNETS.**

Ulrich, A.
Felber, H.

**TROMBONES.**

Stange, G.
Zeller, W.
Nicolini, J.

**BASS TUBA.**

Otte, F.

**TIMPANI.**

Zettelmann, J.

**PERCUSSIONS.**

Wintrich, M.
Wagner, E.
Mittelstaedt, F.

**LIBRARIANS.**

McNicol, Theo.
Whitcomb, W.